AF732385

Adobe® Premiere®

Virtual Classroom

Adobe® Premiere®

Virtual Classroom

Bonnie Blake

Osborne McGraw-Hill

New York Chicago San Francisco
Lisbon London Madrid Mexico City
Milan New Delhi San Juan
Seoul Singapore Sydney Toronto

Osborne/**McGraw-Hill**
2600 Tenth Street
Berkeley, California 94710
U.S.A.

To arrange bulk purchase discounts for sales promotions, premiums, or fund-raisers, please contact Osborne/**McGraw-Hill** at the above address. For information on translations or book distributors outside the U.S.A., please see the International Contact Information page immediately following the index of this book.

Adobe® Premiere® Virtual Classroom

Brainsville.com™
The better way to learn.

1234567890 QPD QPD 01987654321

Book p/n 0-07-2193166 and CD p/n 0-07-2193174
parts of
ISBN 0-07-2193158

Publisher
Brandon A. Nordin

Vice President & Associate Publisher
Scott Rogers

Acquisitions Editor
Gretchen Ganser

Project Editor
Elizabeth Seymour

Acquisitions Coordinator
Emma Acker

Technical Editor
Richard Lainhart

Copy Editor
Ann Grubb

Proofreader
Paul Tyler

Indexer
Valerie Perry

Production Manager
epic/Eric Houts

Computer & Series Designer
epic/Andrea Reider

Illustrator
epic/Qin-Zhong Yu

Cover Series Design
Ted Holladay

This book was composed with QuarkXPress™.

Dedication

This book is dedicated to my father, Edward Blake and mother, Mary Jane Blake, who always sends me her blessings from up above.

About the Author

Bonnie Blake, MFA, has taught at many colleges in the New York metropolitan area and is currently an adjunct Assistant Professor of Digital Media at Ramapo College in New Jersey. In addition, she is a multimedia designer (who has been using Premiere as a tool since the early 90's) and specializes in healthcare communications design. Bonnie is the author *of How to Do Everything with Flash 5* (published by Osborne in 2000) and also co-authored *Flash Deconstruction: The Process, Design, and ActionScripting of JUXT Interactive* (published by New Riders in 2001). In 2000, She authored *Flash 5 ActionScript*, the best selling online course at ehandson.com.

About the Technical Reviewer

Richard Lainhart is Technical Director for Total Training, which produces training videos for digital media applications like Adobe Premiere, After Effects, and Photoshop, and for Atomic Power Corp., which develops plugins for After Effects. As Digital Media Specialist with Novaworks Computer Systems in New York City, he trained hundreds of professional editors, designers, and animators in the use of digital production tools like Premiere, After Effects, Commotion, Electric Image, Media 100, and Final Cut Pro. In addition, he is an occasional demo artist for Adobe Systems; a contributing author to books on digital media production published by CMP Books, IDG, Peachpit Press, and Miller Freeman Books; an Adobe Certified Expert in After Effects and Premiere; and co-founder of the official New York City Adobe After Effects User Group. He has been using Adobe Premiere since it was called ReelTime.

Contents at a Glance

Contents

Acknowledgments

I would like to thank Roger Stewart and Gretchen Ganser for giving me the opportunity to write a book about an application I love so much. In addition I would like to extend my appreciation to Emma Acker and Elizabeth Seymour whose expertise made the process of writing this book run so smoothly. Richard Lainhart, did an incredible job tech editing this book. His knowledge of Premiere is astounding and his input was invaluable.

Adobe Certified Expert Omar Kozarsky provided numerous ideas and input toward the chapter on Premiere Effects. Thank you for your hard work.

Thank you photographer Erlene Healey for contributing your professional expertise on setting up and taking pictures of such difficult subjects. Thanks also for your innovative creation of a makeshift studio.

Thank you Mary Cicitta, for your tireless research on digital video resources and your contribution to the content of the Appendices. Also thank you for all the ideas you gave me regarding this book.

The Brainsville staff, Robert Cowart and Dan Newman, are a pleasure to work with. Brainsville is a great concept and a terrific resource for learning.

Thanks also go to Artbeats (www.artbeats.com) for the use of many royalty stock footage video clips from their collection.

Lastly, I want to acknowledge my daughter Kelly, for being so understanding when I was unavailable an entire summer while writing this book. I hope to make it up to you next summer; that is, if you're still interested in hanging with me when you're a year older.

Introduction

Who Will Benefit From the Book?

Digital video is popping up everywhere nowadays. With the surge in popularity of digital cameras combined with the ability to manipulate digital video clips right on your desktop, it's not surprising that more and more people are becoming interested in a subject that was once the domain of an elite group of video editors. Premiere, as a video editing application, addresses a wide variety of video editing needs. It can be a perfect solution for the independent digital filmmaker, offering a plethora of output options for publishing movies—tape, CD, and the Web just to name a few. From the designer or art director who needs a small budget solution for a client's CD to the employee who suddenly needs to incorporate video on a web site (as more and more companies are starting to do)—many will find Premiere invaluable. So the answer to the above question, "Who will benefit from this book," is clearly anyone who needs to assemble and edit video and is interested in using a terrific, tried and true professional video editing application.

Adobe Premiere Virtual Classroom is geared toward the beginner to intermediate user and it addresses a wide variety of users. Some of these people might include:

- Graphic designers coming from a print or web background who need to hone their skills in order to remain competitive in the workforce.
- The home-based video enthusiast who's looking for a program with a higher level of sophistication than the programs that come pre-bundled with digital video workstations.
- The editor or designer who has a cursory knowledge of older versions of Premiere and wants to jump in and start using all the new features of Premiere 6 without starting from scratch.
- The multimedia designer who needs to incorporate video in popular programs such as Macromedia Flash, Director, Acrobat, and Adobe LiveMotion
- The web designer that needs to incorporate video in their HTML pages
- The aspiring independent filmmaker that uses digital video as his medium

So this book is designed to work for people who have many different reasons for studying Premiere.

How Is This A Virtual Classroom?

When you purchase this book, you won't just read about the bells and whistles in Premiere and have to visualize how to use Premiere's incredible video editing tools. Instead you will have the accompanying CD which transforms this book into a "virtual classroom."

The book and CD are meant to complement each other and as such, you can use them together or separately. However, you will find subjects covered in more elaborate detail on the CD than in the book—and vice versa—so for the ultimate learning experience you'll want to use both. After all, isn't your goal to learn all you can about how to use Premiere? By purchasing the book and accompanying CD you've taken a great first step.

If I were teaching you to use Premiere in a classroom setting, you'd be watching me on an overhead screen because there are certain aspects of Premiere that are best explained in a moving medium. This is where the accompanying CD really comes in handy. On the other hand, there are certain features of the software that are better explained and documented in writing using black and white pictures and screen captures. So, with the Premiere Virtual Classroom, you have the best of all worlds—the classroom environment and support files found on the CD, as well as the book as your constant companion and backup.

Working With This Book

I have organized this book with the intention of making it as helpful and easy to navigate as possible. For instance, if you want to be able to find the topics in each chapter on the CD all you'll need to do is locate CD-ROM icon. It will direct you to the specific CD lesson relating to the chapter you just finished reading.

There will be Tips, Notes, Sidebars, and Warnings throughout the book. These are extra tidbits of information that I felt might be useful or inspirational, providing you with extra tidbits of helpful information. Warnings are specifically directed at activities that could produce negative results, and are usually things that either don't work, create havoc, or both.

The equipment Premiere moviemakers use is as diverse as the group using it. Some readers will have souped-up Macs or PCs with real time graphics cards, while others will be limping along with older models. Some will be using DV cameras for their video clips, and for others, older analog video cameras or stock footage will suffice. Because of this, Premiere is approached from a generic perspective in the book and CD

The screen shots in the book and the lessons on the CD were done on a PC, but all materials are cross platform and most of the dialog boxes will look similar. In examples where the dialog boxes are drastically different, the accompanying text will alert you.

As you read, you'll notice that the book will make reference to lessons. This is what I call all the materials you need to recreate certain projects or concepts discussed in the book. As I've discussed previously, the lesson folders mentioned in the book are located on the CD—and conversely, these lesson numbers directly correlate to the chapters in the book. For example, the lesson 01 folder will contain all the files needed to study a particular concept the related chapter.

One important thing to understand when you're working in Premiere before you begin, is that you'll be working with two elements; the Premiere project file, which will have an extension of .ppj, and associated source files. Source files are media (video clips, sound, etc.) brought into Premiere that is used to create your Premiere production. If you use the lesson files, if the source files or folders with source files have been moved from their original location, Premiere will display a Locate File dialog box asking you to locate these files. Take heart in knowing they are all located within the associated lesson folders and will be just a click away. So if this dialog box appears, simply navigate to the root folder the lesson is located in and search within that folder. Chapters with lessons will indicate the names of the lesson folders and files and where the source files are located for that lesson. The Locate File dialog box has a tendency to frequent PCs then Macs.

I'm very interested your experience in reading this book. If you have questions or comments, you can contact me via email at designod@optonline.net. I will do my best to answer you as quickly as possible.

Adobe Premiere Virtual Classroom CD

This CD contains an exciting new kind of video-based instruction to help you learn Adobe Premiere faster. We believe this learning tool is a unique development in the area of computer-based training. The author actually talks to you, right from your computer screen, demonstrating topics she wrote about in the book. Moving "screencams" and slides accompany her presentation, reinforcing what you're learning. The technology and design of the presentation was developed by Brainsville.com. The content on the CD-ROM was developed by Osborne/McGraw-Hill, Bonnie Blake, and Brainsville.com. Patents (pending), copyright, and trademark protections apply to this technology and the name Brainsville.com.

Please read the following directions for usage of the CD-ROM, to ensure that the lessons play as smoothly as possible.

Getting Started

The CD-ROM is optimized to run under Windows 95/98/ME/NT/2000 or Macintosh using the QuickTime player version 5 (or greater), from Apple. If you don't have the QuickTime 5 player installed, you must install it, either by downloading it from the Internet at http://www.quicktime.com, or running the Setup program from the CD-ROM. If you install from the Web, it's fine to use the free version of the QuickTime player. You don't need to purchase the full version.

To install the QuickTime player from the CD-ROM follow these steps:

On a Windows PC:

1. Insert the CD-ROM in the drive.
2. Use Explorer or My Computer to browse to the CD-ROM.
3. Open the QuickTime folder and the Windows folder within it.
4. Double click on the setup program there.
5. Follow the setup instructions on screen.

On a Macintosh:

1. Insert the CD-ROM in the drive
2. Open the QuickTime folder and the Mac folder within it.
3. Double click on the setup program there.
4. Follow the setup instructions on screen.

Running the CD in Windows 95/98/ME/NT/2000

Minimum Requirements:

- QuickTime 5 player
- Pentium II P300 (or equivalent)
- 64MB of RAM
- 8X CD-ROM

- Windows 95, Windows 98, Windows 2000, Windows ME, or Windows NT 4.0 with at least Service Pack 4
- 16-bit sound card and speakers

The Adobe Premiere Virtual Classroom CD-ROM can run directly from the CD (see below for running it from the hard drive for better performance if necessary) and should start automatically when you insert the CD in the drive. If the program does not start automatically, your system may not be set up to automatically detect CDs. To change this, you can do the following:

1. Choose Settings, Control Panel, and click the System icon.
2. Click the Device Manager tab in the System Properties dialog box.
3. Double-click the Disk drives icon and locate your CD-ROM drive.
4. Double-click the CD-ROM drive icon and then click the Settings tab in the CD-ROM Properties dialog box. Make sure the "Auto insert notification box" is checked. This specifies that Windows will be notified when you insert a compact disc into the drive.

If you don't care about the auto-start setting for your CD-ROM, and don't mind the manual approach, you can start the lessons manually, this way:

1. Insert the CD-ROM.
2. Double-click the My Computer icon on your Windows desktop.
3. Open the CD-ROM folder.
4. Double-click the *startnow.exe* icon in the folder.
5. Follow instructions on the screen to start.

Running the CD on a Macintosh

Minimum requirements:

- A PowerPC processor–based Macintosh computer.
- At least 64MB of RAM
- Mac OS 7.5.5 or later (but not OS X)

As of this writing QuickTime 5 is not compatible with OS X. However, this issue should soon be fixed by Apple, and you can download a free copy of the updated version of QuickTime from www,quicktime.com.

To run the CD:

1. Insert the CD-ROM.
2. Double click on the file "INlesson" to start the introduction.

The Opening Screen

When the program autostarts, you'll see a small window in the middle of your screen with an image of the book. Simply click the book to launch the QuickTime player and start the lessons.

The QuickTime player window should soon open and the Virtual Classroom introduction should begin running. On some computers, after the lesson loads you must click the Play button to begin. The Play button is the big round button with an arrow on it at the bottom center of the QuickTime player window. It looks like the play button on a VCR. You can click on the links in the lower left region of the QuickTime window to jump to a given lesson. The author will explain how to use the interface.

The QuickTime player will completely fill a screen that is running at 800x600 resolution. (This is the minimum resolution required to play the lessons.) For screens with higher resolution, you can adjust the position of the player on screen, as you like.

If you are online, you can click on the Brainsville.com logo under the index marks to jump directly to the Brainsville.com web site for information about additional video lessons from Brainsville.com.

Improving Playback

Your Virtual Classroom CD-ROM employs some cutting-edge technologies, requiring that your computer be pretty fast to run the lessons smoothly. Many variables determine a computer's video performance, so we can't give you specific requirements for running the lessons. CPU speed, internal bus speed, amount of RAM, CD-ROM drive transfer rate, video display performance, CD-ROM cache settings and other variables will determine how well the lessons will play. Our advice is to simply try the CD. The disk has been tested on laptops and desktops of various speeds, and in general, we have determined that you'll need at least a Pentium II-class computer running in excess of 300Mhz for decent performance. (If you're doing serious Web-design work, it's likely your machine is at least this fast.)

Close other programs

For best performance, make sure you are not running other programs in the background while viewing the CD-based lessons. Rendering the video on your screen takes a lot of computing power, and background programs such as automatic email checking, web site updating, or Active Desktop applets (such as scrolling stock tickers) can tax the CPU to the point of slowing the videos.

Adjust the screen color depth to speed up performance

It's possible the author's lips will be out of synch with her voice, just like Web-based videos often look. There are a couple solutions. Start with this one. Lowering the color depth to 16 bit color makes a world of difference with many computers, laptops included. Rarely do people need 24-bit or 32-bit color for their work anyway, and it makes scrolling your screen (in any program) that much slower when running in those higher color depths. Try this (for Windows systems):

1. Right click on the desktop and choose Properties.
2. Click the Settings tab.
3. In the Colors section, open the drop-down list box and choose a lower setting. If you are currently running at 24-bit (True Color) color, for example, try 16-bit (High Color). Don't use 256 colors, since video will appear very funky if you do.
4. OK the box. With most computers these days, you don't have to restart the computer after making this change. The video should run more smoothly now, since your computer's CPU doesn't have to work as hard to paint the video pictures on your screen.

If adjusting the color depth didn't help the synch problem, see the section about copying the CD's files to the hard disk.

Turn off Screen Savers, Screen Blankers, and Standby Options

When lessons are playing you're likely to not interact with the keyboard or mouse. Because of this, your computer screen might blank, and in some cases (such as with laptops) the computer might even go into a standby mode. You'll want to prevent these annoyances by turning off your screen saver and by checking the power options settings to ensure they don't kick in while you're viewing the lessons. You make settings for both of these parameters from the Control Panel.

1. Open Control Panel, choose Display, and click on the Screen Saver tab. Choose "None" for the screen saver.
2. Open Control Panel, choose Power Management, and set System Standby, Turn off Monitor, and Turn off Hard Disks to "Never." Then click Save As and save this power setting as "Brainsville Courses." You can return your power settings to their previous state if you like, after you are finished viewing the lessons. Just use the Power Schemes drop-down list and choose one of the factory-supplied settings, such as Home/Office Desk.

Copy the CD Files to the Hard Disk to Speed up Performance

The CD-ROM drive will whir quite a bit when running the lessons from the CD. If your computer or CD-ROM drive is a bit slow, it's possible the author's lips will be out of synch with her voice, just like Web-based videos often look. The video might freeze or slow down occasionally, though the audio will typically keep going along just fine. If you don't like the CD constantly whirring, or you are annoyed by out-of-synch video, you may be able to solve either or both problems by copying the CD-ROM's contents to your hard disk and running the lessons from there. To do so (on Windows systems):

1. Using My Computer or Explorer, check to see that you have at least 650M free space on your hard disk.
2. Create a new folder on your hard disk (the name doesn't matter) and copy all the contents of the CD-ROM to the new folder (you must preserve the sub-folder names and folder organization as it is on the CD-ROM).

3. Once this is done, you can start the program by opening the new folder and double-clicking on the file startnow.exe. This will automatically start the lessons and run them from the hard disk.
4. (Optional) For convenience, you can create a shortcut to the startnow.exe file and place it on your desktop. You will then be able to start the program by clicking on the shortcut.

Update your QuickTime player

The QuickTime software is updated frequently and posted on the Apple QuickTime Web site, www.quicktime.com. You can update your software by clicking **Update Existing Software**, from the **Help** menu in the QuickTime player. We strongly suggest you do this from time to time.

Make sure your CD-ROM drive is set for optimum performance

CD-ROM drives on IBM PCs can be set to transfer data using the DMA (Direct Memory Access) mode, assuming the drive supports this faster mode. If you are experiencing slow performance and out-of-synch problems, check this setting. These steps are for Windows 98 and Windows ME. only.

1. Open Control Panel, chose System.
2. Click on the Device Manager tab.
3. Click on the + sign to the left of the CD-ROM drive.
4. Right-click on the CD-ROM drive.
5. Choose Properties.
6. Click the Settings tab.
7. Look to see if the **DMA** checkbox is turned on (has a checkmark in it).

If selected, this increases the CD-ROM drive access speed. Some drives do not support this option. If the DMA check box remains selected after you restart Windows then this option is supported by the device.

In Windows 2000, the approach is a little different. You access the drive's settings via Device Manager as above, but click on IDE/ATAPI Controllers. Right-click the IDE channel that your CD-ROM drive is on, choose Properties, and make the settings as appropriate. (Choose the device number, 0 or 1, and check the settings. Typically it's set to "DMA if available," which is fine. It's not recommended that you change these settings unless you know what you are doing.

TROUBLESHOOTING

This section offers solutions to common problems. Check www.quicktime.com for much more information about the QuickTime player, which is the software the Virtual Classroom CDs use to play.

THE CD WILL NOT RUN

If you have followed the instructions above and the program will not work, you may have a defective drive or a defective CD. Be sure the CD is inserted properly in the drive. (Test the drive with other CDs, to see if they run.)

THE SCREENCAM MOVIE IN A LESSON HANGS

If the author continues to talk, but the accompanying screencam seems to be stuck, just click on the lesson index in the lower left region of the QuickTime window to begin your specific lesson again. If this doesn't help, close the QuickTime window, then start the Virtual Classroom again.

VOLUME IS TOO LOW OR IS TOTALLY SILENT

1. Check your system volume first. Click on the little speaker icon next to the clock, down in the lower-right-hand corner of the screen. A little slider pops up. Adjust the slider, and make sure the Mute checkbox is not checked.
2. Next, if you have external speakers on your computer, make sure your speakers are turned on, plugged in, wired up properly, and the volume control on the speakers themselves is turned up.
3. Note that the QuickTime player also has a volume control setting. The setting is a slider control in the lower left of the QuickTime player window.
4. The next place to look if you're still having trouble, is in the Windows volume controls. Double-click on the little speaker by the clock, and it will bring up the Windows Volume Control sliders. Make sure the slider for "Wave" is not muted, and it's positioned near the top.

For Technical Support

For technical support, you can phone Hudson Software at (800) 217-0059. You can also visit www.quicktime.com or www.brainsville.com

1

The Premiere Process

Today, the popularity of desktop digital video is surging. Graphic designers, videographers, multimedia artists, photographers, teachers, filmmakers, entrepreneurs, students, and many more now incorporate digital video into their work. No matter what your background is or what your goals are with Premiere, you can start here on your digital video editing journey. This chapter opens the door to Premiere and introduces basic DV concepts.

What Is Premiere All About?

Premiere is a nonlinear editing program that lets you assemble, edit, and output video clips, music, audio, and still images as a finished video production. You can also apply video and audio effects, titles, video motion, and transitions. We'll cover all these features in subsequent chapters.

There are many facts you must know even before you start to make a video in Premiere.

What's a Nonlinear Video-Editing Software Program?

Knowing what this long term means will help you understand why editing digital video is so easy. You know Premiere is a video-editing program. The nonlinear part means you can jump to any frame in a Premiere movie and manipulate, add clips to, and edit any part of the movie at any time, without having to redo any of the production processes. Nonlinear editing gives you the freedom to make changes easily. If a major change in your movie is necessary, you don't have to completely reassemble the movie to correct that one element.

Linear editing, which is associated with nondigital video, works by assembling your video in chronological order, using multiple video decks. If you edit the video by adding or removing footage, the entire video must be redone from the point of the change. As can be expected, this can be a tedious process. Fortunately, in Premiere you don't have to worry about this.

Editing Offline and Online

It's a good idea to understand the difference between online and offline editing if you'll be working in Premiere. Before you even begin your movie, you must know the movie's final destination—what you intend to do with it once it's finished. You'd be amazed how many beginners forget to consider this. After all, Premiere merely assembles, finishes, and outputs the movie into another format, and the type of output depends on your final goal. Whether your movie is bound for the Web or broadcasting, the production path your movie takes depends on the final goal of your production.

OFFLINE EDITING

NOTE **You can still use clips without timecode for certain projects. However, it's helpful to understand for which types of projects timecode is most appropriate.**

Offline editing is when you use low-resolution video clips to assemble your movie. When assembly is complete, the high-resolution clips and the offline description of the movie (called an edit decision list, or EDL) can be brought to an online video-editing facility. This is where the high-end video (online editing) is assembled and finished. A description or translation of the movie is saved as an EDL. When the EDL and high-resolution source tapes are moved onto the video-editing suite, the EDL recreates the editing process and replaces the low-quality clips with the high-quality versions. Typically, offline editing is associated with analog, or nondigital, video.

The low- and high-resolution clips can be swapped in online editing because of something called timecode. Timecode is a key concept to understand in video editing. When video is recorded with timecode, every frame on the tape is identifiable using a set of numbers, which identify where the frame is in time. A frame shot with timecode is identified by a number consisting of hours, minutes, seconds, and frame number (Figure 1-1).

Have you ever noticed on your home VCR that you can find your way to a certain place on a video if you know at what time it occurs on the tape? So it is with timecode. And, it's because of timecode that you can perform your offline edit. Your EDL records the timecode on the low-quality video and, in the online process,

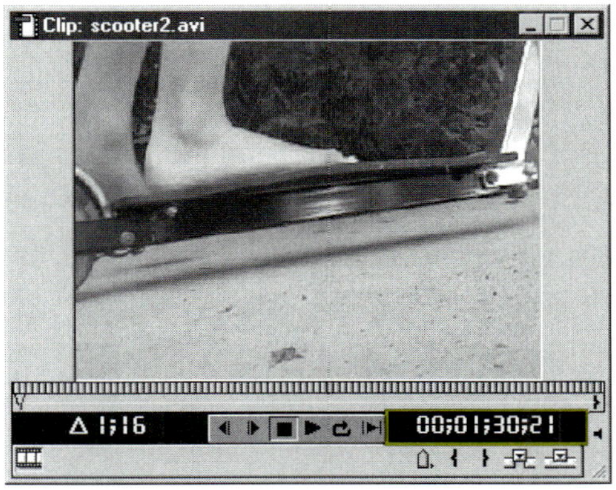

FIGURE 1-1
Timecode on a source clip is indicated in the Source view in the Premiere Monitor window.

replaces the low-quality with the high-quality version. Both versions of the clips have the same timecode, which is what makes offline-to-online editing possible.

DV cameras always record timecode and generally they do this in a drop frame format. This is not true for all cameras, though. Some equipment doesn't read or even record timecode. You should know whether your equipment can record timecode and as drop frame. We discuss drop-frame timecode in Chapter 3 on Premiere project settings.

Theoretically, if you know what the timecode is on your video clips (by watching them on a VCR), you could jot down the In and Out points (the timecode) and the sequence in which you want the clips to appear. All you'd have to do, then, is provide your handwritten list and source video clips to the editing house, which could reproduce the finished video. Thus, offline editing in Premiere is great because you can visualize what a movie will look like before it exists in the final version. In addition, you can generate a thorough list of instructions for exactly how this video is to be done.

ONLINE EDITING

Online editing is when you perform the entire video-editing process using your original footage. This means that the clips used throughout the entire process will be high quality. High-quality video requires a fast computer, lots of RAM, and infinite (well, almost), high-speed disk space. If you want to make videos that are much larger than the samples provided in this book, you really should invest in a fast, external hard drive. Video clips take up a lot of space. DV clips tend to compress nicely, which makes online editing more realistic on a machine that isn't a supercomputer.

Meeting the hardware requirements for the scope of your production is important when working with DV. You must make certain you've invested in a system that can sufficiently support the nature of your work. Appendix B lists resources for hardware, technical support, and training. Appendix C lists the bare-bones, minimum hardware requirements for Premiere. If you intend to be a serious Premiere user, you owe it to yourself to configure your system appropriately for your particular output needs.

Premiere Virtual Classroom hones in on the actual Premiere editing processes and doesn't dwell too much on the before and after issues associated with the art of video editing. After we leave this chapter, we'll examine the editing process in detail to get you up and running in Premiere as quickly as possible. Because Premiere works in conjunction with many other processes, if you're planning to make productions longer, more complex, or more sophisticated than the examples presented in this book, you would greatly benefit from more education in the digital-filmmaking area.

DIGITAL VERSUS ANALOG VIDEO

There are two types of video: *digital* and *analog*. Analog video is the format generated from the camcorders of yesterday. Look in any advertising circular featuring camcorders, and you'll notice cameras that used to be expensive are suddenly affordable. These camcorders record analog video. With analog video, images are recorded on videotape and the actual footage can be captured on your computer only if your hardware configuration is equipped with an analog video-capture card. The capture card digitizes the video. Once the video is in digital format, you can edit it in Premiere.

Digital video that is generated from a digital camcorder is already in digital format. You don't need a video-capture card when using a DV camera because the video digitizing occurs within the camera. The only things you need to transfer footage from a DV camcorder into your computer are a FireWire (Macintosh), i.Link (Sony), or IEEE 1394 (PC) interface and a FireWire (or i.Link, or IEEE 1394) cable. This is simply a high-speed serial interface between your computer and camcorder. DV makes the entire production process incredibly simple. Premiere 6 contains many features that help streamline the DV-editing process.

There are other important issues regarding video production that you must learn in preparation for working in Premiere. We'll discuss these issues using a simple movie as an example.

A PRODUCTION IN PREMIERE

Let's review the Premiere process. Some of the preparation steps for creating a Premiere production will vary from person to person. If you're a beginner, the following section will draw up a blueprint you can refer to.

The elementary process that's mapped out here starts with the movie's concept, which can be in the form of notes or a storyboard. Then it moves on to shooting the footage based on your rough plan. From there, the footage is brought into Premiere, edited, and then enhanced further with transitions, titles, and sound. Let's look at how one might go about creating a short, simple production.

STORYBOARDS

Storyboards can be a great help in bringing your concept to life as well as helping you identify potential trouble spots in the movie. They can also be of great help if you're shooting the movie yourself, rather than using stock photography. Important movie elements such as concept, location, time of day, mood, and camera angles can be annotated in the storyboard process.

Storyboards vary in complexity. They can be as simple as stick figures on a cocktail napkin or as elaborate as a 3-D, full-color rendering of events (Figure 1-2). The most important element of a storyboard is that it guides you toward your vision during the production process.

Storyboards generally depict key events, or *frames*, in a movie. In other words, a storyboard frame is created where there's a change in action or scene. Any information that will help you visualize the movie better while you're producing it is appropriate here. The storyboard becomes your blueprint throughout the production process. You wouldn't think of building an addition to your house without a set of blueprints. Why would you make a movie without a storyboard? Most often, scenes will change throughout the process, but at least the storyboard provides you a springboard from which to base new changes.

FIGURE 1-2
A storyboard can be as simple as a quick sketch with little notations over each scene.

Dialogue, music, and background or ambient sound (if any) are generally also noted in the storyboards. It's important to conceptualize on what frames the dialogue or music begins and ends. A general description of the dialogue or music is helpful, too. This helps you visualize the feeling of the scene.

Provide as much information as you can in the storyboards about the direction the movie will take. Hopefully, drawing it out will alert you to little issues that may crop up. For example, let's say you need some clips of a ball game for your Premiere movie, and the sound of the crowd is an essential part of this shoot. Are there conditions in this location that may affect the outcome of your shoot? Maybe there's an airport nearby that will affect the sound, or noisy traffic. All sorts of conditions come into play when planning a movie.

You also should give major consideration to camera angles, lighting, and sound when you shoot the movie yourself. If you're serious about moviemaking, it's not a bad idea to familiarize yourself with the basics of camera angles and their effects, lighting, and sound. There are some excellent books on the subject, and many of these are recommended for reading in Appendix B.

> **TIP** **Another great feature of Premiere 6 is you can throw together a quick storyboard with the new Storyboard window (see Figure 1-3). Based on the same general concept as a traditional storyboard, this window enables you to visualize a sequence of clips and easily rearrange them to help you decide how you will assemble your movie.**

On the other hand, you could be one of those people who hates to draw storyboards. Did you ever play the game *Pictionary*? Similar to charades, it gives you 60 seconds to render a concept (that might be the name of a book or movie) for your team to guess, based on your drawing. If you happen to be a rotten artist, sometimes your teammates will laugh at you or even worse, try to get you ousted from their team! That same sinking feeling of being inadequate at drawing can intimidate many moviemakers. Although stick figures are perfectly acceptable for a storyboard, some people are more comfortable planning a movie in a table of contents/scripting style. The main goal is to recreate your vision with some form of hard copy to refer to.

Shooting the Footage

When the storyboard is finalized, you acquire video clips either by shooting them yourself with a camcorder or by using stock video. Filming your video is an art

FIGURE 1-3
A Storyboard window in Premiere can be used like a hand-drawn storyboard to give you a rough visual outline of your movie.

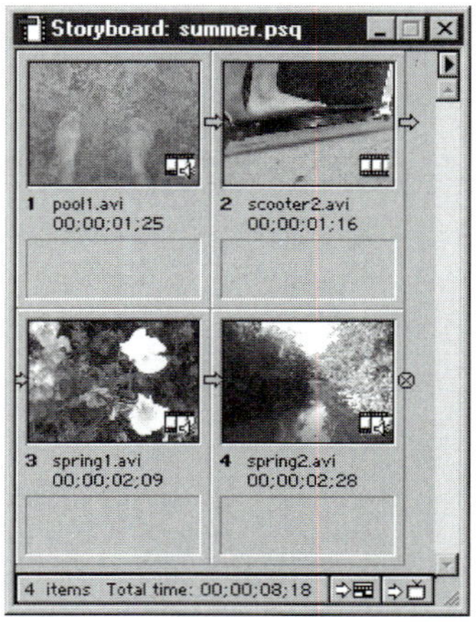

unto itself. After all, your final cut will only be as good as the original input. You should acquire some knowledge about the basics of filming before you just go out and shoot video. Otherwise, you could be disappointed with the results.

One bit of advice: Always shoot more footage than you need. It's better to have too much footage and trim it down rather than to have left something out. Sometimes it's hard to go back and re-create the identical circumstances. Many ideas may be only a one-shot deal. For example, you may catch something unexpected on tape that will happen only once. If you're prepared, chances are you'll be able to use this footage. Otherwise, you'd have to trash it if the lighting, sound, or focus was bad.

Other pieces, or *assets*, to be included in the video are gathered at this time. For example, you may want to incorporate logos created in vector programs such as Adobe Illustrator, still pictures, or sound, to name a few. Ideally, all the pieces you'll use to assemble your video will be in order before you began to edit in Premiere.

Capturing Video

To edit a movie in Premiere, you must transfer it from your camera to your computer. This is known as *capturing video*. Although you can do this with other programs, it's most efficient to capture your video in Premiere. The video clip assembled in Figure 1-4 was captured from a DV camcorder and transferred directly into the computer. Using DV to capture clips in Premiere is virtually a plug-and-play operation. Capturing video is discussed in more detail in Chapter 6.

FIGURE 1-4
The video clip in this sample was captured directly into Premiere via a FireWire/IEEE 1394 interface.

If the device controls are set correctly in Premiere (and assuming your computer is equipped with this feature), when the video camera is plugged into the computer via the FireWire or IEEE 1394 interface, Premiere can take control of the DV camcorder and actually run its VCR capabilities.

The clips in the sample were contained on a single mini DV tape, so capturing the video was merely a matter of playing through the tape, identifying random clips at various points in the footage, and capturing them.

You could theoretically capture each clip exactly where you wanted it to begin and end. However, in general you'll shoot more footage than actually needed, and then in Premiere you'll trim off the excess. The extra footage is referred to as *handles*. Handles allow editors more creative leeway in the trimming process. In the simple production we examine in this section, each clip was captured with additional footage before and after the clip. Then, the extra footage was trimmed off using the editing tools in Premiere.

Clips in the Project Window

After capturing the clips for our sample movie, I assembled the movie. To do this, I created a new file and established its location in relation to the captured clips, then chose the appropriate settings from the Load Project Settings dialog box.

The first process was to import the clips into the Project window so I could see all the pieces I had collected or created for my movie (Figure 1-5). The Project window is a place where all the elements used to assemble a movie are stored. This window makes it easy to manage these elements. The Project window is discussed in Chapter 2.

Adjusting the Clips

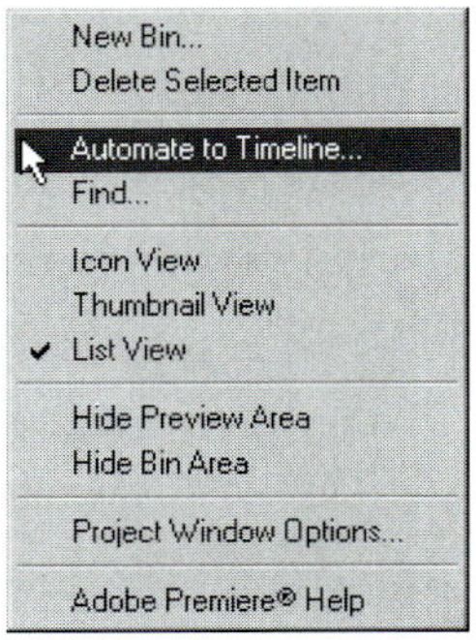

At this point, I could have dropped all the clips sequentially from the Project window into the Timeline, and my movie would by partially constructed. To automatically dump the contents of the Project window into the Timeline, I could click Automate To Timeline… in the Project window pop-up menu.

The clips needed a little more manipulating before I could bring them into the Timeline. Specifically, I had to set new In and Out points on the video clips. The In and Out points determine where a clip begins and ends in your movie. Remember when you shot your footage that you shot more than was needed? Here is where you tweak each clip and trim the excess footage. We'll discuss this process in more detail in Chapter 4 on editing in the Monitor window. To set the new In and Out points, I dragged the clips from the Project window into the Source view Monitor window (in Dual Monitor mode, the monitor on the left). Each clip was previewed individually, and new In and Out points were set (Figure 1-6).

Creating the First Rough Cut

Once the video clips were edited to my liking, I dragged them individually from the Source view Monitor window to the Timeline, in the sequence I wanted them to appear, as shown in the illustration on the next page.

FIGURE 1-5
The Project window contains all the source materials, or assets, you'll use to assemble your movie.

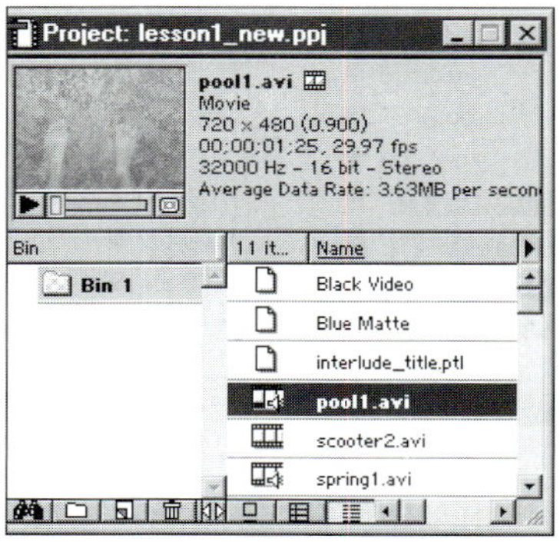

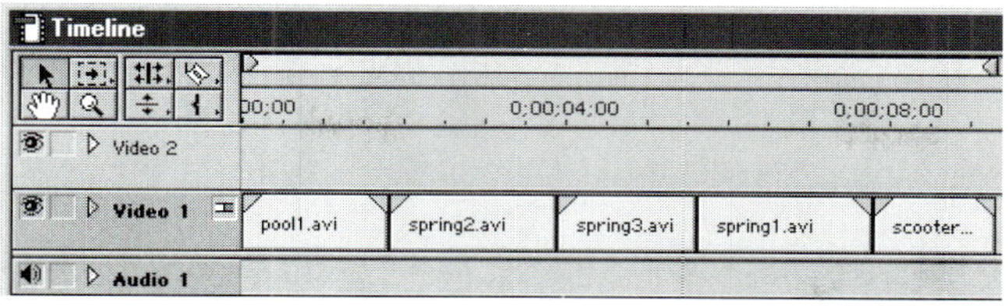

Doing this created a rough, unfinished version of the final movie. It still needs much finishing, but from the Timeline window, I can play back the clips to get an idea of how the final movie will look as a whole.

To review the movie in the Program Monitor window (the Monitor view on the right in Dual Monitor mode in the Monitor window), I dragged the Edit line, which is the little triangle at the top of the Timeline with a vertical line coming out of it. I forced the Edit line to the beginning of the Timeline by either dragging the triangle to the beginning or pressing the A key. I played through the movie by manually dragging the Edit line (referred to as *scrubbing*) or pressing the L key.

After the movie was previewed, it still seemed to need additional adjusting. This time, I edited the In and Out points right in the Timeline. You can edit in the Monitor window as well as the Timeline at any point in the editing process.

For editing purposes, I set my Window view set to Dual view, letting me see both the Source at the left (the individual video clips being edited) and the Program at the right (the sum of my editing efforts). You can change the Window view to Single or Dual view using the little icons at the top left of the window (Figure 1-7).

NOTE When you mark In and Out points on your clips, the source clips are never altered; they remain intact. You're just recording the final editing instructions for these clips in your Premiere files.

FIGURE 1-6
Setting In and Out points on a video clip in the Monitor window

FIGURE 1-7

The Monitor Window set to Dual view

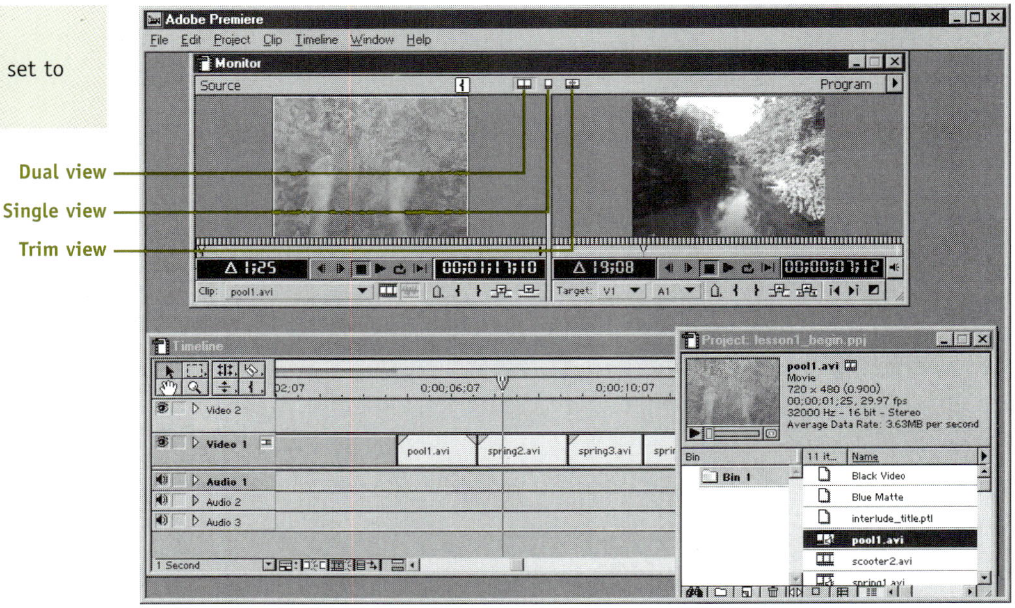

Adding Transitions

As I tested the movie in the Program Monitor window, I noticed that the clips changed in a way that appears visually abrupt. To give the movie a smoother appearance, I added transitions in between certain clips. In Premiere you can choose from many different kinds of transitions, such as dissolves and wipes, from the Transitions palette.

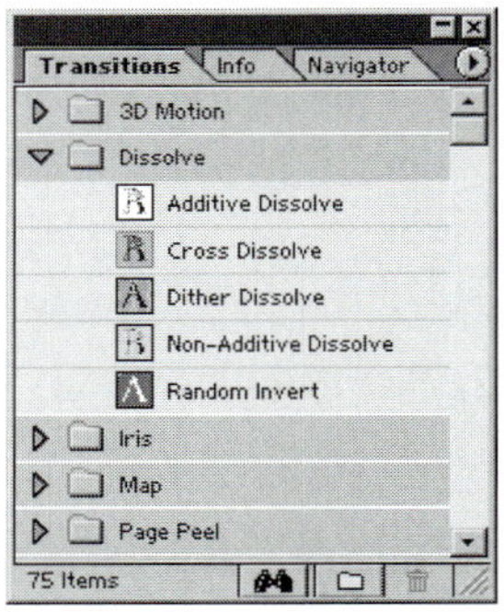

Furthermore, you can customize these transitions to set the mood of your movie. Transitions are discussed in detail in Chapter 7. The following illustration shows a cross-dissolve transition between two clips. Transitions are depicted on the Timeline as a blue rectangle between clips.

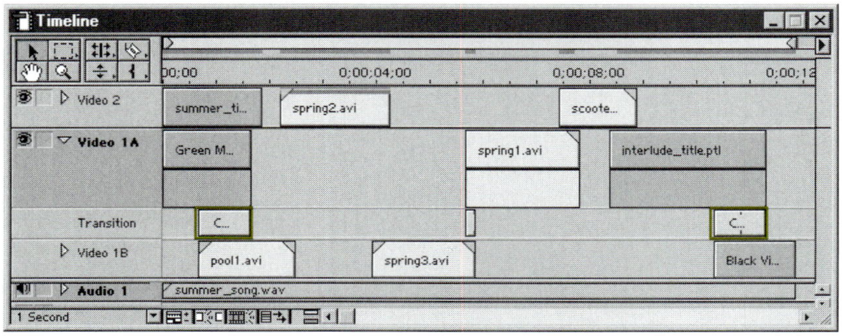

When the Timeline is displayed in A/B Editing mode as it is in the preceding illustration, you can actually see how the transitions sit in Video Track 1A and Video Track 1B. Notice also that the video tracks work in a similar manner to the way a layer works in Adobe Photoshop or Illustrator. They stack on top of one another, with the top video tracks overlaying the bottom video tracks in sequence. Thus, elements on a higher layer block out objects on a lower layer. You can also view the Timeline in Single-Editing mode where only Video Track 1 is displayed. Working with the Timeline in both modes is discussed in Chapter 5.

> **NOTE** **Cross dissolves aren't visible when you play back a movie by pressing SPACEBAR or the letter L. To see them, you must either render the movie (Timeline | Render Work Area) or drag (scrub) the Edit line over the area while pressing either ALT (in Windows) or OPTION (Macintosh).**

ADDING A TITLE TO THE VIDEO

Graphics and text created in other programs can be imported into Premiere, and you can also create simple graphics and text in Premiere to enhance your production.

> **NOTE** **The Windows version of Premiere ships with two character-generator plug-in modules, Title Deko and Inscriber.**

Although the title tools in Premiere are limited, you can create vector text and shapes from within Premiere very easily.

Titles are created in the Title window, as shown here.

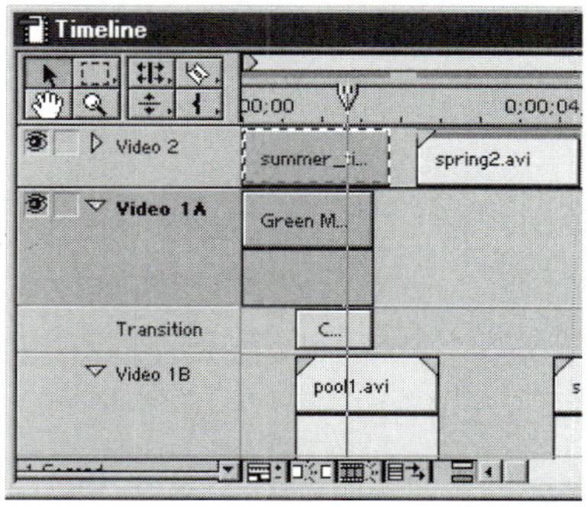

In this window, you can type your text or create simple geometric shapes. You can also use a frame as a sample background for your text or graphic so you can position it correctly. The title was saved as a separate file and is stored in the Project window. This text becomes an additional element you can use, just like the video clips, to assemble your movie in Premiere.

Because the background image is only a guide for your title text or graphic, it can be trashed after you've determined your text or image placement by selecting Window | Remove Background Clip. Creating titles is discussed further in Chapter 8.

In the Title window, you can choose a font, color text, adjust leading, and even kern the text. You can place a title on the main track, Video Track 1, or a superimpose

track (all tracks above Video Track 1). You can make title backgrounds opaque or transparent in Premiere to control superimposing. This process, known as *keying out* color, is discussed in Chapter 9.

After titles are created and saved, just as with clips, you drag them to the Timeline and tweak them further. You can additionally modify titles by changing their opacity with the fade in and out handles or add special effects to them. The transparency of elements on the superimpose track can change from opaque to transparent over time, as well. What's more, you can control when and how this effect happens. This process is discussed in Chapter 9.

Adding Sound to the Video

If you're reading this book, it's assumed you're somewhat of a novice in Premiere. As such, you probably don't have much experience with audio files. You can create sound yourself using sound-editing software, or you can buy stock audio files from many different sources. If sound is an important part of your future productions, you might want to peruse the sound resources listed in Appendix B.

For those of you who just want something quick and simple, Adobe has included a SmartSound Quicktracks CD with Premiere 6. With SmartSound, you can make simple sound tracks quickly and easily. You can further tweak the sound and remix it with Premiere's new Audio Mixer window (Figure 1-8). SmartSound is a bit limited, though, so if you're looking for a particular sound, you may not find it here. Sound in Premiere is covered in Chapter 11.

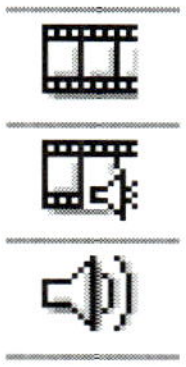

To bring audio into Premiere, you use the File | Import command. Sound appears in the Project window along with all the other assets of the movie. Also note that in the Project window List view, sounds are represented by a speaker icon, movie clips by a filmstrip icon, and movie clips with sound by both a filmstrip and speaker.

SAVING AND COMPRESSING

When you are satisfied with the results of your movie, you prepare to output it to its final destination. You've known what your output goal was from the beginning of the process. Your final production can be printed to tape or exported to CD-ROM, DVD-ROM, a web file, or to a file format that can be imported into another application.

If you're saving your file to be used on the Web, you might want to use one of Premiere's new plug-ins. There's a Save For Web feature in Premiere driven by the Cleaner EZ plug-in. This dialog box offers a quick and simple solution

FIGURE 1-8
The Premiere Audio Mixer is used to balance the sound tracks in Premiere.

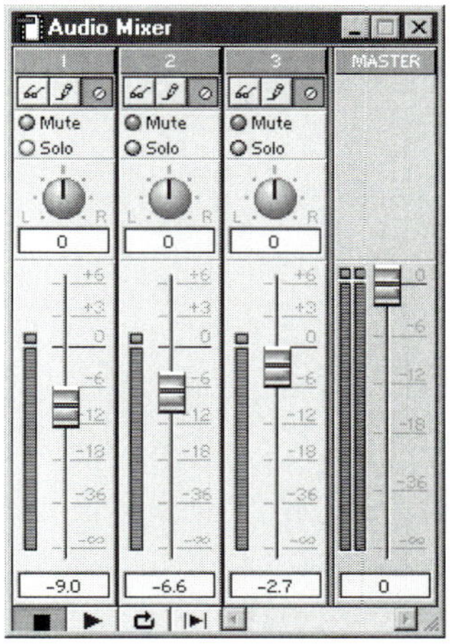

for web export, helping you select the proper balance of quality versus size in your output (Figure 1-9).

Premiere also offers an Advanced RealMedia Export feature that lets you hone in on just the right settings if you're outputting in RealMedia format. Outputting is discussed in Chapter 12.

That's all there is to creating a basic movie in Premiere. After you have a better understanding of the Premiere workspace and how the different tools work, you'll be able to breeze through the creation of a simple movie. In the next chapter, we examine each component of the Premiere workspace so you can become acclimated to your new surroundings.

NOTE Your working file in Premiere never actually affects your original video clips. Source clips stay intact no matter how much you chop them up and manipulate them. Thus, each time you open your Premiere file, the source files are located and loaded into the program. Sometimes you have to help Premiere find the source files, especially when folders have been moved from one location to another. On these occasions, Premiere displays a File Locator dialog box, seeking a particular file. If Premiere can't find the source clips or other assets assembled in your movie, they won't show up in the movie.

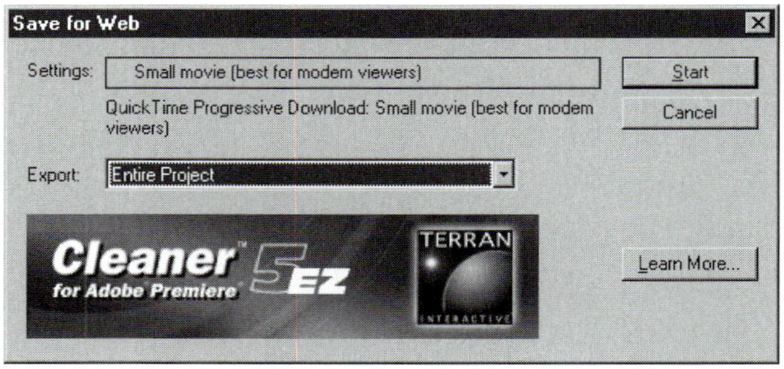

FIGURE 1-9
The Save For Web dialog box, with settings for exporting video output to the Web

2

Navigating Through the Premiere Workspace

In this chapter, we navigate through the Premiere workspace, which will give you a solid foundation on which to build major Premiere skills. Once you develop a comfort level with this workspace, you'll be better prepared to make movies. If it's the first time you've ever worked in a program like this, the interface may look puzzling and unfamiliar. We will examine all the windows in the workspace so you'll know why they exist and how they're used.

Creating a New Project

When you create a new production in Premiere, it's called a *project*. A project is a collection of files, including movies, audio, and information used to edit those files into the final production. The extension for a Premiere file is .ppj, which stands for "Premiere project."

The project file contains complete editing information about your finished movie and it can be used for both online and offline editing. It's important to remember that the project file references only the external *assets*. Assets are elements used to assemble a Premiere production such as audio clips, still graphics, titles, and video clips.

Your First Time in Premiere

The first time you open Premiere, which most of you have probably done already, you see the Initial Workspace dialog box. This box determines the display (editing mode) of your Premiere workspace.

In this box, you select between two displays: A/B Editing or Single-Track Editing (Figure 2-1). The A/B Editing workspace is recommended for beginners because, among other things, you can visualize how transitions superimpose over one another. We discuss transitions in Chapter 7. Pressing ENTER makes A/B Editing your default workspace.

FIGURE 2-1
The Initial Workspace dialog box appears the first time you launch Premiere on your computer

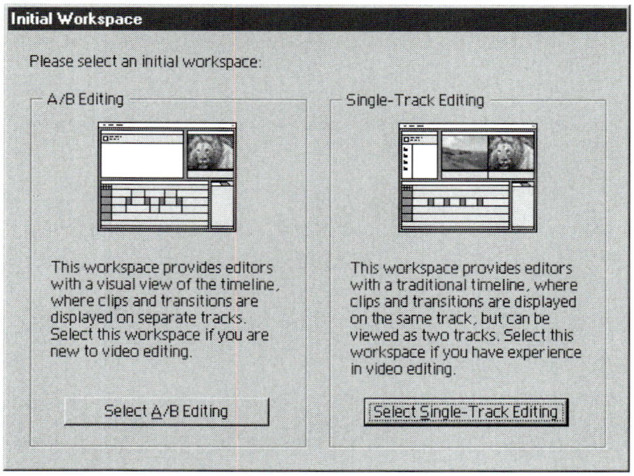

Single-Track editing, on the other hand, is often used by more-experienced Premiere users because they may not need the visual reassurance of seeing exactly how one clip transitions into another. Also if you're working in a single screen environment with limited screen real estate, a single track timeline will take up less screen space. You can easily change the editing mode at any time during production. In the section "Single-Track and A/B Editing," we'll look at these two editing modes and learn how to change the settings.

NOTE **When you open an existing project in Premiere, often you are prompted to locate the folder in which the assets are located. The Project file merely contains specific instructions for these assets, so each time you open the file, they must be located again. Make sure you pay careful attention to how you organize your project so these assets can be easily located whenever the project file is opened.**

- To create a new file in Premiere: Select File | New Project from the menu.
- To open an existing project: Select File | Open and navigate to the folder where the Premiere file is located.

THE PROJECT SETTINGS DIALOG BOX

You've probably figured out by now that when you begin a new file in Premiere, it's known as a project. You'll see this term used in different parts of the Premiere workspace and interface. A finished Premiere movie is known as a "production." This is the goal you're working toward as you assemble and edit all the various assets into a finished movie.

Before you start working on your new project, you must define the parameters of your workspace in the Load Project Settings dialog box (Figure 2-2).

This dialog box contains presets (suggested settings) for a variety of editing environments. For example, if you want to capture video from a DV camcorder attached to your computer via FireWire (IEEE1394) and you live in the U.S., chances are you'll select one of the DV-NTSC presets. Or, if you want to use QuickTime stock footage clips for a web production, you'd probably select one of the multimedia presets. The nice thing about presets is that if you're a beginner, you can choose one and be reasonably assured your production will turn out okay. But to have full control over your production, you still must know what all the settings mean.

FIGURE 2-2
The Load Project Settings dialog box contains various preestablished settings for a workspace

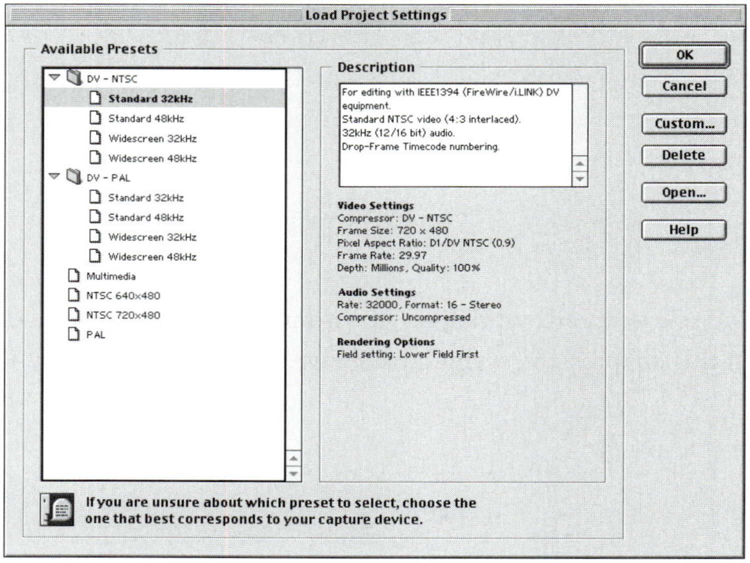

The settings you choose in this dialog box will ultimately affect the outcome of your final movie and, as such, are important. We discuss the settings in more detail in Chapter 3. It's important to select the proper settings for your project at the beginning, so you don't have to restart from scratch. Let's become familiar with some settings.

The Available Presets at the left side of the dialog box consist of many DV-NTSC, DV-PAL, and multimedia settings. When you select any of these, the description of the preset appears at the right side of the dialog box. Also included are the preset's properties, such as video settings, audio settings, and rendering options.

After you choose a preset and check out its contents in the right column, you can modify the preset by clicking the Custom button to access the Project Settings window.

NOTE **DV always stands for digital video, referring generally to your camcorder type. NTSC stands for National Television Standards Committee. PAL stands for Phase-Altering Line. These terms probably don't mean much to you if you're a beginner. The most important concept to understand at this point is that NTSC format is used in the U.S. and PAL format is used in Europe and other countries. Video equipment, such as camcorders, televisions, and VCRs, will conform to one format or another, depending on the country in which you bought it. Suffice to say, you should stick with the format (selected in your Premiere settings) familiar to your country of origin, or your Premiere movie won't play back correctly on your equipment.**

These settings are important for your project because they set the stage for the future properties of your movie, like the size of the frames and the rate at which they will play. For the next few chapters, we'll use the settings I instruct you to use for tutorial purposes. After that, you'll understand settings better and will be able to choose your own with confidence.

THE PREMIERE WINDOWS

Once you've selected your workspace environment, the Premiere workspace appears. In this chapter, the spring.ppj file we reviewed in Chapter 1 is used as an example to walk through the Premiere workspace. You can either follow along using this movie as a reference, which is located on the CD in the chapter 02 folder, or you can use the movie file Ztour.ppj located on your hard drive in the Premiere 6.0 folder\Sample Folder (see the following illustration). Alternatively, you can refer to the figures in this book.

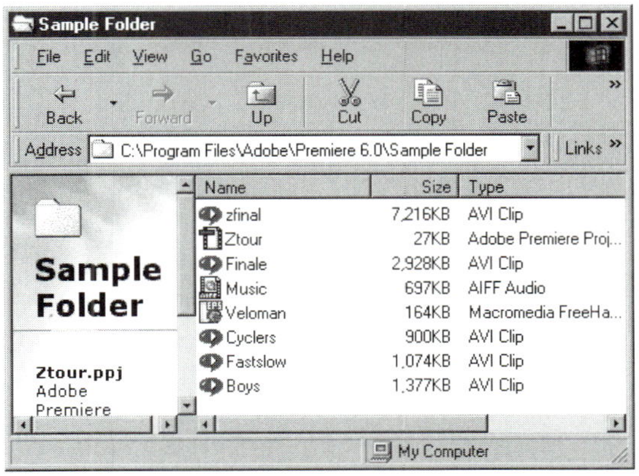

- If you use the spring.ppj file, copy the folder from the hard drive to your hard disk.
- If you decide to refer to a Premiere file (.ppj) to follow along with this chapter, first launch Premiere and then open the file (spring.ppj or ztour.ppj) by selecting File | Open from the menu.

Navigate to the appropriate folder. Once you locate the file, click Open. You will see a Locate File dialog box if any source files, or files linked to the project,

> **NOTE** Premiere users often use two monitors when they assemble a video: one for the workspace and the other for the Program view. The Program view is the movie that's been assembled and edited. For people who do heavy editing, it's easier to view the results of the movie being assembled apart from the rest of the workspace.

have been moved outside their folder (as in the following illustration). If you do see this, navigate to the file's current location or click on the Find button on the Mac.

TIP **The Introduction in this book explains how to copy lesson folders from your CD to your hard drive.**

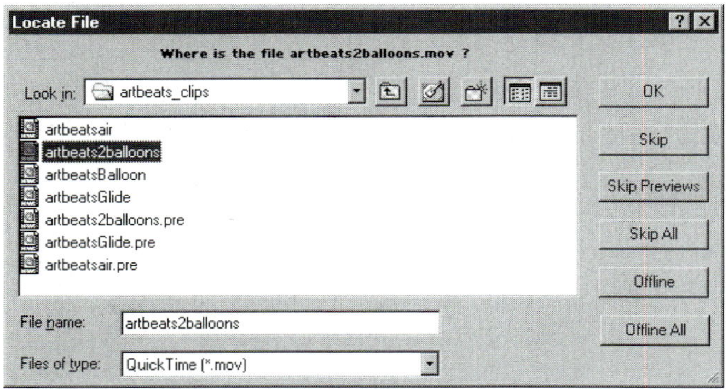

The main Premiere workspace consists of three windows used to assemble a Premiere movie: the Project window, the Monitor window, and the Timeline window (Figure 2-3). In all three windows, information about individual clips, or other assets, such as name, duration, and timecode, are displayed in easy-to-find locations.

NOTE **You may arrange the Premiere windows on your desktop any way you like. If your desktop looks crowded, you can close the windows by clicking the little box in the upper-left corner of the window. If you close the Timeline and Monitor windows, you can reopen them by selecting the window (Timeline and Monitor) from the Window menu. Closing the Project window closes the Premiere project file. In the figures and accompanying video CD, the workspace appears crowded to show all windows in the same area. However, when you create your Premiere movie, you'll probably use dual monitors or at least work in a higher screen resolution. Most likely you will be less crunched for workspace.**

The Project Window

Although all windows can be dragged anywhere in your workspace to personalize the display, the Project window's default display is in the upper-left corner of the desktop.

The Project window acts as a storage area for all the assets you'll use to assemble and edit your movie. These assets don't actually become a part of your video until they are placed in the Timeline window. However, it's much easier and neater to keep track of all the assets when you have a special area in which to organize them.

FIGURE 2-3

The three main windows in the Premiere workspace

Navigating the Project Window

As shown in Figure 2-4, the Project window for the spring.ppj movie has been extended so you can see all the fields of information. Ordinarily, you won't stretch the window out this much, but if you want the full story on any of your assets, you'll have to extend it. In fact, this window is navigated the same way you'd nav-

FIGURE 2-4

The Project window displayed as a list, extended horizontally to view all its information fields

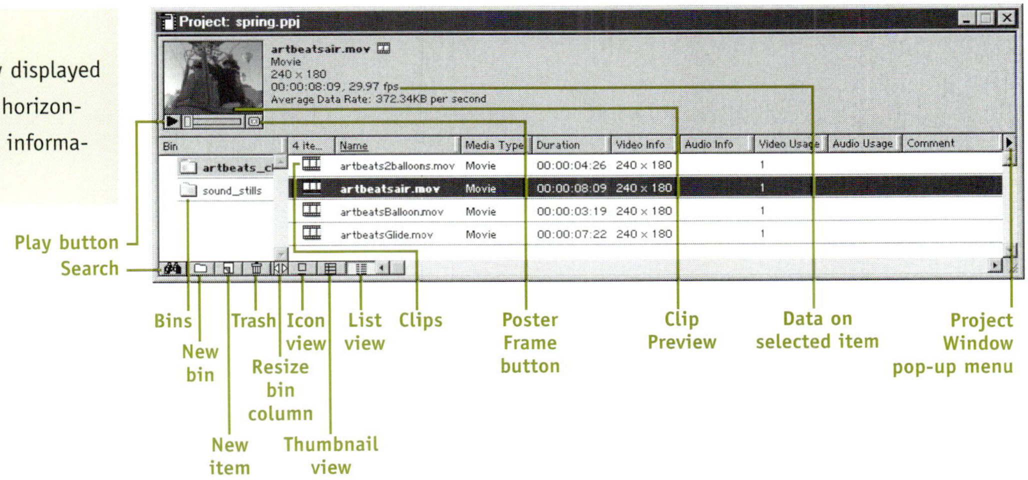

igate any window on your system's desktop. In addition to extending the window, you can customize the view, expand it, collapse it, and scroll through it.

The List view in the Program window is the default view. You can change this view by clicking the little icons at the bottom of the window. In fact, selecting these icons gives you an idea of what the view will look like.

To Change the view in the Project window, click any one of the following icons:

1. **The List view, which depicts assets as little black and white icons with information fields to the right of the icons**
2. **The Icon view, which depicts asset as large icons with title and timecode listed underneath the icon (see the top illustration)**

3. **The Thumbnail view, which depicts assets as a list with small color icons to the left and information fields to the right (as in the illustration to the right)**

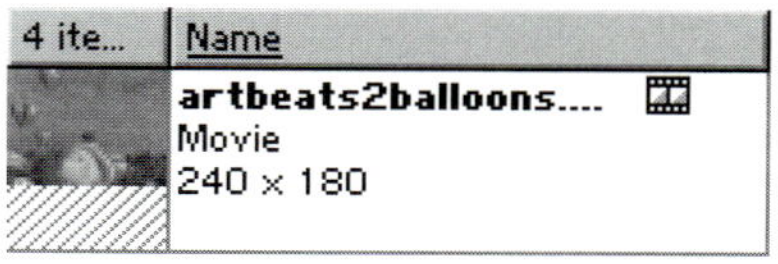

If you click individual assets in the right column of the dialog box, a Preview window appears at the window's upper left. Here, you can preview a clip by using a mini play button at the bottom of the poster frame. The poster frame refers to the sample frame used to preview the clip or frame of a still image in the Thumbnail and Icon views in the Project window. You can change the poster frame in this preview by using the play button to select another frame and the slider to identify a new frame. Once you've selected the frame, click the Poster Frame button. A new frame will appear Figure 2-5.

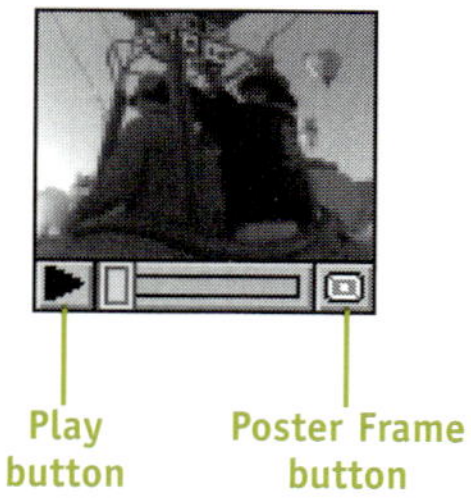

FIGURE 2-5
Preview of a clip in the Project window

BINS IN THE PROJECT WINDOW

> **TIP** **Bins can have subfolders, or nested bins.**

Bins are stored in the far-left column in the Project window. Similar to folders on a desktop, bins are another way to organize clips within the Project window. This is a great feature because sometimes your Project window can contain hundreds of assets. It's much simpler to browse through windows that are displayed in a logical manner relating to your project.

Notice in the previous figures of the Project window, there are two bins:

- artbeats_clips
- sound_stills

As you click each bin, the contents of the selected bin open in the right column of the Project window. When a bin is selected, the contents of the bin are displayed at the right side of the window.

CREATING AND MANAGING BINS Because bins help you organize your project, you must know how to manage them. You can create or manage a new bin several different ways. You can access bin and asset management options

- From the file menu
- From the Project window pop-up menu (see the illustration)
- From the context menu in the Project window
- From the buttons on the bottom left of the Project window

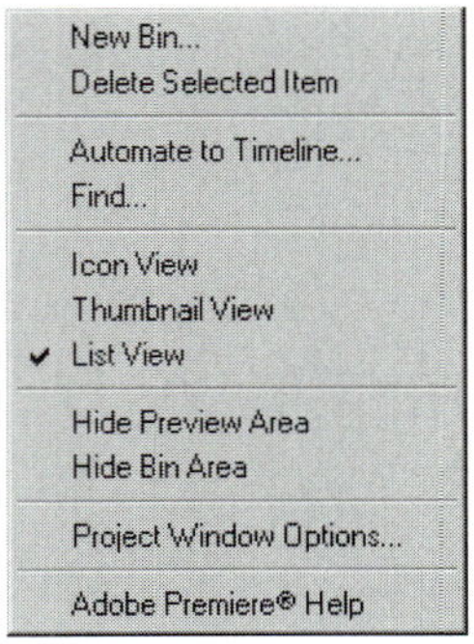

Probably the easiest way for a beginner to manage bins and their contents is to click the buttons at the bottom left of the Project window. Context menus also provide an easy way to select options.

Let's quickly review the bin management options:

- To create a new bin, click the New Bin button at the bottom left of the window.
- To delete a bin, drag it into the trash at the bottom left of the Project window.
- To drag the contents of one bin into another, click the bin you want to drag from, click the item to the right (press SHIFT and click to select more than one), and drag the items into the bin of choice at the left.

- To nest a bin inside another bin, drag one bin onto another.
- To hide bins, select Hide Bin Area from the context menu or the Project window pop-up menu.

TIP A context menu is a menu you can access within many programs. It provides a customized menu that lists all the menu elements relative only to the selected item or area. To use context menus, right-click (in Windows) or press CONTROL and click (on a Macintosh) in an area or on a specific object.

MODIFYING THE PROJECT WINDOW DEFAULT OPTIONS You can further customize the Project window's Icon, Thumbnail, and List views to accommodate your work style.

To display the Project Window Options dialog box, select Project Window Options from the Project window pop-up menu or context menu. In Figure 2-6, if you select List View from the pop-up menu, you can display or make invisible the Project fields that appear above the assets. The options available for the Thumbnail and Icon views both relate to the size and display of icons.

ADDITIONAL FEATURES IN THE PROJECT WINDOW If you peruse the pop-up Project menu, you'll notice a few other tasks you can perform in the project window.

- **Automate to Timeline** Displays the Automate to Timeline dialog box. You can automatically place all the items or selected items from the Project window in the Timeline, thus creating a rough cut of sorts. Although this method of making a movie has limitations, it might be appropriate for something very simple.

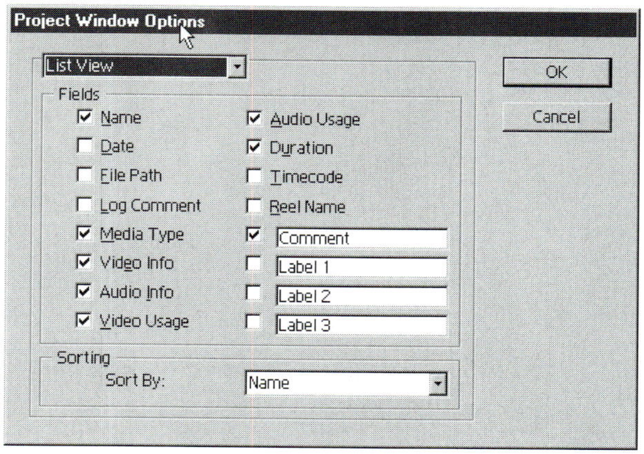

FIGURE 2-6
The Project Window Options dialog box, where you customize Icon, Thumbnail, and List views

- **Find** Displays the Find dialog box that searches and locates specific types of items.
- **Show Preview Area/Hide Preview Area** Lets you hide the Preview if you need more workspace.
- **Import File/Folder/Project (available only in context and top menus)** Lets you import, or bring assets, into your movie. When you import a video clip, still image, sound, or graphic, it always appears in the Project window.

As you can see, the Project window plays a major role in the making of a movie in Premiere. This is the area in which all assets are stored and managed. From here, they are brought into the other two windows, Monitor and Timeline.

In the next sections, we discuss these windows, describing their purpose and when and how to use them. In chapters 4 and 5, we'll delve further into the Monitor and Timeline windows and learn how to edit and assemble movies using these two windows as our primary tools.

Clip Windows

If you press Alt and double-click (in Windows) or press Option and double-click (on a Mac) any assets you've stored in the Project window, you can display them in their own clip windows. Video and audio clips can appear in clip windows (Figure 2-7).

The clip windows are free-floating replicas of the Source view, discussed in the next section. If you double-click a clip, it appears in the Monitor window's Source view. You can set a general default that opens a clip in its own clip window

FIGURE 2-7
A clip window appears when you double-click a video or an audio clip in the Project window

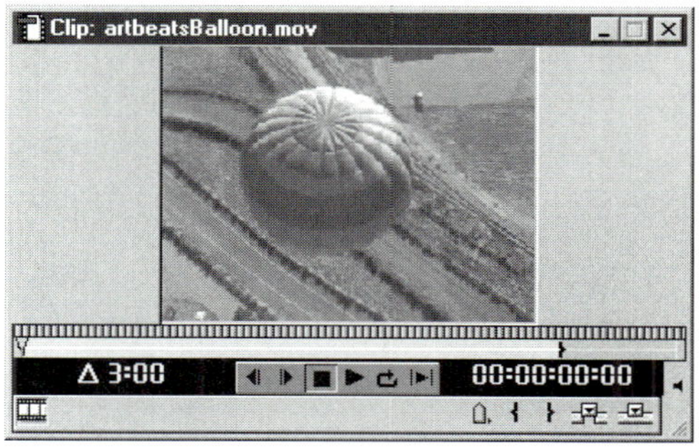

each time you double-click it. To do so, from the menu select Edit | Preferences | General and Still Image. If Open Movies in Clip Window is checked, clips will always open in their own windows (as in the illustration). This is true of clips in the Timeline as well.

TIP **The same process you use to open a clip in its own window from the Project window (ALT and double-click in Windows or OPTION and double-click on a Mac) can be used in clips in the Timeline, too.**

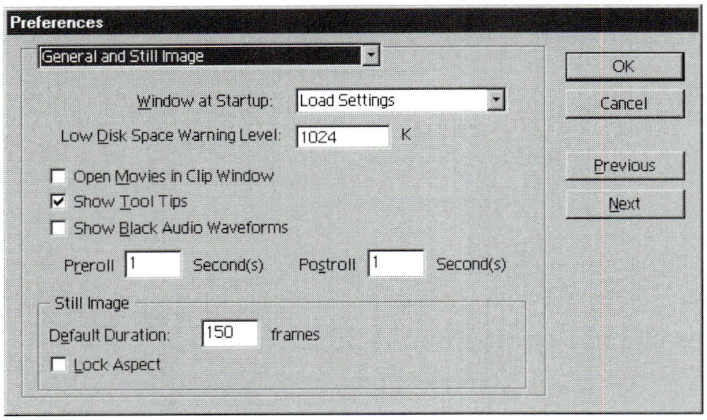

When the Monitor is in single-view mode, you view only the Program window as shown. If you view only the project in the Program window, to preview a source clip you'll have to open the clip in a clip window.

NOTE **You can also open a clip in its own window by right-clicking (in Windows) or pressing CONTROL and clicking (Mac) the clip In the Project window and selecting Open in Clip Window from the pop-up context menu.**

THE MONITOR WINDOW

The Monitor window is chock-full of features; use it to do much of the editing on your video clips. When you begin a new movie, the default Monitor window appears in the workspace (Figure 2-8). You preview your source clips and program in this window. It's important to understand the difference between the source clips and program before you begin editing because they appear almost identical to the beginner. They actually serve very different purposes and I'll explain the differences between both views in this section.

Source clips consist of your original video footage. You view them in the Source window. The Program is your final edited output; you view it in the Program window.

FIGURE 2-8
The Monitor window, where you preview your source clips and program

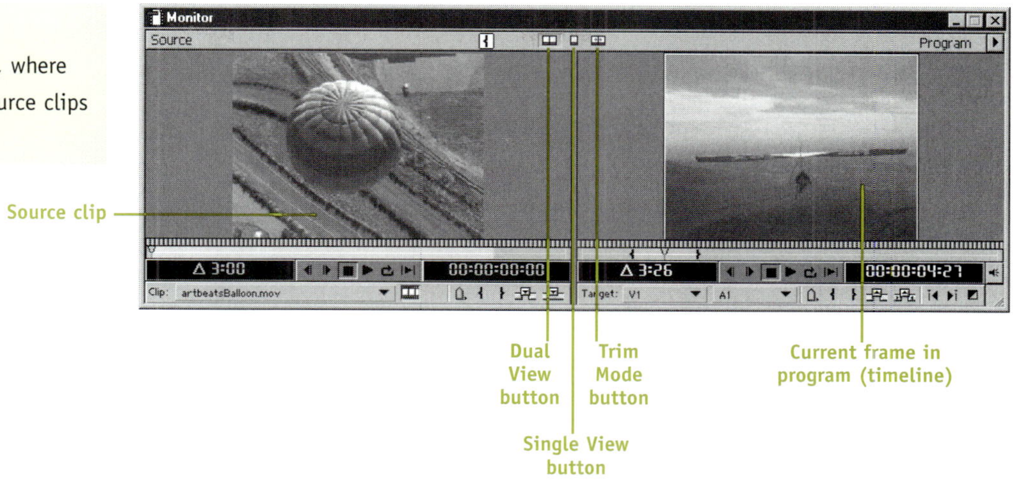

The time display in the production used in this chapter (spring.ppj) is 30 fps non–drop-frame timecode. Timecode counts the frames in your footage. This method of counting footage was developed by the Society of Motion Picture and Television Engineers, more commonly referred to as SMPTE, and is used for NTSC video. PAL video uses a different timecode.

Timecode counts hours, minutes, seconds, and frames of footage. The timebase for NTSC video is 29.97 frames per second, or fps, which is not a whole number. Because of the odd timebase of NTSC video, SMPTE timecode is counted in two ways: non–drop-frame and drop-frame.

Non drop-frame timecode counts 30 fps (the NTSC video timecode). With non drop-frame timecode, as time passes, a discrepancy begins to occur between the actual elapsed time versus the timecode readout. If you're a beginner or your production is very small, this discrepancy may not be an issue for you. This format is commonly used on source tapes. In the Monitor window, the timecode for non-drop frames is displayed with colons between numbers.

Drop-frame timecode fixes timecode so the NTSC timebase of 29.97 reads out accurately. It makes an adjustment by counting 30 fps and then skipping two frame numbers at the end of every minute, except every 10 minutes. This slight adjustment makes the timebase accurate to 29.97. Most DV cameras record in drop-frame timecode. Drop-frame timecode is displayed in the Monitor window with semicolons between numbers.

In the Monitor window, you can play both the source and program clips with control buttons located at the bottom of each view. You can also drag, or scrub, the Frame Locator to manually control playback. As you play back the clips in the Source and Program views, the frames in these views depict their timecode under each view. In the Source view, the timecode reflects the current position of the Frame Locator in this view. In the Program view, the timecode represents the current position of the Frame Locator in this view and the current position of the Edit line in the Timeline.

SOURCE VIEW

The Source view appears at the left of the Monitor window when the Monitor is in dual-view mode. The Source view is used to test, preview, and edit source clips. Source clips are stored in the Project bin and are the ingredients that will be used for your recipe, the production. In this window, they are prepared and then assembled in the Timeline (Figure 2-9).

FIGURE 2-9
The Source view in the Monitor window

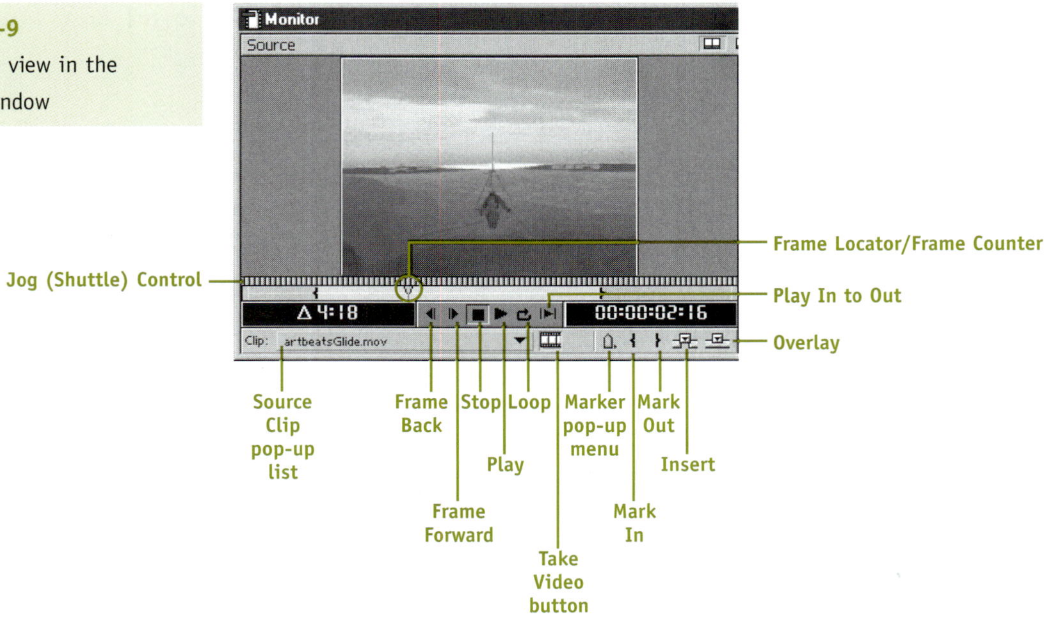

PROGRAM VIEW

The Program view (Figure 2-10) is where you preview your final production. Here you can see how all the ingredients of the production flow together after being assembled in the Timeline. In fact, the Program view represents what's in the Timeline. The difference between the two is that the Timeline lets you see the entire movie laid out, almost like a progress chart—a physical representation of where the movie is coming from and where it's going. In the Program window, the movie plays back the sum of the Timeline's contents.

NOTE **The clips used in the Monitor window are similar to those in the Project window in that the physical clip on your hard drive is not altered when you edit or delete a clip in this window. Only the instructions on each clip become part of the project file you're generating.**

In the next section, we cover the Timeline window features. The Timeline window works hand-in-hand with the Monitor window. Both windows perform many of the same functions in different ways.

FIGURE 2-10
The Program view in the Monitor window

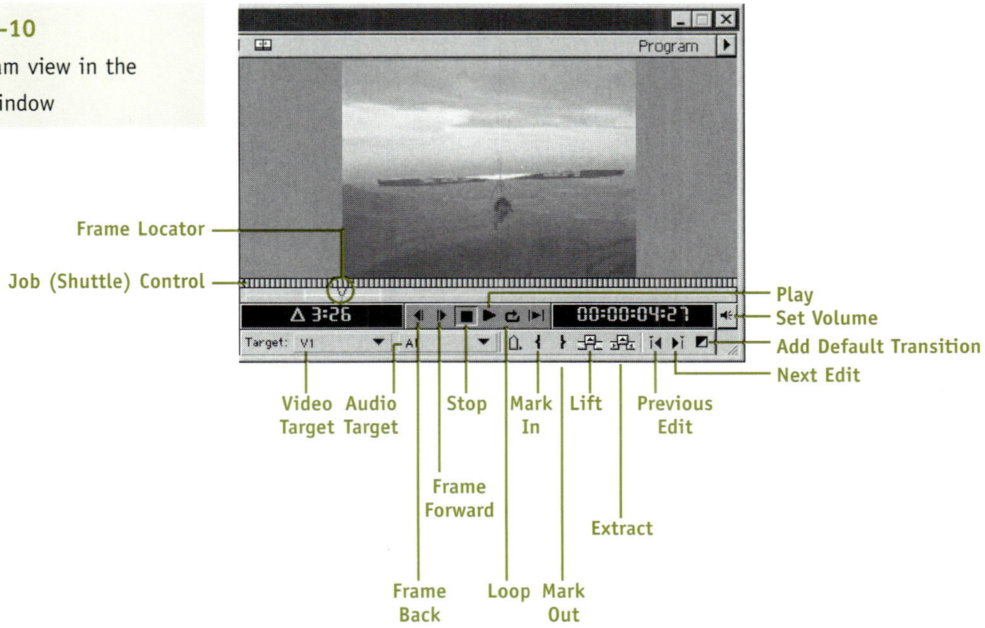

THE TIMELINE WINDOW

The Timeline window gives you a visual representation of the shape your movie is taking. It also lets you see how all your clips move sequentially in time. This makes it easier to make editing decisions during the production process.

The Timeline is packed with many features, as shown in Figure 2-11.

The Timeline is composed of video and audio tracks. Audio clips, video clips, and still-image graphics are visually represented on these tracks.

The main track is Video Track 1. The Timeline also gives you a Video Track 2 and three audio tracks under Video Track 1. Video tracks numbered greater than 1 take precedence over lower-numbered tracks. You can create up to 99 tracks in Premiere. To create a new track, access the pop-up Timeline menu in the upper-right corner and select Add Video Track or Add Audio Track.

All the assets that make up your movie will appear in the Timeline. In the Timeline, you can arrange and edit clips just as you can in the Monitor window. The Timeline gives you a more visual representation of the process than does the Monitor window. Often, more-experienced video editors opt to assemble and edit their source clips in the Monitor window. However, many people use both the Monitor window and the Timeline in combination to achieve the same outcome.

FIGURE 2-11
The Timeline window (Single-Track Editing mode)

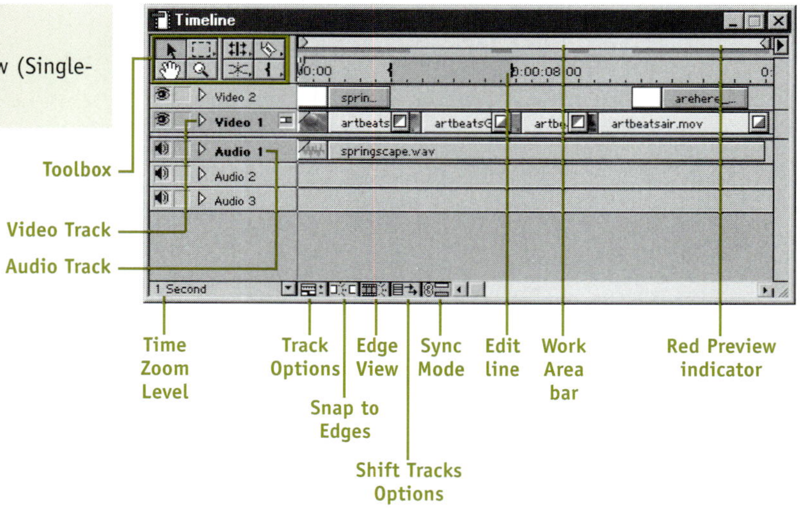

Single-Track and A/B Editing

Remember the dialog box that was displayed the first time you launched Premiere? The results of your choice in this dialog box are depicted in the Timeline. Recall that you had to select either Single-Track or A/B Editing. Now you understand what a track is. But what's the difference between a Single and an A/B Track? You'll be amazed at how simple the answer to this question is.

In Single-Track Editing, the Timeline displays Video Track 1 as a single track when in fact it's composed of a Track A and B. Track 1A is the base track and Track 1B is where clips live that transition into one another. There is also a third track where the actual transition clip lives. This is called the Transition Track.

> **TIP** Premiere uses Tool Tips in windows. Tool Tips are little labels that appear when you place your mouse over icons in windows, telling icon names. This is a great feature when you're learning a new program. For Tool Tips to work, though, the icons must reside in the currently selected window. To select a window, just click it. If you don't see a Tool Tip when you place your cursor over an icon, select Edit | Preferences | General and Still Image. In this dialog box, make sure Show Tool Tips is checked.

The movie in Chapter 1 used Transition techniques on a few clips. The transitions used a dissolve technique, which gave the soft illusion of one clip melting into another. If you click the expandable Track mode button in Video Track 1, you can see how the transition transforms one clip into one another.

In contrast to Single-Track Editing, A/B Track Editing visually displays both Tracks A and B on Video Track 1 (see the illustration). If you're a beginner and have a hard time visualizing what transitions do, you may be more comfortable starting with the A/B mode.

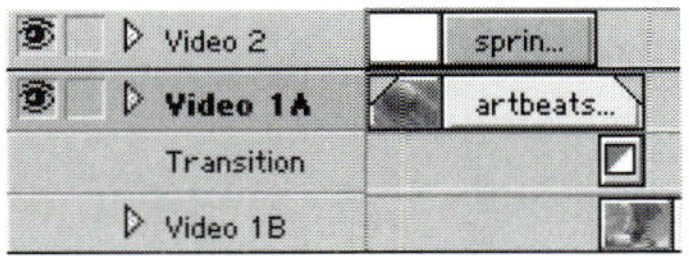

If you change your mind, you can easily switch between Single-Track Editing and A/B Editing in the Timeline pop-up menu.

Moving Around the Timeline

The Timeline gives you a visual representation of where each frame is in time, how long it is, and where every element sits in relation to other elements within your movie.

Generally, you'll be working with the Monitor window and Timeline closely together, especially when you need to go back and polish your movie to bring it closer to the final production.

THE TIME RULER At the top of the Timeline window is a Time Ruler, which lets you see where your clips exist in time. You can easily modify it to reflect a different zoom and timecount.

To modify the Timeline's zoom, click the Time Zoom Level pop-up menu located at the bottom left of the Timeline (see the illustration on the right). You can view the Timeline in different frame, second, or minute increments.

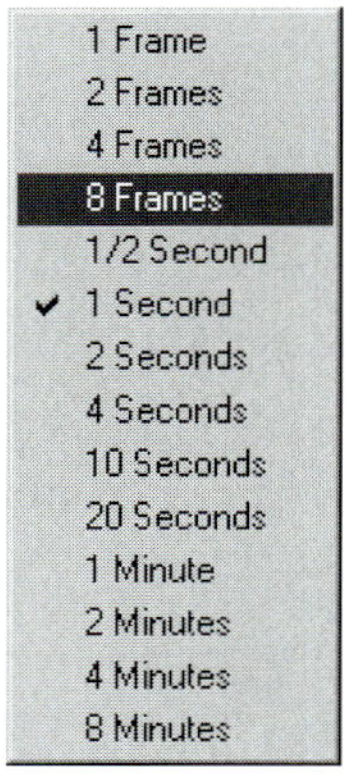

You can also zoom in the Timeline using the Zoom tool in the Timeline toolbar (see the illustration below). In zoom mode, the magnifying glass displays a plus (+) sign. To use this tool, click the magnifying glass and bring the icon to the Timeline. Click near the area on which you want to zoom.

To reduce the zoom level, press ALT and click (Windows) or press OPTION and click (Mac). The magnifying glass displays a minus in the center when reducing the zoom.

Notice that when you zoom in and out of the Timeline, the ruler is always visible to orient you to where you are at any given time.

In the Timeline Window Options dialog box, you can customize the Timeline by changing the display of icons on clips and clip format on a track (Figure 2-12). You access this dialog box from the Timeline pop-up menu or context menu.

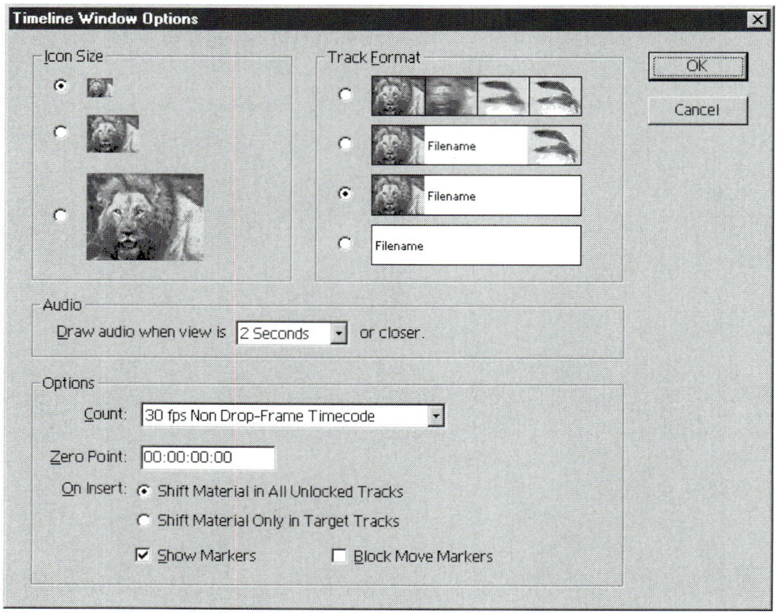

FIGURE 2-12
The Timeline Window Options dialog box

THE EDIT LINE The Edit line is the little upside-down triangle with a thin, vertical black line extending from it (see the illustration). As you scrub this triangle across the ruler area, the movie plays back, frame by frame, in the Program view. The Program view provides a good example of how both windows work well together. The Program view not only gives you a motion version of the movie, it also tells you the exact frame number you're scrubbing over in the Timeline.

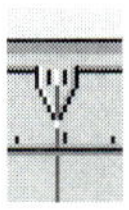

ADDITIONAL TOOLS

There are many additional tools, windows, buttons, and menus within the Timeline. Some of the editing tools won't make much sense this early in the book, so we'll review just a few of the simple navigation tools.

TIMELINE TOOLBOX In the upper-left section of the toolbar is a small grouping of tools (Figure 2-13). The first tool is the Selection tool, used to physically select and/or move a single clip. The tools to the right of this are various clip-editing and selection tools. On the right side of the toolbar, each one contains a fly-out panel listing additional tools. Whatever tool you've selected becomes the current icon.

The bottom-left tool is the Hand tool used to scroll through the timeline. To use the Hand tool, select the tool and bring it into the Timeline. Drag the hand to navigate quickly and scroll through the Timeline.

The Zoom tool, discussed in the earlier Zoom Tool section, lets you zoom in and out on the Timeline.

The Link tool lets you link video and audio clips together or unlink them. For example, if you decided to delete the sound that was linked to a video clip, you could use this tool to unlink the audio track from the video track so you could then delete the audio without deleting the video. Like the other editing tools, this tool has a fly-out panel that includes additional editing icons.

FIGURE 2-13
The Toolbox in the Timeline

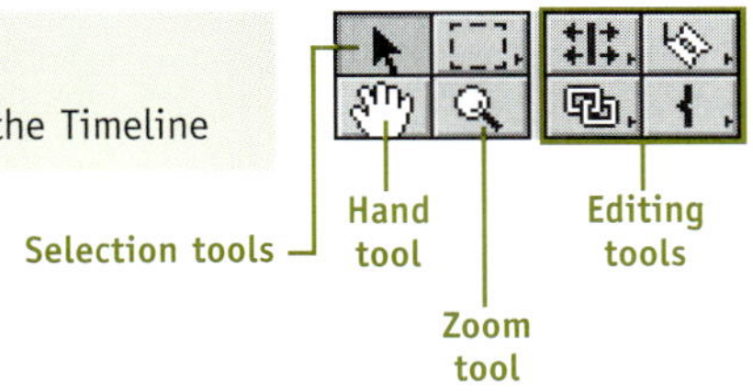

Timeline Tracks

Under the Toolbox in the Timeline are the Tracks. When you're learning how to navigate the Timeline, it's important to understand the icons on the tracks. Following is a list of some of the major icons on the tracks:

- **Eye icon** The Shy video track (visibility) icon (see the illustration). If the eye is showing, the track is visible in the Program window; if the eye is gone, the track won't appear in the Program window. Use this feature to turn off other tracks if you want to view a track alone.

- **Lock/Unlock Track icon** The box at the right of the eye icon. When a track is locked, a lock appears. When it's unlocked, it remains blank. When a track is locked, you cannot manipulate it.
- **Speaker icon** Resides on the audio tracks (see the illustration). When a speaker is showing, the sound (if any) on that track is audible. If there is no speaker, the sound is inaudible (if there are clips on the track).

Adding and Deleting Tracks

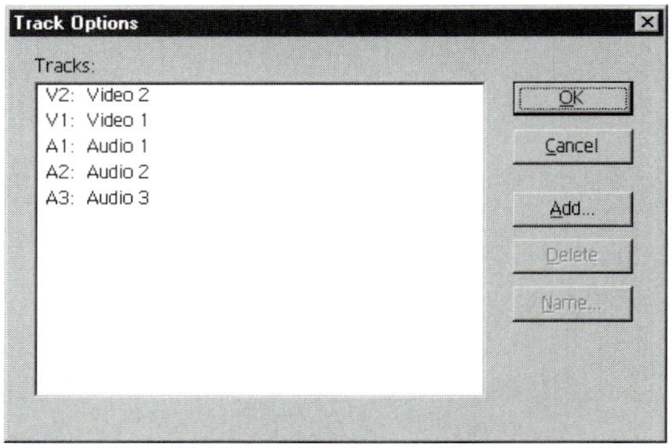

Adding and deleting tracks is an easy task in Premiere. As with many other Premiere features, you can choose from a variety of ways to do this.

To add tracks, you can select from the context menu or pop-up Timeline menu. But probably the easiest, most visual way for a beginner is the Track Options dialog icon in the bottom-left corner. When you click this, it displays a dialog box from which you can add and delete tracks (as in the illustration). You can also name a track in this dialog box.

The Storyboard Window

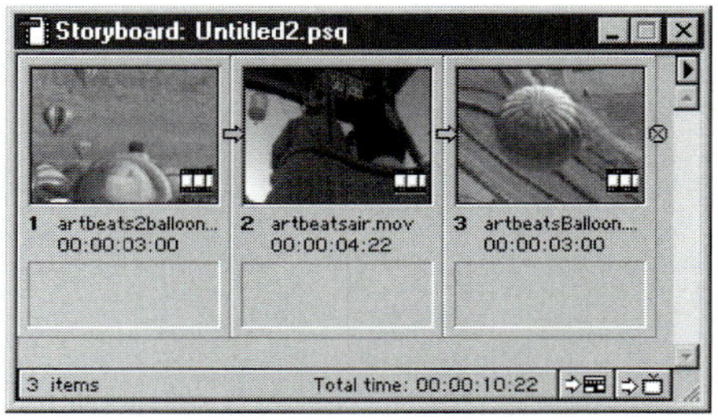

The Storyboard window is new to Premiere 6 (see the illustration). This window lets you create a visual storyboard from the clips in your Project window.

Not only is the Storyboard window great for depicting a real storyboard, it helps you decide how to sequence your clips in the Timeline.

Making a Storyboard

Create a storyboard for your movie by selecting File | New Storyboard. You can create and edit the storyboard by dragging the source clips from the Project window into the storyboard. Then you arrange them in the sequence that you want them to appear in the Timeline.

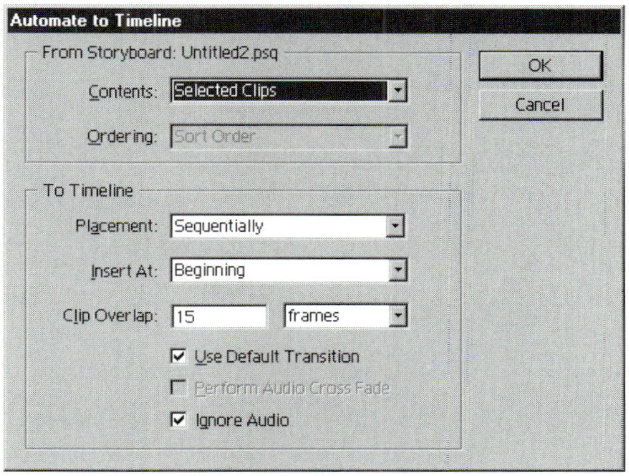

From there, you can select the Automate to Timeline button to access the Automate to Timeline dialog box (as in the illustration). Access this dialog box from either the icon at the bottom of the Storyboard window, the pop-up Storyboard menu, or the context menu. In the Automate to Timeline dialog box, you can custom-select how you want the contents of the storyboard to appear in the Timeline.

After you click the OK button, the contents of the storyboard (as per your customized set of instructions in the Automate to Timeline dialog box) appear in the Timeline.

Note that the same feature is available via the Project window. If you view the contents of the Project window in Icon mode, the icons can be positioned in the same way they can in the Storyboard window. You can access the Automate to Timeline dialog box for the Project window in that window's context and pop-up menus.

Managing Your Storyboard

Storyboards are saved just like any other file in the folder where your movie is located.

To Save a storyboard:

- **Select File | Save from the menu. Storyboards are saved with a .psq extension.**

To Close A STORYBOARD:

- **Click the box in the upper-left corner of the window, or select File | Close from the top menu. Make sure if you want to close only the Storyboard that only the Storyboard window is selected.**

To Open AN EXISTING STORYBOARD:

- **Select File | Open from the menu.**

THE AUDIO MIXER WINDOW

In the earlier Timeline Window section, we looked at the audio tracks in the Timeline. In the Audio Mixer window, you can adjust the sound on each individual sound track. The Audio Mixer window looks similar to a professional mixing board and has an easy-to-use interface. This is a useful window because it gives you complete control over the sound levels on each track.

Figure 2-14 shows the Audio Mixer window. This window mirrors the tracks in the Timeline. The corresponding audio track number appears at the top of each mixing column and the Master track includes all audio tracks. If you add more audio tracks, the Audio Mixer will indicate the additional tracks by adding them

FIGURE 2-14
The Audio Mixer window, where you adjust the volume level of sound tracks

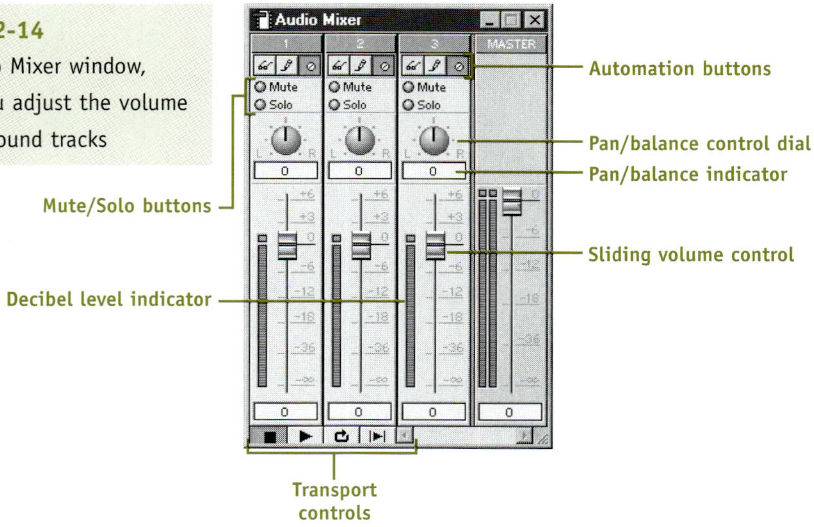

to the right of the window. From this window, you can adjust the volume level of clips on each track. The volume is measured in decibels (dB) and is indicated as a number at the bottom of each audio track. You can enter this number manually or by dragging the sliding volume fader control up and down. The higher the number, the louder the audio, and vice versa. You can also adjust the pan/balance between speakers.

The three automation buttons appear as eyeglass, pencil, and slashed circle icons, respectively, at the top of each track. These buttons let you record or store audio adjustments or ignore them.

At the top of the window, you can also make tracks mute or solo. This lets you selectively listen to certain tracks while turning off others. Clicking the Mute button turns off the audio for that track. Clicking the Solo button turns off the audio for all the other tracks and lets you hear the soloed track by itself.

In Chapter 11, when we discuss sound in Premiere, we'll experiment more with the Audio Mixer window.

ACCESSING THE PREMIERE PALETTES

You can expand the Premiere workspace to include a number of smaller windows, which are accessible in the window menu. The smaller windows are known as floating palettes.

These palettes give you instant access to a myriad of different features, including information about your movie, effects, and audio mixing (see the illustration). If you're working in a single-monitor environment and aren't using any of the palettes at a given moment, you'll probably want to display palettes on an "as-needed" basis.

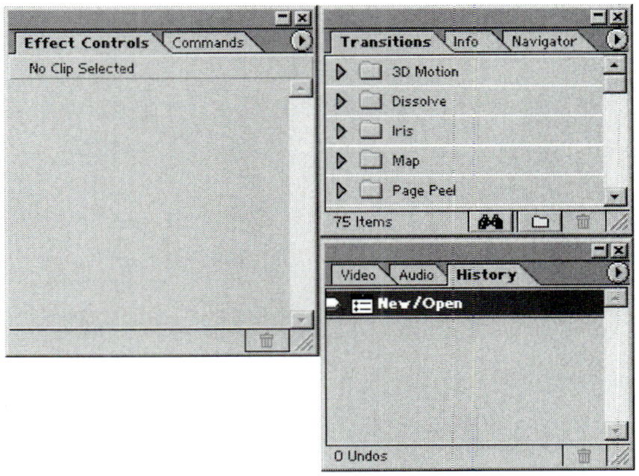

You access the palettes from the window menu. By default, some palettes are grouped together in one large palette to economize on desktop space. To access a palette, simply click a tab with the name of the palette you want to view. As you do this, the palette's contents appear at the bottom of the window.

Palettes can be moved anywhere within the Premiere workspace, and just like any window, they can be expanded, collapsed, and navigated. You can tear off any palette from a grouping by clicking its tab and dragging the palette out onto the workspace. You can also regroup palettes by clicking a tab and dragging it to another palette. Thus, you can arrange palettes in any way that suits your working style.

The following palettes are available in Premiere:

- **Navigator** Gives you a thumbnail representation of the Timeline. You can drag the green rectangle in the box to navigate to a specific point on the Timeline. This palette also contains zoom controls at the bottom.
- **History** Lets you jump to a specific point in your project and undo a move. This provides a great way to correct mistakes.
- **Commands** Lets you select commands right from a palette as opposed to using the menus, pop-up windows, or shortcut keys. You can load additional commands or delete them from this palette.
- **Transitions** Select Transitions and special effects for audio and video in this palette. When a clip replaces another in your Timeline, you can use Transitions to make the change more gradual and apply a customized effect to the way this transition occurs. Transitions include effects such as dissolve features that give the appearance of one clip melting into another.
- **Audio and Video Effects** Add special effects to your audio and video. For example, with the video effects, you can manipulate the brightness, contrast, or tint of a clip and add textures to it, among many other selections. Audio effects include standard effects found in audio-editing programs.
- **Effect Controls** Lets you customize effects. Different settings and dialog boxes can be accessed through this panel, depending on the effect you've selected.
- **Info** Gives you information about a selected element. It indicates what type of object you've selected, its name, and properties associated with the element.

As we begin making movies in Premiere, we'll use the features from these palettes. There are numerous additional features in the Premiere workspace, many of which we'll use throughout the rest of the book.

> **ON THE VIRTUAL CLASSROOM CD-ROM** **In Lesson 1, "Using the Project Window," the instructor introduces you to the features of the Project window and discusses how to navigate through it.**

3

The Project Settings Dialog Box

The Project Settings dialog box is one of the most important windows you'll encounter in Premiere because this is where your production begins to take shape. The settings you choose will be based upon your final output goal, whether that be a production for the Web, CD-ROM, or one of the other myriad of output options available in Premiere. These settings let you customize your video's properties. You can change most settings at any time during the movie-making process. Nevertheless, it's prudent to plan the entire process and decide ahead of time what settings will work best for your production. This way, you can avoid revising major portions of your production late in the game.

If you're a beginner, many of these settings will look strange You don't have to deal with this dialog box at all if you can locate a preset that's suitable for your production when you begin a project. The presets are available in the Load Project Settings dialog box that appears when you begin a project in Premiere.

NOTE In Windows, this dialog box is called the New Project Settings dialog box. On the Mac, it's called the Project Settings dialog box.

If you decide to select a preset from the Load Project Settings dialog box, you don't have to worry about customizing settings in the Project Settings dialog box because Premiere does it for you. For a beginner, the presets make life easy. When you're more comfortable with the process, you can wander into the numerous settings in the Project Settings dialog box and tweak them to your liking.

Many third-party manufacturers of video cards that work with Premiere provide presets specifically for that hardware in the card's installation software. Because of this, you should install Premiere first so the video card's software can locate Premiere on your system and install these presets. This way, you'll find presets in the Load Project Settings dialog box that match your card. Using these custom presets for your video card avoids potential configuration problems.

Load (New) Project Settings

In Chapter 2, you learned that when you begin a new movie in Premiere, the Load Project Settings dialog box appears. This dialog box offers several common preset combinations. Not knowing what these settings mean is like living in a foreign country and not speaking the language. You may get by for a little while, but to fully function, you need to speak the language. Ultimately in Premiere, you have to control what you're selecting to obtain your desired results.

Customize Project Settings

In the Load Project Settings dialog box (accessed by selecting File | New Project) is a button at the right labeled "Custom..." (see Figure 3-1). Click this button to access the Project Settings dialog box.

In the Project Settings box, you can customize your settings before or during your project (see the illustration on the next page). Settings are available in five

FIGURE 3-1
Load Project Settings dialog box with a customized preset called "virtual classroom book"

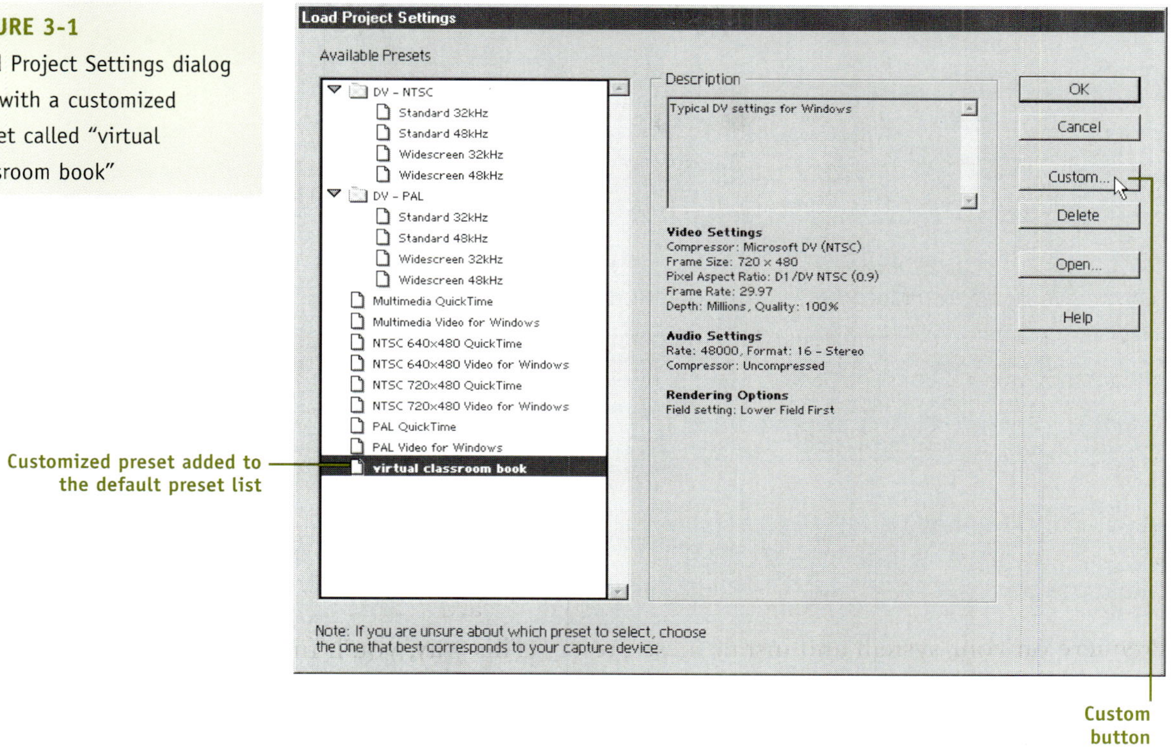

categories: General, Video, Audio, Keyframe and Rendering, and Capture. When you select a settings category from the pop-up menu in the top left of the Project Settings dialog box, a panel will appear within the Project Settings dialog box with settings pertaining to the category you selected. You can also access these categories by clicking on the Next button in the bottom right corner. We'll be covering the different settings in each category throughout this chapter.

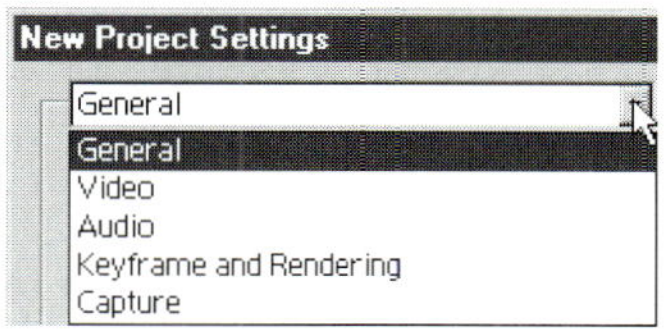

In the Load Project Settings dialog box in the previous figure, you'll notice I've created a custom preset called "virtual classroom video," which is now listed with all the default presets in the bottom of the left column. So you can create a custom preset, save it, and reuse it, instead of making new custom settings each time you begin a new movie. This is a convenient feature if you often create productions with the same settings.

Later in this chapter, we review the process of making and saving your own customized settings.

PROJECT SETTINGS DIALOG BOX

Although this dialog box looks small, it isn't. It lets you navigate to dialog box after dialog box right in the current window. Why does Premiere offer so many setting choices? Many people develop video for professional broadcasting in different countries with various video standards. Others are developing multimedia projects and still others are outputting video to the Web. Resolution, size, frame rate, and other aspects of these projects vary widely. Premiere provides many different video settings to accommodate the program's many different users and applications.

In addition to being able to access the Project Settings dialog box from within the Load Project Settings window, you can also access it from the main menu. If you select a preset, then change your mind and want to adjust a customized setting, go to Project | Project Settings | General in the menu (see Figure 3-2).

When the Project Settings dialog box is first displayed, the settings selected from the last project worked on are reflected in this box.

If you've never worked in Premiere before, the settings may seem foreign to you. Let's discuss what they mean.

GENERAL SETTINGS

In the General Settings box, you can select the Editing Mode, Timebase, Time Display, and review the Current Settings (see Figure 3-3). Following are descriptions of each setting.

EDITING MODE The Editing Mode is the video format you'll use. Typically, QuickTime format is used for the Mac, and Video for Windows format is used for Windows. Various compression methods will become available to you in the Project Settings Video Settings panel depending on which editing mode you select. Video must be compressed because digital video files are enormous. Digital video

FIGURE 3-2
You can also access the Project Settings dialog box from the Premiere menu

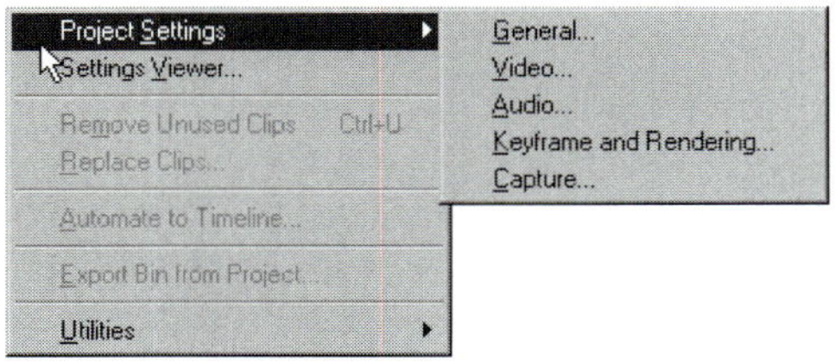

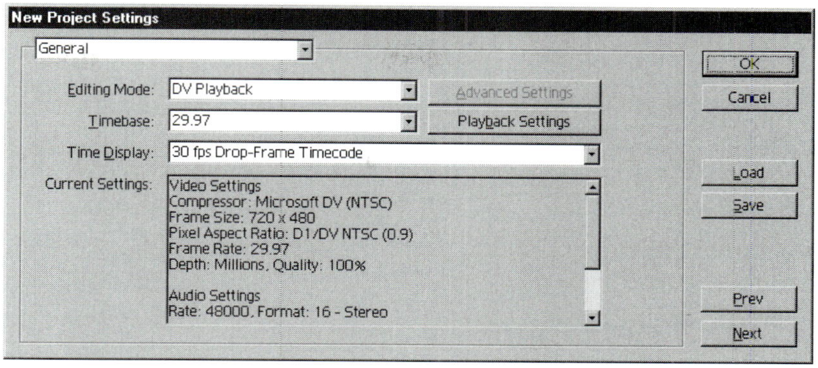

FIGURE 3-3 In the General Settings panel, you can set the editing mode, timebase, and time display

and audio use something called a "codec" (short for compression/decompression) to compress and decompress clips.

Many different codecs are available for compression and some methods enable you to compress digital video into smaller file sizes than others and sometimes at the expense of image quality. Compression is used when capturing and rendering video. In the Project Settings Video Settings panel, you can change the compression type. We'll be taking a closer look at the Video Settings panel more closely in the next section.

TIMEBASE Timebase is a pop-up menu in the General Settings panel with several selections. Timebase simply refers to time divisions in frames. When editing video, you can calculate an exact position for your edit because of the timebase. You can actually see the timebase on the front of many camcorders. It looks like a little stopwatch with digital numbers that count when a tape is running (see Figure 3-4).

> **NOTE** ***Capturing*** **refers to the process of getting your video from a tape in your camcorder or VCR to the desktop.** ***Rendering*** **refers to the mathematical calculation performed on frames that have transformations or other special effects applied. Rendering enables you to preview the playback of these effects in the program.**

The following selections are the most commonly used settings for video timebase:

- 29.97 fps for NTSC (North American standard)
- 25 fps for PAL and SECAM (European standard)

TIME DISPLAY Time Display is another pop-up menu in the General Settings panel with several selections to choose from. As you probably guessed, *time display* refers to the way in which time is displayed in a project. Because time is an

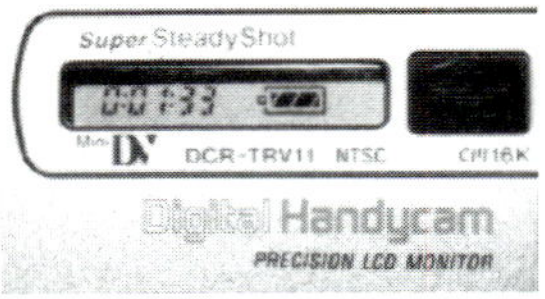

FIGURE 3-4
Many DV camcorders display the timebase (timecode) right on the camera as on this Sony TRV11

essential element in your editing process, this, like Timebase, is an important setting. Here are the most commonly used settings:

- 30 fps drop-frame timecode. Use this setting for standard NTSC broadcast video.
- 30 fps non–drop-frame timecode. Use this setting for web, CD, and DVD projects.
- 25 fps timecode. Use this setting for PAL and SECAM projects.

The timecode helps identify clips from your source video to your program. This is what makes frame-accurate editing possible in Premiere. With timecode, all information is recorded permanently to a specific time.

CURRENT SETTINGS The Current Settings box lists all the settings currently selected for your project. Once you change these settings in the Project Settings dialog box, the changes are reflected in the Current Settings box.

VIDEO SETTINGS

To navigate to the Video Settings panel in the Project Settings dialog box, either select Video from the top-left pop-up menu in the Project Settings dialog box or click the Next button at the bottom right of the dialog box. Let's review some of the key settings in this box (see Figure 3-5).

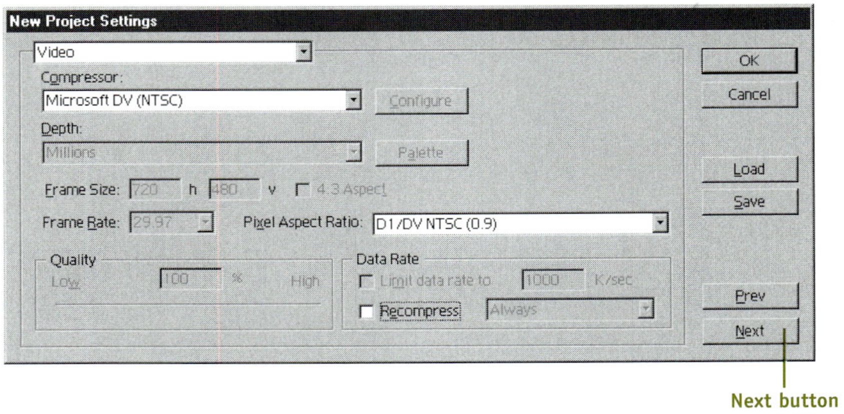

FIGURE 3-5
The Video Settings panel in the Project Settings dialog box

- **Compressor** Depending on which format you've selected in the General Settings dialog box (QuickTime or Video for Windows are the two most commonly used formats), the codecs available to you in this dialog box will change. Depending upon what platform you're working on (Windows or Mac), the settings will also vary. Microsoft DV-NTSC is selected for the settings in the dialog box in Figure 3-6. If I click in the drop-down menu for Compressor, I can view the other compression options available for QuickTime format. The drop-down menu depicted in Figure 3-6 is a Windows-based system using a DV preset.

NOTE **Compression, or codec, technology, is one of the most important aspects of digital video production and is a science unto itself. Compression is what enables you to use an application such as Premiere to edit videos on your desktop. Full-screen, uncompressed video is too large to work on even the biggest and fastest systems. Full-screen video is typically 1MB per frame. So even for a 30-second movie at 30 fps, the file size would be off the charts. This is why compression is necessary. One of the reasons digital video is so efficient is because the DV compression occurs in the camera, even before it gets to the desktop. DV compression offers high-quality output and manageable file sizes.**

- **Depth** Although this is not an option for DV, it is for other common compression formats such as Animation, Cinepak, and Sorenson Video. *Depth* simply refers to the amount of color (color bit depth) you want your video to display. This directly relates to the video's resolution as well as file size. For example, a file set to a depth of 256 colors would create an 8-bit color palette, making the video appear low resolution.
- **Frame Size** Select the pixel dimension of your final output here. Your source clips should match the dimensions of your frame size. It's very important that if you're capturing video, you want to make sure the capture dimensions are the same as the frame size you set in your video settings. If you're unsure of what size to select, sticking with the preset frame sizes are consistently a safe bet. For example, the preset size for DV is always 720 pixels in width by 480 pixels in height. Larger frame sizes dramatically increase file size but

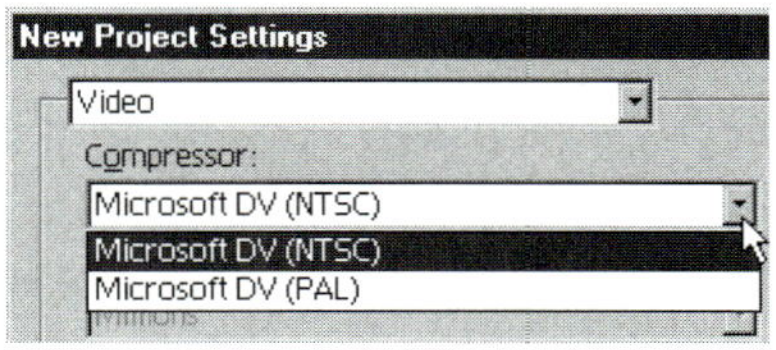

FIGURE 3-6
Various compression formats (codecs) can be selected from the Compressor pop-up list in the Video Settings panel

ensure a high quality level of output. Most often, video on the Web is sized on the small side at 320 × 240 pixels, or 240 × 180 to expedite loading time.

- **Aspect** This refers to clip-size ratio. Standard (analog) broadcasting video has a 4:3 size ratio. The exception to this rule is DV, which has a slightly different aspect ratio.
- **Pixel Aspect Ratio** This refers to the aspect ratio of the source clips. If your source clips are DV, your aspect ratio will be D1/DV NTSC (0.9). If your source clips are from an analog device, most likely the setting you choose will be Square Pixels.
- **Quality** A lower-quality setting reduces the quality of your final movie but also reduces the file size. You need to achieve a delicate balance of quality versus size. Certain compressors (codecs) are not affected by adjusting the picture quality setting. Such is the case with DV, which maintains a high picture quality regardless of the selected setting.

AUDIO SETTINGS

The audio settings determine the quality of the audio and ultimately the final file size. For example, selecting stereo settings can greatly increase file size compared to mono settings. To navigate to the Project Settings Audio Settings panel, either select Audio from the Project Settings pop-up menu or click the Next button at the bottom right of the Project Settings dialog box. Let's review some of the main settings in this box (see Figure 3-7).

- **Rate** The Rate setting refers to the sampling rate frequency of the sound in the movie. The Rate selections appear in a pop-up menu (see the illustration).

FIGURE 3-7
The Audio Settings panel

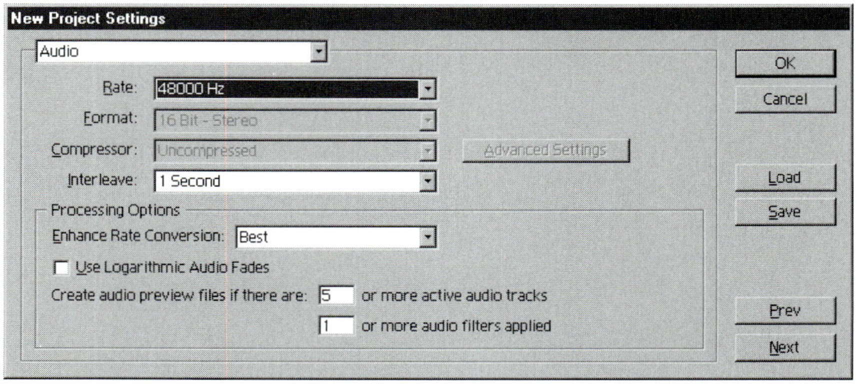

Digital frequencies, such as the sound you'll use in Premiere, are measured in hertz and kilohertz. Because sampled sound is a complex topic, for our purposes it's most important to know that the higher the rate, the better the sound quality. Higher sound quality also dramatically increases file size. Typically, CD quality is associated with a rate of 44,100 Hz (44.1 kHz). DV video is often associated with a rate of 48,000 Hz (48.0 kHz). Sound for general use is acceptable at a rate of 22,050 Hz (22.05 kHz). Voice or AM radio quality is generally around a range of 11,025 Hz (11.0 kHz).

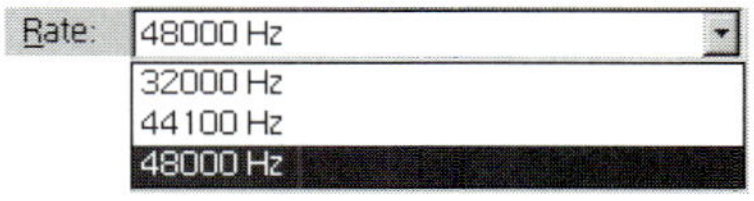

- **Format** Because the sound you'll use is digital, you can select a bit depth just as you can with video. The higher the bit depth, the better the sound quality. Sixteen-bit sound is twice the quality of eight-bit. Stereo sound is also larger in file size than is mono. Sixteen-bit sound is generally used for CD quality, and eight-bit sound is used for FM-broadcast quality.
- **Compressor** This lets you select an audio codec. Sound, like video, can take up an enormous amount of disk space, so it must be compressed. Different codecs are available to you in this pop-up menu, depending on the format you selected in General Settings. It's advisable to compress audio only for exporting your movie, not for playback in the Timeline. We'll discuss audio codecs in Chapter 11 on Audio.
- **Interleave** This pop-up menu normally doesn't need adjusting because the setting is determined by your preset selection. It refers to the frequency in which audio information is loaded into RAM and inserted (interleaved) between video frames. Smaller values mean more RAM usage because the segments of video stored are longer and are processed less often. Sound problems during playback may be solved by adjusting the Interleave setting.

Keyframe and Rendering Settings

The settings in this dialog box relate to the way your video will look when the frames are rendered (built) for preview. Most of the time, to see what your movie looks like, you simply use the playback buttons in the Monitor window or press SPACEBAR. Either method provides a quick, no-frills glimpse of the movie.

When you preview a file (click Timeline | Preview from the menu), it renders the audio and video either to disk, screen, or RAM. If you're using transitions, effects, or superimposing elements on higher video tracks, you can preview these effects only if you render the file. You can't see these effects merely by pressing SPACEBAR or by using the control buttons in the Monitor window. The settings in the Keyframe and Rendering dialog box let you customize the way your video will be previewed.

> **TIP** In order to see a portion of your timeline that needs to be rendered, such as frames with titles, transitions, and video effects, depress the Alt key (in Windows) while you drag the pointer over that part of the video in the timeline. On the Mac, depress the Option key while you drag the pointer over that portion of the timeline. This process is known as "scrubbing" and you'll be using it frequently to preview the timeline.

If you're rendering on a system configuration that isn't equipped with a realtime video card, it can take a long time to build a preview. Realtime video cards are additional pieces of hardware (boards that have special processors) you can add to your system configuration to accelerate the rendering process. One frame of video can contain up to one megabyte of data. So several frames that need to be rendered at a frame rate of 30 frames per second could take hours to process on an average configuration. So if your system is of the average, consumer variety, you could adjust some rendering options in this box to accelerate the rendering process.

To summarize, these settings let you customize how your movie is rendered. They also work in conjunction with the video settings, so whatever you've selected for video determines the keyframe and rendering settings. The following settings are available in this dialog box (Figure 3-8).

- **Rendering Options** Check boxes are provided for ignoring audio, video, and audio rubber band effects. Select these if you want a quicker preview. You won't be able to see the "ignored" effects when you preview the movie.

FIGURE 3-8
Selecting keyframe and rendering settings

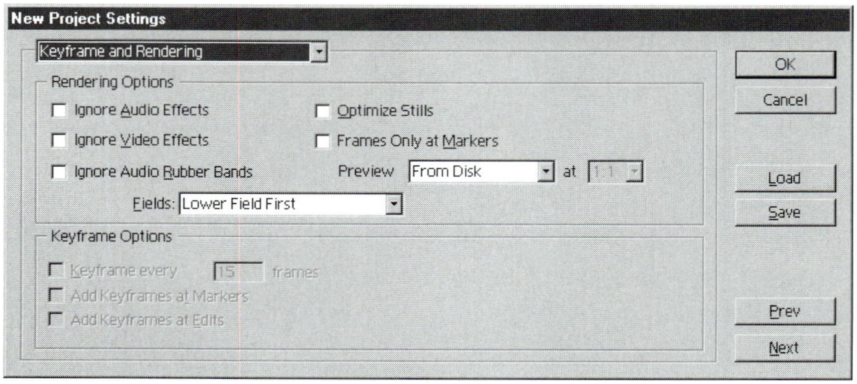

- **Fields** Fields relate to the way Premiere processes video fields—that is, how televisions and computers display video. The default for this setting is No Fields. Selecting the wrong field setting creates a flicker or jagged effect in the movie when rendered.
- **Keyframe Options** These options become available if the codec you've selected in the video settings supports compression keyframes.

Capture Settings

By now, you probably know that capturing refers to getting video from your tape onto a computer. The capturing process requires exact settings in the Capture Settings dialog box before the capturing occurs. Specifically, what you're doing here is setting the properties of the clips, such as format and frame size, among other things (Figure 3-9). There are also separate Audio and Video buttons to further customize the capture.

As with many of the other settings, your choices here relate directly to your video settings. Your capture settings should generally mirror your video and audio settings. As with the other project settings, you can navigate to the Project Settings capture box either by selecting Capture from the Project Settings pop-up menu or clicking the Next button at the bottom right of the Project Settings dialog box.

Capture settings are covered in detail in Chapter 6 on Capturing Video.

Saving Settings

After you've devised the perfect custom setting for your production, you can save it so it appears in the Load Project Settings dialog box as shown at the beginning

FIGURE 3-9
The Capture panel in the Project Settings dialog box

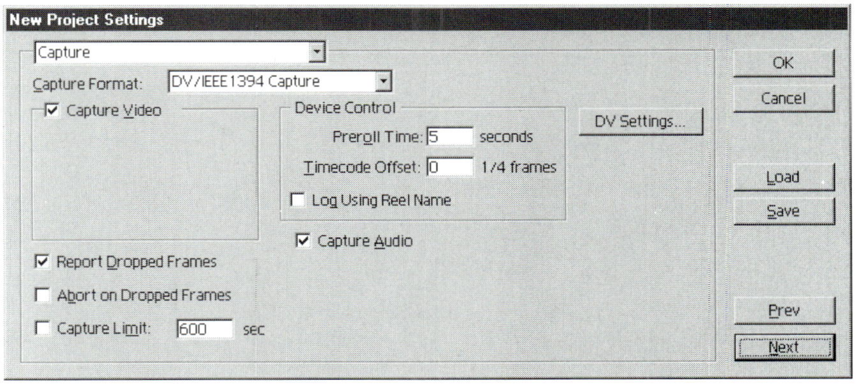

of this chapter. Thus, each time you start a new project, the custom setting you named will appear in the dialog box along with all the available presets.

To Save the settings you've selected in the Project Settings dialog box:

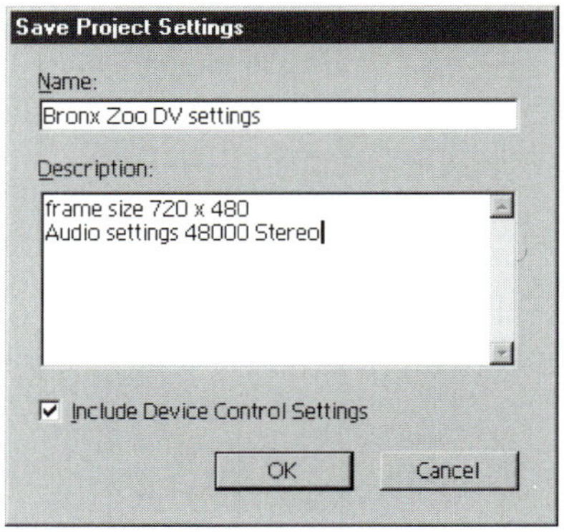

1. Click the Save button.
2. In the Save Project Settings dialog box (see the illustration), type a name and description of your new setting.
3. Click the OK button to return to the Project Settings dialog box.
4. Click the Load button. You'll see your new setting at the bottom of the Load Project Settings dialog box.

The Settings Viewer

The Settings Viewer is a window in which you can preview and compare all the current settings on your project at a quick glance.

To access the Settings Viewer, select Project | Settings Viewer from the menu as shown in Figure 3-10.

In the Settings Viewer, you can view all the data on a clip by using the pop-up menu in the third column. You can also edit settings in this window by clicking any of the settings categories (Capture Settings, Project Settings, Export Settings)

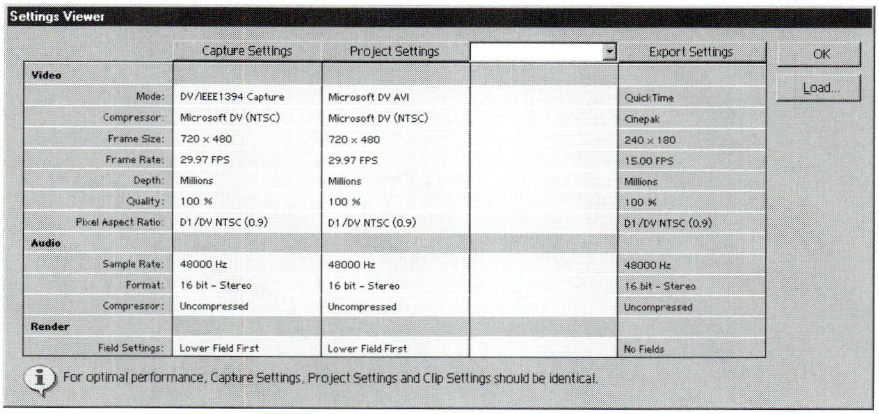

FIGURE 3-10 Use the Settings Viewer to compare and edit project settings

at the top of the table. Doing this opens the appropriate settings dialog box for the settings category you've chosen.

Also note the message at the bottom of the window that says, "For optimal performance, Capture Settings, Project Settings and Clip Settings should be identical." This provides a reminder for you on how the settings work best.

From this window, you can also access the Load Project Settings dialog box by clicking the Load button. In this window, you can return to edit any settings dialog box with a simple click.

In the next chapter, we'll assemble a simple movie. This will let you start playing with some of the cool tools you've been reading about.

4

Edit in the Monitor Window

Now we start making videos! The Monitor window is where your movie comes alive for the first time. Here, you can look at the clips you stored in the Project window and decide whether they fit into the scheme of the overall movie design. If they do, you can decide what frame you want each clip to start on and where you want it to end. You can even insert clips from the Monitor window into the Timeline. In Chapter 2, we reviewed the Monitor window and some of its major components. In this chapter, we actually use these components so you can get the feel of how Premiere works. If you want to follow along with the accompanying files associated with this chapter, copy chapter 04 folder from the CD to your hard drive. In addition, copy the folder named artbeats_clips into the chapter 04 folder. From your hard drive, open the file in this folder named chapter04_finished.ppj. Premiere may ask you to locate files because assets associated with a Premiere movie exist outside of the program. The files you need to locate are either in the artbeats_clips folder or in the chapter 04 folder. When prompted to locate a file, simply navigate to one of these folders, choose the correct file, and click the Select button.

You can either use this file to help familiarize yourself with the Monitor window, or just refer to the figures in this chapter.

You also want to keep in mind that if a file from the chapter 04 folder has been moved since the last time the project was opened, Premiere will also display the Locate File dialog box prompting you for its location. If this is the case, simply navigate to the file's proper location again. This dialog box typically appears more often in the Windows version of Premiere than in the Mac version. In fact, sometimes in Windows users will see this dialog box even when a file's location has not changed. Once Premiere locates a file in a folder, it can generally recognize other files associated with the project stored in the same folder.

Let's look at the Monitor window in chapter04_finished.ppj. The Monitor window plays an important part in the Premiere movie-making process because you can perform most of your trimming and even create the program here. Typically, the sequence of events that occurs in the making of a movie proceeds as follows:

1. Clips are imported into the Project window.
2. From the Project window, clips are brought into the Source view in the Monitor window.
3. In the Source view, the clips are checked out and often trimmed.
4. From the Source view, clips are assembled in sequence in the Timeline.

With this sequence of events in mind, let's start editing!

Monitor Window Views

A view refers to the way the Monitor window appears. The Monitor window is actually set up to resemble the monitor configuration in a traditional editing suite where you view and edit video using two separate monitors. Like a professional video-editing workstation, Premiere gives you one "monitor" (i.e., source view) on which you prepare the raw footage that becomes part of the project and another monitor (program view) that represents the project itself, with all the components that make up the movie as a whole.

Let's say you were assembling a patchwork quilt. You would have several patches you've prepared to sew together to make the whole quilt. The quilt patches are analogous to the Source view. These are the pieces that will eventually make up the final quilt. The actual quilt is like the Program view—the sum of all the patches that becomes the finished piece.

You should also remember that the Monitor window works hand in hand with the Timeline window. The Timeline is where you visualize and arrange the sequence of the assembled clips, and in the Program view, the contents of the Timeline can be played back.

In the Monitor window, you can display clips in dual mode, where you see both the Source and Program, or you can view only the Program in single-view mode. There is also a third view, the Trim mode, where you can visualize adjacent clips while you trim them.

You can access these different views by clicking one of the three icons at the top of the Monitor window (Figure 4-1).

Clicking the Single view button lets you view only the Program (Figure 4-2). Use this view to save on screen real estate if your configuration consists of only one monitor.

FIGURE 4-1
Views buttons in the Monitor window

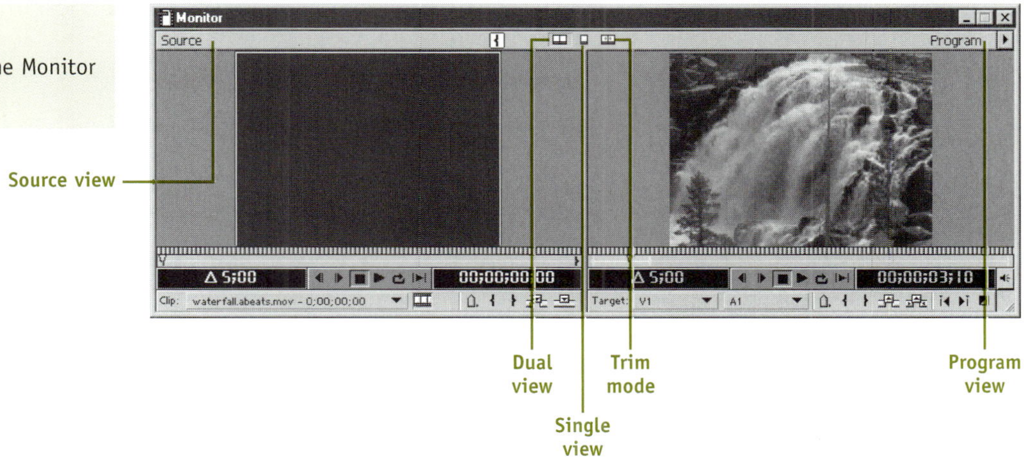

FIGURE 4-2
Setting the Monitor window to Single view displays only the Program view.

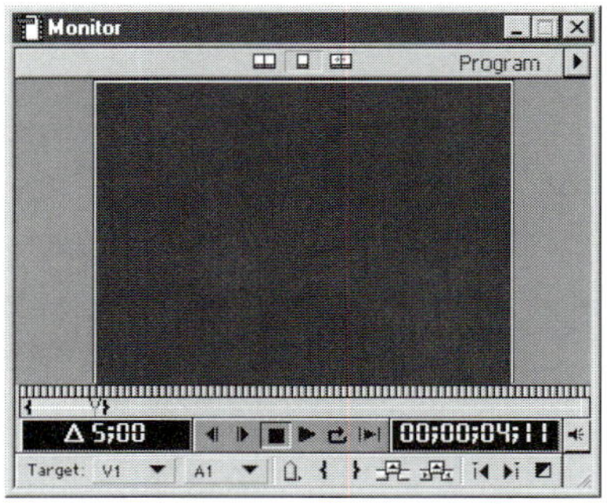

You can also open clips on the Timeline in their own clip windows. This is particularly helpful when you use a single view in the Monitor window. A clip window is analogous to the Source view but, unlike the source, it can be moved anywhere on screen because it's a window. Clip windows are discussed in the section "Source Clip Windows" later in this chapter.

SAFE MARGIN GUIDES IN THE MONITOR WINDOW

The safe margin guides are white outline boxes around the Source and Program views. The outside margin is the action safe margin; the inner margin is the title safe margin. These margins indicate safe boundaries within which you can place your elements if you're outputting to a video monitor (Figure 4-3). Video monitors can overlap the edges of your frame. These margins help determine where the edges of the frame should end.

FIGURE 4-3
Safe margins in the Source and Program views

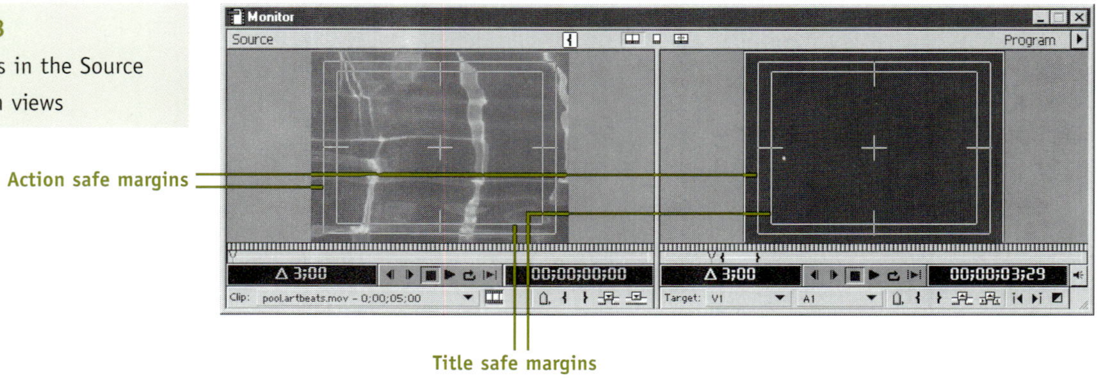

If you will output your final movie as full-resolution video, make sure any text you add to the production sits inside the title safe area; otherwise, its edges may be cut off when you view your movie on a television screen.

Display the safe margins by clicking the pop-up menu in the Monitor window as shown in Figure 4-4. Check Safe Margins for Source Side or Safe Margins for Program Side. You can display margins for both boxes simultaneously. These margins don't play back in the movie; they are just guides for you to follow. You don't even need to worry about the safe margins if your final video will be viewed on a computer screen. Safe margins apply only to full-resolution NTSC or PAL video displayed on a video monitor.

To review, the Source view is used to test and edit individual clips before they're assembled in the Timeline. The Program view, on the other hand, is a representation of the contents of the Timeline—the sum of your project.

Examining the Source View

Let's examine some clips in the Source view and play around with the various controls.

If you're following along with the chapter files provided on the CD, close file chapter04_finished.ppj and open file chapter04_begin.ppj located in the chapter 04 folder. If you're not following along with the chapter files, you can always refer to the zTour.ppj file in the Sample Folder within Premiere.

This project (chapter04_begin.ppj) is empty except for some elements in the Project window. In the Project window are two bins: one for the video clips (the bin called artbeats_clips) and the other for the audio clip (sounds). Four video clips were imported as a folder called artbeats_clips. The sounds bin is

FIGURE 4-4
To turn on safe margins, click the Monitor window pop-up menu

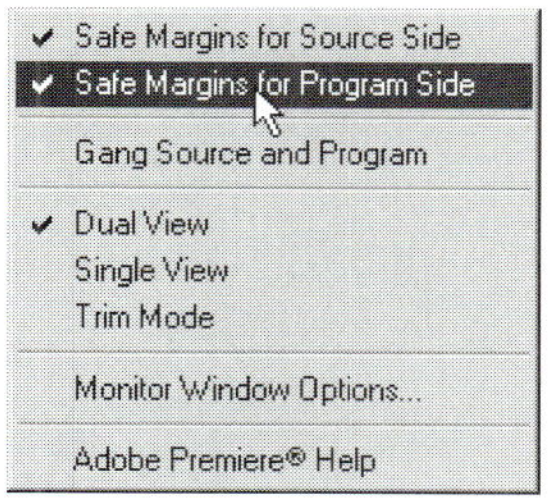

empty. We'll import the audio into the Project window and store it in the sounds bin. We'll then trim and assemble the movie primarily in the Monitor window.

BRINGING CLIPS INTO THE SOURCE VIEW

First, we'll import a sound into the Project bin. Then we'll move the clips from the Project window into the Source view so we can view them and decide how we want to edit them.

To Bring an audio file into the Project window:

1 **In the Project bin, click a bin. In this file, audio files are to be stored in the bin named sounds.**

2 **Right-click (in Windows) or press CONTROL and click (Mac) in the Project window to display the context menu. Select Import | File to display the Import dialog box (Figure 4-5). You can also select File | Import | File from the menu or press CTRL-I (Windows) or COMMAND-I (Mac).**

3 **In the Import dialog box, locate the sound you want to import. For the file we're working with in this chapter, we'll import the sound named Rays.aif from chapter04 folder. To do this, in the Import dialog box, navigate to chapter04 folder and locate the sound file Rays.aif. Select it and click the Open button.**

4 **Rays.aif now appears at the right side of the window and is in the sounds bin. You can navigate the contents of both bins by clicking them. When you click a bin, the bin contents appear in the right column of the Project window (Figure 4-6).**

FIGURE 4-5
Import dialog box

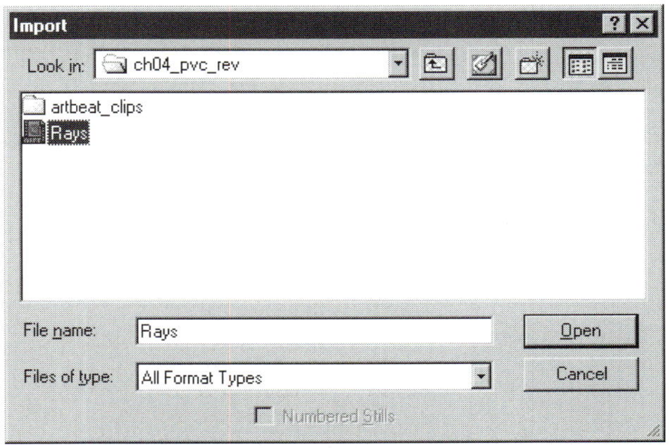

FIGURE 4-6
The sounds bin contents are displayed in the right column of the Project window

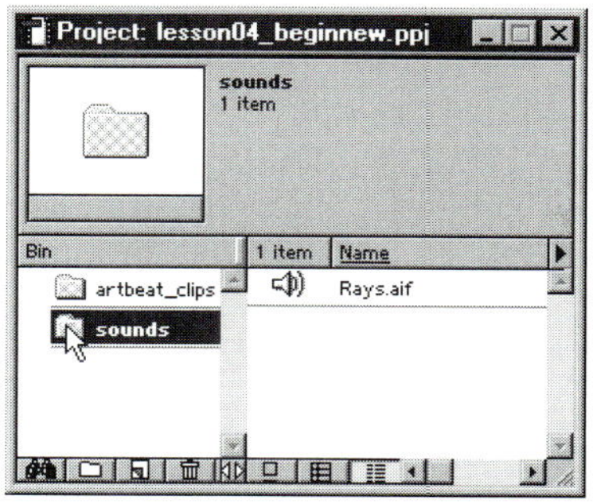

After files are organized in the Project window, generally the next step is getting the video clips into the Source view. Now let's bring all the video clips from the artbeats_clips bin into the Source window for trimming.

> **NOTE** Entire folders can also be imported in Premiere. Clicking File | Import | Folder lets you select a folder (as opposed to a file). Folders will be imported, with all their contents, as a bin in the Project window.

To Bring clips from the Project window into the Source view:

1. For individual clips, click a clip in the Project window and drag it to the Source view. Or, you can simply double-click the clip in the Project window. The double-click method works only if you've unchecked Open Movies in Clip Window in the Edit | Preferences | General dialog box.

2. We will now bring multiple clips into the Source view. Click the artbeats_clips bin and press SHIFT and click the first and last video clips in the right column of the Project window. Doing this selects all the clips in this bin. Once they're all selected, drag them into the Source view (Figure 4-7).

FIGURE 4-7
Use SHIFT-click to select consecutive clips in the Project window

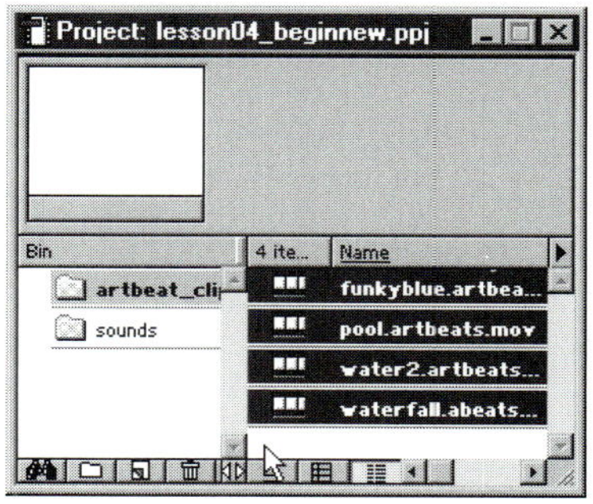

If you're following along with the Chapter 4 lesson, drag all the clips into the Source view. When you drag clips into the Source view, you can access them individually by clicking the Clip pop-up menu at the bottom of the Source view. This menu displays an expandable list of all clips in the Source view (Figure 4-8).

To view a clip in the Source view, select it from the pop-up menu. The clip will then appear in the Source monitor window.

> **TIP** To select non-consecutive clips, press CONTROL and click (Windows) or COMMAND-SHIFT and click (Mac) on the clips.

> **TIP** To delete clips from the Source view, select the clip in the pop-up menu and press ALT-BACKSPACE (Windows) or COMMAND-DELETE (Mac).

NAVIGATING IN THE SOURCE VIEW

The Source view offers many ways to view the contents of your clip. You can use the controller buttons at the bottom of the window or shortcut keys to perform various functions (Figure 4-9). When you become adept with Premiere and you're moving around quickly within the interface, you'll probably want to take advantage of the many shortcut editing keys. Throughout the book, when relevant to the topic discussed, we'll cover some of the more commonly used shortcut editing keys.

When a clip is displayed in the Source window, you can navigate through the Source view with the controller buttons located at the bottom of the view.

FIGURE 4-8
When you click the Clip pop-up list in the Source view, you can select the current clip in the Source view

FIGURE 4-9
Controller buttons at the bottom of the Source view

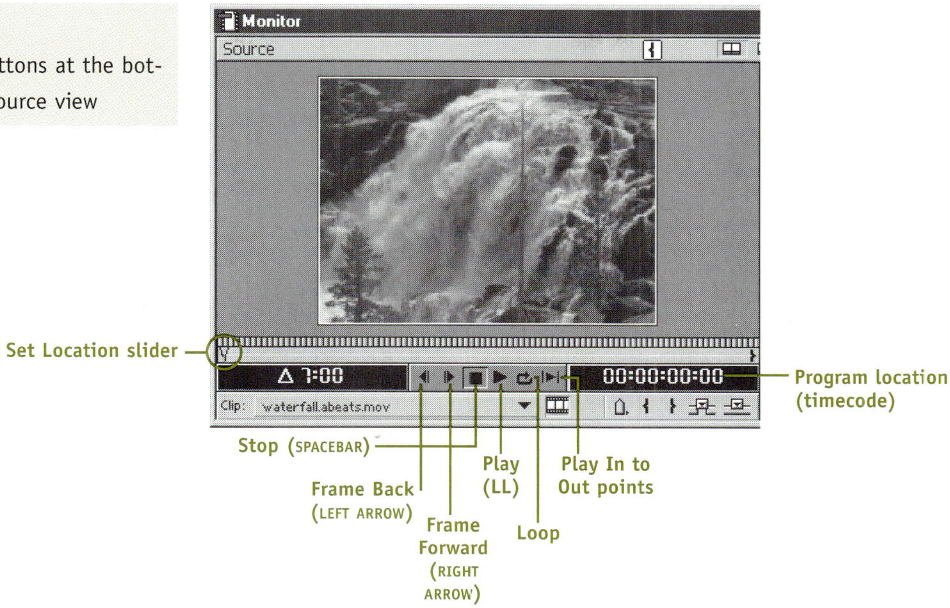

To Use THE CONTROLLER BUTTONS:

1. Starting at the left, the first two buttons move one frame back and one frame forward. Notice when you position the pointer over these keys, Tool Tips (descriptions of the icons) pop up. Tool Tips not only indicate what an icon's purpose is, they also indicate the equivalent shortcut key that performs the same function. For example, pressing the left and right arrow keys also performs the frame forward and backward functions as the corresponding icons. Shortcut keys can save a tremendous amount of time in Premiere. If you don't see a Tool Tip when you position your pointer over an icon, select Edit | Preferences | General & Still Image... and make sure Show Tool Tips is checked.

2. The center rectangle is the Stop button; pressing the spacebar toggles between Stop and Play of the clip.

3. The next button is the Play button; the shortcut is the L or the TILDE (~) key.

4. To the right of the Play button is the Loop button, and next to that is the Play In to Out button. The Loop button continuously replays the area where you want your clip to begin and end (between the In and Out points).

> **TIP** More About Shortcut Keys: The UP and DOWN arrows move to the first and last frame. The K key stops playback of frames, and the J key reverses playback. Pressing the J, L, or ~ key repeatedly increases the speed of the clip's playback.

5 **The Play In to Out button plays only the part of the clip that has the In and Out points marked. (We cover setting In and Out points in the Source view in the section "Setting In and Out Points.")**

TIMECODE IN THE SOURCE VIEW

To the left and right of the controller buttons are digital readouts of the clip's duration and timecode displayed in green digital text. It resembles the digital readout on your VCR (Figure 4-10).

The number at the left shows the total or trimmed duration of the clip in hours, minutes, seconds, and frames. The number at the right indicates the current clip location (based on the position of the frame counter) in hours, minutes, seconds, and frames.

To navigate through a source clip, click and drag the Set Location slider (sometimes referred to as the frame counter) to the left and right. The Set Location slider is an aqua blue triangle with a red, vertical line coming out of the bottom. Notice that the numbers to the right of the controllers, which indicate the frame's position, change as you drag the Set Location slider, or the frame counter.

> **NOTE** **In addition to the control buttons in the Source view, you can navigate a source clip using the gray and white toothed bar above the triangle. This is known as the Frame Jog control, or sometimes called the Shuttle control. To use this method, click and drag the bar. This is an effective method of scanning the clip to pinpoint one frame at a time on very long source clips. You can also use this to shuttle quickly or slowly back and forth through the clip.**

The timecode displayed in Figure 4-10 is based on a 30 fps non-drop frame rate setting. (Frame rates are discussed in Chapter 3.) You can change the frame rate in the Monitor Window Options dialog box (Figure 4-11). You access this dialog box either by right-clicking (Windows) or pressing CONTROL and click (Mac) in the Monitor window and selecting it from the context menu, or selecting it from the pop-up menu in the Monitor window. Don't change the

FIGURE 4-10
The Timecode in the Source view

FIGURE 4-11
Monitor Window Options dialog box

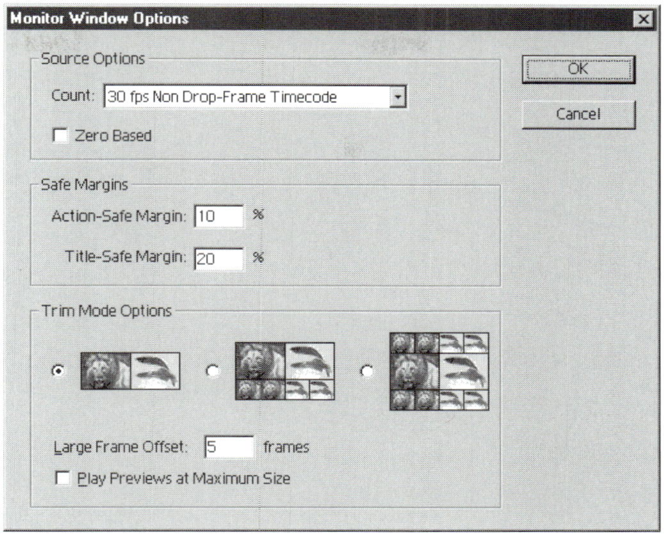

timecode count unless you've also changed your Project Timebase settings. Otherwise, the timecode displayed in the Source window will no longer match the timecode of your original footage.

Setting In and Out Points

In Figure 4-12, notice that in the Source view there are two brackets to the far left and right of the Set Location slider. These icons resemble brackets; one pointing to

FIGURE 4-12
In and Out points in the Source view

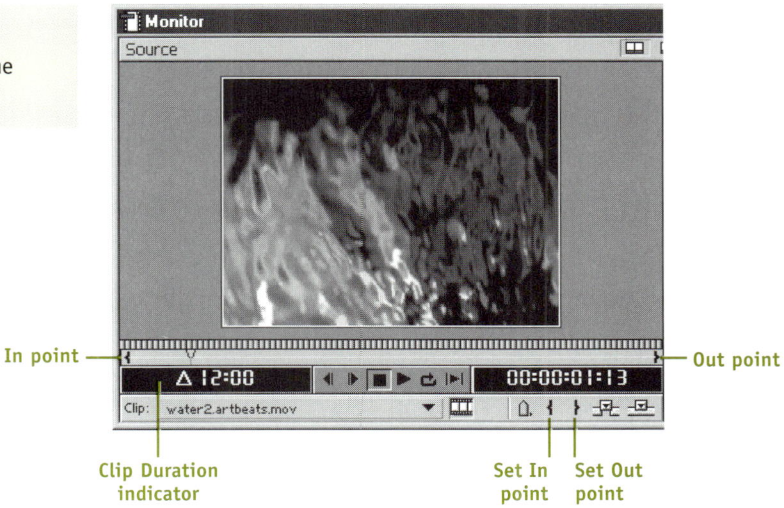

the left and the other pointing to the right. These are the In and Out points used for trimming clips. When you set these points, you decide where you want the clip to begin and end.

Setting In and Out points is easy. Once you know the shortcut keys, you can speed through this process. You can do it visually in the Source view or zero in on a particular frame in time using the timecode.

NOTE When you set an In and Out point on a clip, you're not actually modifying the original clip on your hard drive. You're indicating in the project instructions that when your final movie is rendered, you want to show only the footage between the In and Out points you've set on that clip instance.

If you're following along with the chapter lesson, select a clip in the Clip Source view pop-up menu named waterfall.artbeats.mov. Otherwise, use any source clip to perform the same task. This is footage of a waterfall. According to the Clip Duration readout at the left of the Source view, this clip is seven seconds long. Let's shorten it to one second by adjusting the In and Out points in the Source view.

NOTE You can also set In and Out points in the Timeline and Program view.

To Change THE IN AND OUT POINTS ON THIS CLIP:

1. **Drag the Shuttle Location slider to the right until the Current Clip Location Timecode reads "00:00:01:00."**
2. **Click the Mark In point at the bottom right of the Source view (the little bracket icon that points to the left). The bracket icon appears in the bar with the Shuttle Location slider.**
3. **Now, set the Out point. Drag the Shuttle Location slider to the right until the Timecode reads "00:00:02:00." Click the bracket icon that indicates the Out Point at the bottom right of the window. The Out Point now appears where the frame counter head is located (Figure 4-13). Now the clip's duration is one second.**

To test your edit, click the Play In to Out Button in the Controller (last button). Only the edited portion of the clip plays. Pretty easy, huh?

You'll no doubt notice the yellow fill that appears between the In and Out point icons in the Source view as shown in Figure 4-14. This yellow fill visually indicates the length of the clip in the Source view. Another way you can adjust the

FIGURE 4-13
The In and Out points set in the Source view on the clip waterfall.artbeats.mov

trimmed clip is to click and drag either the In or Out point right in the Source view, above the Controller buttons.

Let's lengthen the clip a little to "00:00:04:00" by changing the Out point. Doing this lengthens the clip's duration to three seconds.

To lengthen the duration of a clip:

- Drag the Out Point to this number frame in time using the timecode

OR

- Click the Frame Back/Frame Forward control buttons until the timecode reads "00:00:04:00" (Figure 4-14).

FIGURE 4-14
The Out point on this clip has been adjusted so the clip plays two seconds longer

In the chapter lesson file, there are a total of five clips in the Source view. For extra practice, you can set the rest of the clips' time to approximately three seconds using the In and Out points in the Source view.

You can also use the shortcut keys to trim your clips instead of clicking the Set In and Out point icons. In fact, this is probably the most efficient way to trim clips once you become comfortable with them. Click the "I" to set the In point and "O" to set the Out point. Use this in combination with the other shortcut keys (e.g., LEFT ARROW, RIGHT ARROW, J, K, L, ~, SPACEBAR) to trim expeditiously. The idea here is to work efficiently and to trim your clips down to more manageable lengths, both to tighten your edit and focus on only the best shot or series of frames in each clip.

Source Clip Windows

If you prefer to work in a lone clip window, you can access one by pressing ALT and double-clicking (Windows) or pressing OPTION and double-clicking (Mac) any of the icons in the Project window (Figure 4-15). You can also use this key combination to click on a clip in the Timeline and Source view to open a clip in a clip window. This window has all the same features as the Source view. Why edit in this window instead of the Source view? If you need to conserve on screen real estate, you can use the Monitor window in Single view mode and just access the clip window when you need to trim a source

NOTE **In the Edit | Preferences | General & Still Images... dialog box, checking the option Open Movies in Clip Window lets you open a clip in its own window simply by double-clicking the clip in the Project window.**

FIGURE 4-15
Single clip window of a source clip

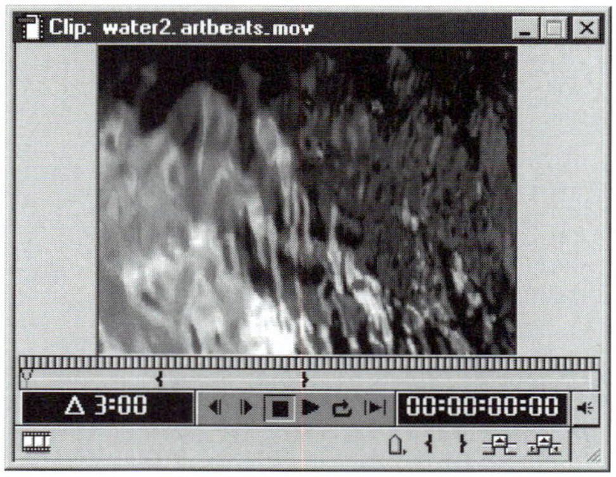

clip. Then you can close it up when you're done, giving you additional workspace. Also, in older versions of Premiere that didn't have the Source view, clips were edited in clip windows.

You can adjust the In and Out points in the Source view easily using these techniques. There are a few other buttons at the bottom right of the Source view (markers, Insert and Overlay buttons) that relate to the Timeline. We'll cover these later in this chapter.

Moving Source Clips from the Monitor Window into the Timeline

Once your clips look perfectly trimmed, there are two ways to move them into the Timeline so you can start to put the pieces of your movie together. Let's experiment with both ways.

Before the clips are brought into the Timeline on video track 1, you must establish a clip sequence. You can change the clips' order at any time by using the tools in the Monitor window and Timeline. If you're following along with this chapter lesson, you can assemble the movie too. Otherwise you can use any video clips to experiment with the process. The order of the clips as they will appear in the movie from this lesson are as follows:

1. waterfall.artbeats.mov
2. pool.artbeats.mov
3. water2.artbeats.mov
4. funkyblue.artbeats.mov

An easy way to bring clips from the Source view into the Timeline is simply to drag them in proper order.

To Drag clips from the Source view into the Timeline:

1. **Select the first clip (waterfall.artbeats.mov) in the Select Source Clip pop-up menu. It will then appear in the Source view.**

2. **Click the actual clip in the Source view and drag it to the far left of Video 1 Track (00:00) in the Timeline (Figure 4-16). Notice that the clip now appears in the**

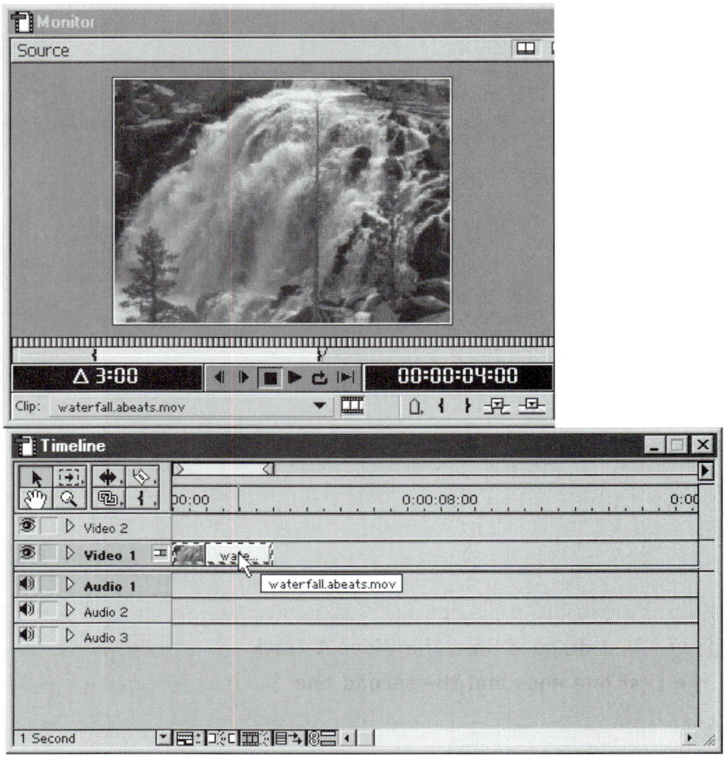

FIGURE 4-16
Source clip moved into the Timeline

Timeline as well as the Program view in the Monitor window. (Remember, the Timeline and Program view are interrelated.)

3 **Repeat this process for the second clip, pool.artbeats.mov, butting the head of this clip up with the end of the waterfall.artbeats.mov clip.**

We can try another method of moving a clip from the Source view into the Timeline. This involves a button in the Source view that we haven't used yet, called the Insert button (Figure 4-17). The Insert button inserts a clip into the Timeline at the designated Edit line location and shifts all other clips forward in time to accommodate the new clip.

If you use the Insert button to place a clip on the tail of the last clip on the track, it falls in place and lengthens the program. If you use the Insert button to insert a clip in the middle of a clip, it splits the clip in two and moves the clips to the right forward in time. Thus, using the Insert button to insert a clip lengthens the duration of a program.

FIGURE 4-17
The Insert and Overlay buttons in the Source view

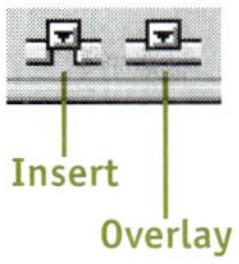

Let's move the third clip into the Timeline, only this time we'll insert the clip in between the first two clips.

To Insert THE CLIP NAMED WATER2.ARTBEATS.MOV INTO THE TIMELINE:

1. Select the third clip, water2.artbeats.mov, in the Source view using the Select Source Clip pop-up window.
2. In the Timeline, place the Edit line in between the two clips you just dragged onto the Video 1 Track (where the first one ends and the second one begins). If you're having a hard time locating the area where one clip begins and another ends, use SHIFT-+ to zoom up in the Timeline and SHIFT-_ to zoom down.
3. Click the Insert button (or use the shortcut comma key). The third clip is inserted where your edit line is located and shifts over the last clip forward in time.

For additional practice, continue to place the remainder of the clips in the Timeline using the methods we've just reviewed.

NOTE The Overlay button, located to the right of the Insert button, also inserts clips. It differs from the Insert button in that it overlays, or covers up, any clip that occupies the same space as the new overlay clip. The result is that the clips to the right are shortened in length to accommodate the original length that is the sum of all the clips. For example, if you had a total of five clips that played out to 30 seconds on the Timeline and you overlayed a 5-second clip in between the first two clips, the Timeline duration would still be 30 seconds. The other clip's duration would be adjusted accordingly to reflect the original duration time.

TESTING THE ASSEMBLED VIDEO

Now that the clips are assembled on the Timeline, you can test them to see how they look as a rough cut using any of several methods. Because this chapter is about editing in the Monitor window, we'll hone in on the controls in the Monitor window.

Control Keys in the Program View

By now, you've probably noticed that the Program view bears an amazing resemblance to the Source view. Indeed, the control buttons (e.g., Stop, Play) work the same way. Not only do the control buttons work the same way, the shortcut keys associated with them are identical as well (Figure 4-18).

To complicate matters, the buttons that control the Source and Program views (and the shortcut keys) work in the Timeline, too. How do you know what's controlling what? The buttons control the element that is selected, as do the shortcut keys. If you've selected a clip in the Source view and want to play it, clicking the Play button or pressing the L key (or ~, or SPACEBAR) will play the clip. On the other hand, if you've selected a clip in the Program view and you click the Play button or use the same shortcut key, the contents of the Timeline (the current compilation of assets in the Timeline) will play. Because the Timeline and Program

FIGURE 4-18
Control keys in the Monitor window Program view

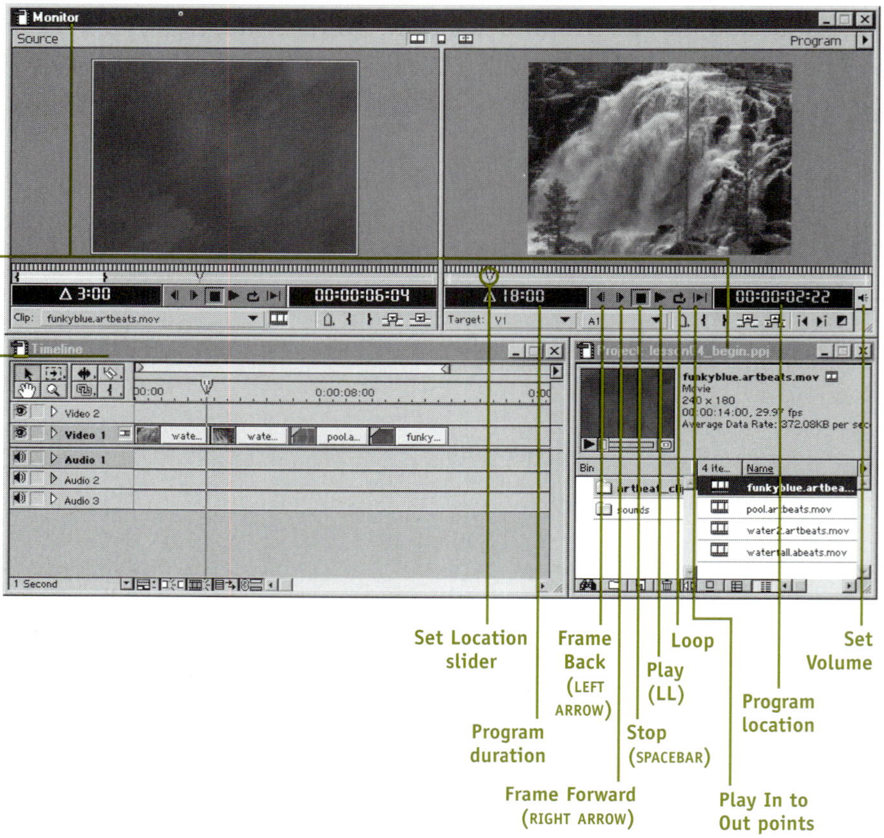

view work together, the control keys in either window control both these elements. When a clip is selected in either the Source or Program view, a blue rectangle appears around the selected clip, and the timecode and In/Out points in the other clip are dimmed.

The same control buttons and shortcut keys work when you play a program from the Timeline. The Timeline is a little trickier on playback than the Source and Program views in the Monitor window, so we'll save that topic for the next chapter.

NOTE **When you work in the three main windows (Monitor, Project, and Timeline), the top window bar of the current window is highlighted with color or horizontal stripes (depending on how your operating system displays windows) and the other window bars are dimmed. You can work in only one window at a time. To select a window, simply click on it to make it the current window. Toggle from the Monitor window to the Timeline with CONTROL-TAB.**

The Program View

By now, you probably have a good idea of the difference between the Source and Program views in the Monitor window. To reiterate, the Source view is for preparing the clips that will go into the Timeline. The Program view displays the results of the Timeline.

Editing in the Program View

You can do a few other cool things in the Program view besides previewing the movie. You can edit the video right from the Program view; the tools at the bottom of the Program view perform these edits (Figure 4-19).

Three- and Four-Point Editing

In the earlier section "Examining the Source View," we set In and Out points on the Source clips and dragged the clips into the Timeline. You can edit the contents of the Timeline in the Monitor window by setting In and Out points in the Program view, as well. Setting In and Out points affects the program in the Timeline as opposed to the source clips. This method of editing is known as Three-Point Editing and Four-Point Editing.

Basically, three-point editing refers to identifying an In and Out point on a source clip, and identifying an In point in the program where the source clip is going to be located. Thus, you're editing with the two points from the source clip (In and

FIGURE 4-19
Editing tools in the Program view

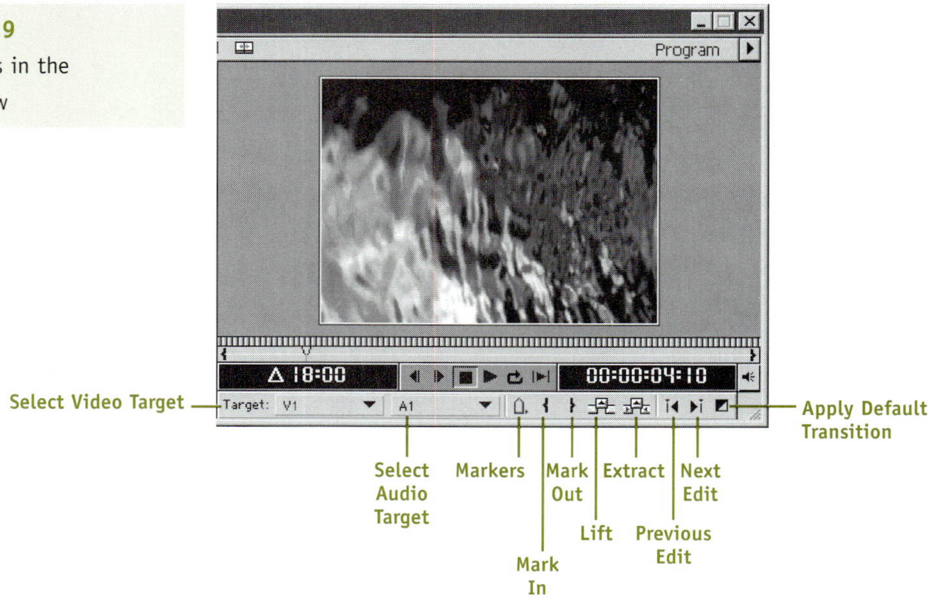

Out points) and the In point in the program. In four-point editing, you identify an In and Out point on a source clip as well as an In and Out point in the program where you want the source clip to reside. Thus, you're identifying two points in the source clip and two points in the program to create a four-point edit. You use the Insert and Overlay buttons in the Monitor window in combination with the Target track popup list to do three- and four-point editing. The program can also be edited in the Timeline, which is discussed in Chapter 5.

Lift and Extract in the Program View

The Lift and Extract buttons are located in the Program view and are similar to the Insert and Overlay buttons in the Source view.

Instead of inserting clips into the Timeline, the Lift and Extract buttons take clips, or ranges of clips, out of the Timeline. The difference between the two is that the Lift button leaves empty space where the clips once were, whereas the Extract button closes up the empty space by moving all the clips to the right of the edit over to the left to fill the gap.

Let's perform an experiment on the movie we've been making and lift a clip sequence from the Timeline using the Lift button in the Program view.

To Use the Lift button from the Program view:

1. Click the Program view and make sure V1 is selected in the Select Target Video pop-up menu.

2. In the Program view, get ready to set an In and Out point. In Figure 4-20, the In point is set to 00:00:02:00 and the Out point to 00:00:04:00. This was done in the Program view using the identical methods (set In and Out point buttons, or I and O) used in the Source view. Notice now, the In and Out points are being set on the assembled program as opposed to an isolated clip in the Source window. Once you set the In and Out points in the Program view, they are simultaneously indicated in the Timeline over the associated footage.

3. In the Program view, click the Lift button. In the Timeline there is now a gap where the In and Out points were set in the Program view. Similar to the Insert button in the Source view, the Lift button leaves the footage the same length it was before the lift was performed (Figure 4-21).

The Extract button works the same way to remove footage according to the location of your In and Out points. The only difference is it yields different results.

To Edit in the Program view using the Extract button:

1. Click Edit Undo (or press CONTROL-Z in Windows or COMMAND-Z on the Mac) twice to undo the Lift command you just performed.

FIGURE 4-20
In and Out points have been set in the Program view before performing a lift

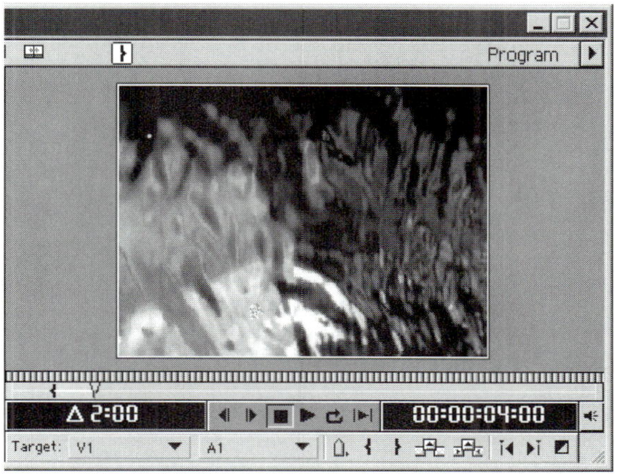

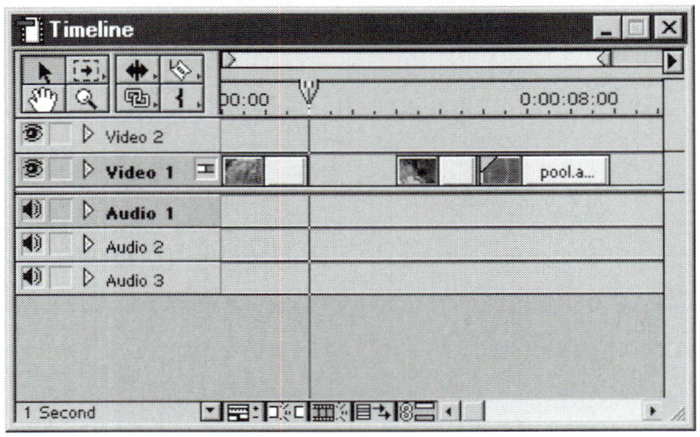

FIGURE 4-21
The Lift button leaves a gap where the lifted clip sequence once resided in the Timeline but maintains the program's original duration

2 **Reset the In and Out points using the same method we used with the Lift button (step 3). This time, set the In point to 00:00:04:00 and the Out point to 00:00:08:00 (Figure 4-22).**

3 **Click the Extract button. Notice the additional footage is now joined together in the Timeline and the duration of the total video is now shorter (Figure 4-23).**

To review the results of your edit in the Program view, click in the Program view and either drag the frame counter all the way to the left and click the Play button or click the A and L keys to rewind and play forward. Try to play with a few of the other shortcut keys and control buttons to familiarize yourself with navigating in the Program view.

CONTROLLING SOUND IN THE PROGRAM VIEW

At the far right of the Program window is a volume icon. Click this icon to mute the sound in the program. Note that this button controls only local playback volume.

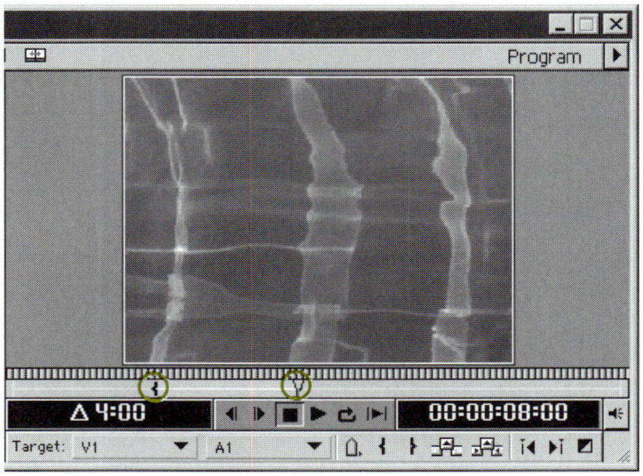

FIGURE 4-22
The In and Out points reset in the Program view before performing an extract

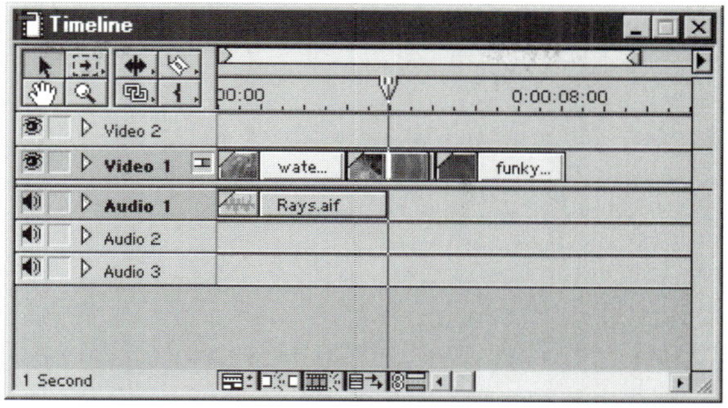

FIGURE 4-23
Extracting a clip joins additional footage left on both sides of the extracted footage.

Controlling a project's audio for an exported movie is done differently. We discuss audio in Chapter 11.

Notice that there are varying degrees of a sound wave emanating from the icon as you click on it multiple times. It ranges from no sound wave (mute) to two rings of a sound wave (maximum sound). You can control the volume of sound locally in your program by clicking this button. Let's learn what this button does by importing a sound into the movie and seeing what happens when we click several times on the button.

To Bring AUDIO INTO THE SOURCE VIEW:

1. **Click the sounds bin and drag the sound (Rays.aif) into the Source view.**
2. **Notice you see the waveform representation of the sound. Here you can play the sound to review it by pressing the Play (L) button (Figure 4-24).**

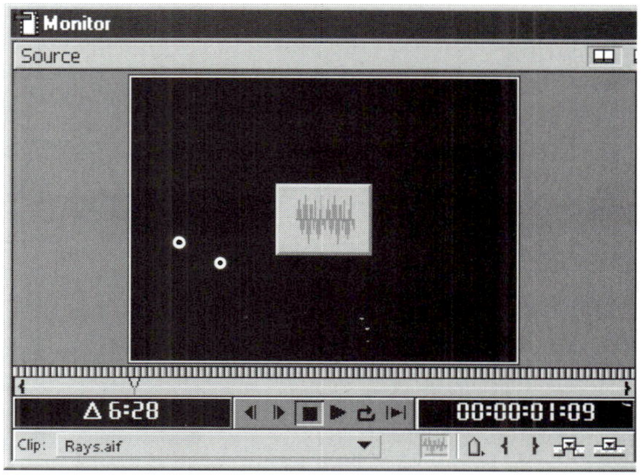

FIGURE 4-24
A sound called Rays.aif dragged from the sounds bin onto the Source view

3. Drag the sound from the Source view into the beginning of the Timeline, Audio 1 Track.

4. Click the Program view and drag the frame counter back to the first frame (or press the A key).

5. Play the movie to hear the audio using the L key or the Play button.

6. Click the Set Volume icon in the Program view to make the audio louder, quieter, or mute.

TIP You can turn on and off local sound from the Timeline by alternately clicking the sound icon to make it visible and invisible (Figure 4-25). When the icon is white, it's shy. This means a track becomes hidden. Do this if you need to economize on screen space. To make an audio track shy, press CONTROL and click (in Windows) or COMMAND and click (Mac) an audio icon in the Timeline. To make a video track shy, press CONTROL and click (Windows) or COMMAND and click (Mac) a video icon in the Timeline.

Our production needs a lot more work. But it's beginning to take shape as we use a few editing tools.

The Program and Source views provide additional editing tools, such as Markers and Default Transitions, which we'll cover in Chapter 7. But by now, you're probably feeling a lot less intimidated by the Premiere workspace.

If you've been following along with the lesson files in this chapter, keep the file you've been working on (chapter02_begin2). In the next chapter, we'll augment this movie using the Timeline more extensively. This will give you a complete selection of editing options both in the Monitor views and Timeline window.

FIGURE 4-25
You can turn on and off local sound by clicking the sound buttons in the Timeline.

ON THE VIRTUAL CLASSROOM CD-ROM Follow along with the instructor in Lesson 2, "Trimming Clips in the Source View," as she shows you how easy it is to set In and Out points in the Monitor window.

5

Editing in the Timeline

In Chapter 4, we briefly discussed editing in the Timeline and had a glimpse of its features. As was demonstrated, the Program view and Timeline work together closely in editing your movies. Not only do they work together, the Program view lets you play the entire movie (or any part of it) according to its sequence in the Timeline. You can also play back the movie directly in the Timeline and view it concurrently in the Program view. In fact, the same shortcut keys you use to control the Monitor window playback can be used in the Timeline.

Think of the Timeline as a map, with the length and location of the video physically depicted with bars (clips and still images). If the Timeline is the map, the Program view is the physical, moving picture of the route you're taking. You could reach your final destination using either method alone, but using both together, you can reach your destination—in this case, your finished video—far more efficiently.

Getting Started in the Timeline

As with the Project and Monitor windows, you should feel comfortable with all the Timeline features to make the best use of Premiere. This way, you can have complete control over what you're doing and design your project knowing which editing methods work best for you.

In this chapter, we'll enhance a project that's partially completed. We used some of these clips in Chapter 4, so they'll look familiar to you.

The finished version of this file, chapter05_finished.ppj, can be found in the chapter 05 folder on the CD. This file contains five video clips, three tracks of audio clips, transitions, and superimposed vector art (Figure 5-1). In later chapters, you'll learn how to apply these special effects. In this chapter, we focus mostly on the actual Timeline itself.

Notice in the Timeline of this figure, the project is in Single-Track Editing mode. The Timeline can be displayed in two different modes: Single-Track and A/B Editing. Later, we'll see what the project looks like when we switch over to A/B Editing mode, and we'll discuss the differences between the two modes. For now, just know that each editing mode makes the Timeline appear slightly different.

If you're following along with the book, open up chapter05_begin.ppj in the chapter 05 folder. Save it to your hard drive along with the artbeats_clips folder. This is the partially finished version of the previous file you looked at, chapter05_finished.ppj. We will work with chapter05_begin.ppj to better understand the many functions of the Timeline. If you want, refer to the screen shots in the book for reference instead of working with the project files.

Moving Clips into the Timeline

In the preceding chapter, we inserted clips in the Timeline using the Source view in the Monitor window. By doing this, we actually created a rough cut of a movie.

FIGURE 5-1
The finished video we examine in this chapter contains trimmed video clips, transitions, superimposing, and audio tracks

In this chapter, we'll add and edit elements primarily using the Timeline. You'll see that making a movie in Premiere requires some sculpting as you go along, no matter how much you've planned it out.

In the preceding chapter, we used the Insert and Overlay buttons from the Source view to move clips into the Timeline. In the following example, we'll use the drag-and-drop method to move a clip from the Source view to the Timeline and then trim the clip to fit it perfectly on Video Track 1.

Adding a Clip and Simple Trim in the Timeline

In the Chapter05_begin, in the Project window is a bin named artbeats_clips. This is the bin where all the movie clips used in this project are stored. In addition, audio has been stored in a bin called audio, and all other graphics are in a folder called stills. Using bins helps organize projects.

In the chapter 05 folder, the video clips are stored in the bin artbeats_clips. In fact, this entire folder was imported directly into the Premiere Project window using the File | Import | Folder command from the menu. The folder, initially created outside of Premiere, is now a bin in the Project window. The other two bins were created right in Premiere, and their contents were also added in Premiere.

If you double-click on this bin, you can find clips named purple.artbeats.mov and funkyblue.artbeats.mov. Select both clips while holding down SHIFT and drag them both into the Source window to test them. From here, we'll move these into the Timeline.

To Insert a clip from the Source view into the Timeline:

1. **Select a clip in the Source view. In this case the clip is purple.artbeats.mov.**
2. **Click the Source view and drag the new clip (purple.artbeats.mov) from the Source window into the Timeline so that the head (front) of this clip butts up against the end (tail) of another clip (see the illustration). The current tool now is the Selection tool from the Timeline toolbox. The Selection tool is the default navigation tool in the Timeline, used for selecting and moving individual clips.**

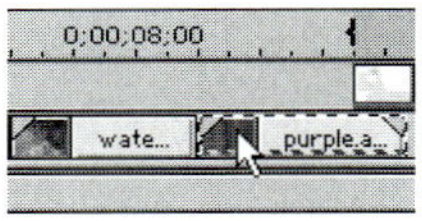

Because the default view of the Timeline is small, sometimes using the Zoom tool in the Timeline toolbox is helpful for identifying the exact position where two clips meet. To use the Zoom tool, select it in the Timeline toolbox, bring the tool in the vicinity of the place you want to magnify, and click. Each time you click, the magnification increases. To zoom down, hold down the ALT (Windows) or OPTION (Mac) key while clicking. Notice also that when you zoom in and out, the Time Zoom Level changes (the bar at the bottom left of the Timeline window) and is reflected on the Timeline ruler.

> **NOTE** In the Preferences dialog box (Edit | Preferences | General and Still Images), the option Open Movies in Clip Window should be deselected for this lesson. This will make the clips open in the Source view instead of their own clip window. There's nothing wrong with viewing them in the clip window, but for this lesson, we want to view them in the Source.

Let's trim the clip in our example. It can be trimmed in the Source view, but let's see how we can use a simple trimming method right in the Timeline.

> **NOTE** Pressing SHIFT+ (plus) or shift– (minus) also lets you zoom up and down in the Timeline.

To Trim a clip in the Timeline:

1. **Click the clip named purple.artbeats.mov (or any clip) in the Timeline, and mouse over the end, or tail, of the clip. Notice that a red, right-pointing bracket with a double-headed arrow appears. This is the Trim Out tool, and it lets you edit the Out point right**

in the Timeline. The Trim-In tool would appear if you moused over the beginning, or head, of the clip. This technique provides a quick way to change the In and Out points on a clip right in the Timeline.

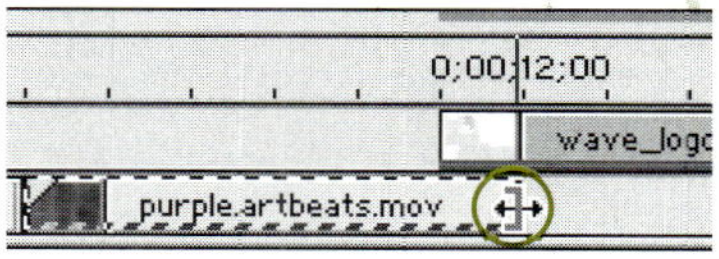

2 **Display the Info palette to view statistics about this clip. To do this, select Window | Show Info from the menu. We can use this window to obtain information about the clip we'll trim. Display the panel to the right of the clip. This way, we can monitor the panel while we adjust the clip.**

3 **Drag the tail of the purple.artbeats.mov clip to the left to trim the clip about an eighth of an inch. Notice that in the Info panel, as you drag the Trim Out point, the duration of the clip changes. Adjust the Trim Out point so that the Info palette indicates a clip duration of 00:00:03 seconds. This is one way you can adjust the Out point on a clip in the Timeline.**

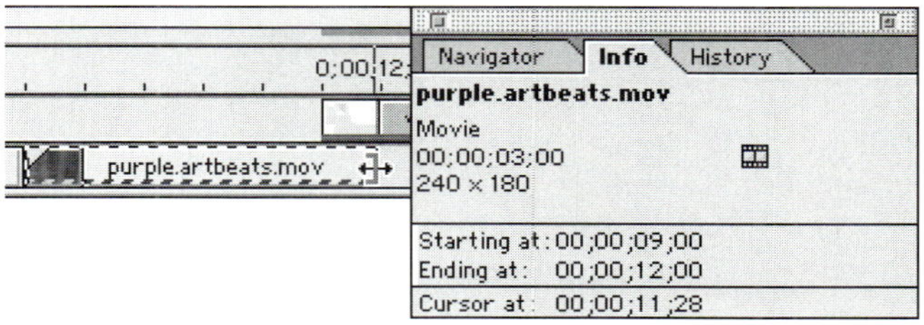

As you can see, trimming this way is a very visual method.

> **TIP** **The Info palette comes to life when you select any element in the Timeline, Monitor, or Program window. You can obtain information about any object in this palette. Depending on the type of object you select, the properties in the Info palette will change.**

If you double-click the purple.artbeats.mov clip, you'll notice that a few things have happened. The first is that the new In and Out points you just set by dragging the trim handles in the Timeline are indicated in the top of the panel. The second thing you'll notice is that the In and Out points for this clip are indicated in the Program view with a green fill between them. The third thing that happens is that the newly trimmed clip now appears in the Source window and in the Select Source Clip pop-up menu. Also in the Source view, you'll see the new clip duration time indicated at the left of the controls.

To Finish off the clips on Video Track 1:

1. **Drag the clip named funkyblue.artbeats.mov from the Source view into the Timeline so the head of the clip butts up against the tail of the clip named purple.artbeats.mov.**

2. **With the Info palette displayed, trim the Out point of this clip so the duration of the clip is 00:00:03 seconds, using the same technique we used on the purple.artbeats.mov clip.**

> **NOTE** If the Toggle Edge Viewing button is turned on (at the bottom left of the Timeline), you can see the trim happen in the Program view.

If you're following the lesson along with the book, do a Save As on your file and save it in the chapter 05 folder on your hard drive. Name the new file chapter05_begin2.ppj. We'll use this file to experiment with the many other editing tools in the Timeline. Otherwise, you can just follow along using figures and illustrations in the book for reference.

Before we continue exploring the editing tools in the Timeline, let's review some ways you can move around in it.

Navigating the Timeline

To edit effectively in the Timeline, you must be able to move around quickly. We discuss how to do this in the following section, including using the toolbox, Navigator palette, markers, and shortcut keys.

The Left Side of the Timeline Toolbox Tools

We've already had some experience using the Zoom and Selection tools in the previous section's exercise. Now we examine the other navigation tools at the left side of the Timeline toolbox (Figure 5-2).

> **NOTE** All the tools in the toolbox can be accessed using letter keys as a shortcut. For example, clicking the letter z always accesses the Zoom tool. For a complete list of all the keys associated with the tools, go to Help | Keyboard Shortcuts in the Premiere menu.

The Hand Tool

The Hand tool appears as a gloved hand. Similar to such tools in other graphics programs, the Hand tool lets you drag and move backward and forward through the Timeline. Because parts of the Timeline are often out of your viewing area, this

FIGURE 5-2

Tools at the left side of the Timeline toolbox let you select and navigate the Timeline

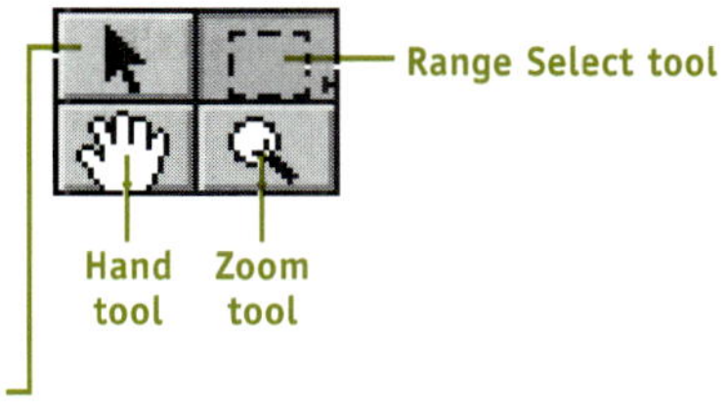

is a convenient feature. It's the equivalent of clicking or dragging the scroll bars. To use it, select the hand from the toolbox, and click and drag in the Timeline.

The Range Select Tool

The Range Select tool is used to select a range of clips in the Timeline. To use this tool, select it and bring the tool into the Timeline. When you do this, it turns into a crosshair with a box in the lower right corner. Click and drag over the clips you want to select. Once you've selected them, you can move this selection to another place in the Timeline.

The Range Select tool is in a flyout menu in the Timeline toolbar with three other tools (see Figure 5-3). You access the flyout tools by clicking on an icon that has a little arrow in the bottom right corner of the icon. This group of tools helps you select clips in different ways. These tools include the following:

- **Block Select tool** This tool lets you create virtual clips. Virtual clips act as a container for a sequence of clips. Almost like making a group out of selected clips, once selected clips are made into a virtual clip, they appear as one clip. You can reuse virtual clips as additional instances, too. You can also apply different settings, transitions, and effects to virtual clips. To use this tool, select it and click and drag over the clips you want included in your virtual clip. You'll see a marquee around the clips as you drag. Select the grouping and drag them

FIGURE 5-3

The Range Select tool is in a flyout menu in the Timeline toolbar

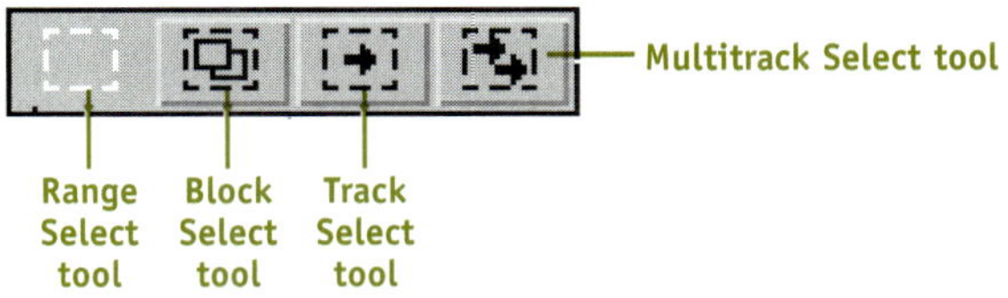

to another part of the Timeline. They turn into a single green bar, and the original clips stay intact.

- **Track Select tool** This tool selects all clips on a track.
- **Multitrack Select tool** Similar to the Track Select tool, this tool lets you select clips on multiple tracks.

That's it for the Select tools. Now let's look at ways we can navigate the Timeline.

Navigating the Timeline

If you know what you're doing, it's easy to navigate the Timeline. This is especially important for finding your way around when you're making a lengthy video, where the Timeline goes on and on. You want to be able to move to a frame or an area as quickly as possible. As a beginner, instinct probably tells you that you can get around simply by dragging, or scrubbing (with the Selection tool) the Edit line backward and forward in the Timeline. This does, in fact, work, and you'll probably use it often. Another convenient feature for navigating is the Navigator palette.

The Navigator Palette

The Navigator palette gives you a miniature version of the Edit line and Timeline (Figure 5-4). To access the window, select Window | Navigator from the top menu.

If you click and drag the green rectangle in the box, you can move backward and forward in the Timeline. Notice when you do this, the scroll bars at the bottom of the Timeline window move, too.

FIGURE 5-4
The Navigator palette provides an easy way to get around the Timeline

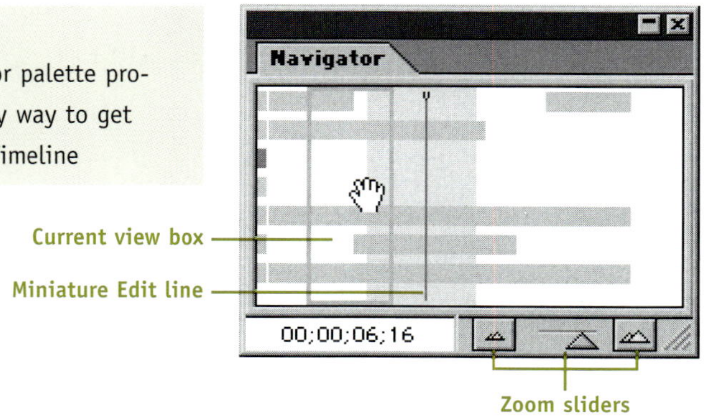

If you hold down the SHIFT key and drag the miniature representation of the Edit line in the Navigator, you can control the Edit line in the Timeline. The miniature Edit line appears as a red line. This is a quick and easy way to move to a particular spot in the Timeline.

You can also use the little icons at the bottom of the window—the zoom sliders—to change the zoom of the area in the Timeline you're navigating.

SHORTCUT KEYS

After working a while in Premiere, you'll yearn for some shortcut keys to make your project move more efficiently. Because we're discussing navigation, let's review some common navigation shortcuts:

- Move to first frame: A or HOME
- Move Edit line marker to last frame: S
- Play: SPACEBAR, tilde (~), or L
- Preview: ENTER (Windows) or RETURN (Mac)
- Reverse: J
- Stop-spacebar: K
- Move Edit line forward one frame: 2 or right arrow
- Moving Edit line backward one frame: 1 or left arrow:
- Moving Edit line forward five frames: 4 or SHIFT + right arrow
- Moving Edit line backward five frames: 3 or SHIFT + left arrow
- Deselect elements: CONTROL-SHIFT-A (Windows) or COMMAND-SHIFT-A (Mac)

There are many more keys you can use to help you navigate and edit. In fact, many of the shortcut keys are exactly the same as those used in professional editing workstations. Refer to the Quick Reference card that came with your software or Help | Keyboard Shortcuts in the menu for a complete list of shortcuts.

THE WORK AREA BAR

The work area bar spans the area of the Timeline in which you're currently working. This area is defined in the Timeline by a thin, yellow bar with two sliding arrows on both ends that resides on top of the Timeline.

The work area bar defines the area of the Timeline you want to preview. Previewing a program is discussed later in the section, "Controlling Tracks in the Timeline."

You can reposition the bar by clicking and dragging it backward and forward. You can shorten and lengthen this bar to change the range of your work area.

To Change THE RANGE OF YOUR WORK AREA:

1. **Click and drag the end markers until your work area is the length you want it to be.**
2. **To set up the work area on a continuous series of clips, press ALT and click (Windows) or OPTION and click (Mac) on the work area bar.**
3. **To set up the work area so it spans everything in the current view of your Timeline, double-click the work area bar.**
4. **To preview your defined work area, press ENTER (Windows) or RETURN (Mac).**

You'll notice other bars that appear in the top of the Timeline from time to time. If the program contains transitions and special effects on certain clips, you'll see a red bar at the top of this area, indicating areas that must be rendered so they can be seen in the Program view.

SETTING MARKERS IN THE TIMELINE

"What's a marker?" you may wonder. In and Out points are a type of marker because they mark the trim points of a clip. You can also create markers in Premiere to help find your way around the Timeline when it becomes too long and complex to handle.

You can also use markers to designate important things occurring in your movie at different points. Both the Timeline and individual clips can have their own markers.

You can add markers from the Monitor window and the Timeline (Figure 5-5).

FIGURE 5-5

You can set markers in both the Source and Program views of the Monitor window

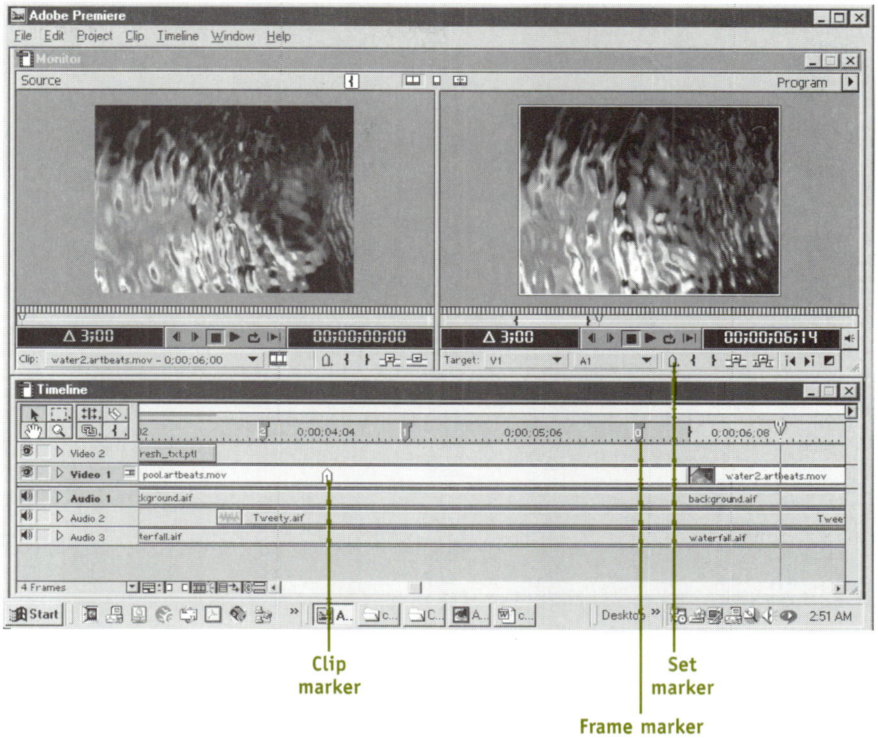

To Add A MARKER TO A CLIP:

1 Move the edit line to a place on a clip where you want to add a clip marker. Right-click (Windows) or press OPTION and click (Mac) a clip in the Timeline to access the pop-up context menu. In the pop-up menu, select Set Clip Marker. From the flyout menu, select a numbered or an unnumbered clip. Select a number from zero to nine.

2 You can have up to 10 numbered markers and 999 unnumbered markers on a clip.

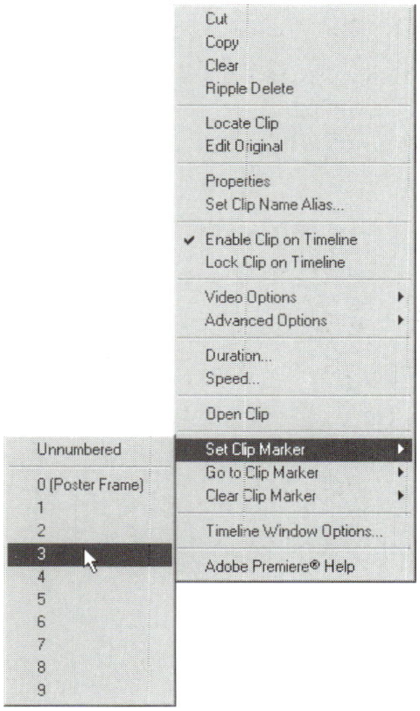

> **TIP** You can press ALT and double-click (Windows) or CONTROL and double-click (Mac) on the clip in the Timeline to display the clip in a clip window. In the clip window, you can use the marker icon to display a pop-up menu. and set clip markers right in the Source view. If Edit | Preferences | General and Still Images | Open Movies in Clip Window is selected, a clip window will open as the default when you double-click.

To Add MARKERS TO THE PROGRAM VIEW IN THE TIMELINE:

1. Navigate to the point in the Timeline where you want to place a marker.
2. Right-click (Windows) or press OPTION and click (Mac) the top of the Timeline in the time ruler to access the pop-up context menu.
3. In the pop-up menu, select Set Timeline Marker.
4. From the flyout menu, select a numbered or an unnumbered clip. Just as with a clip marker, you select a number from zero to nine for a numbered clip marker, and you can have up to 999 unnumbered markers. You can clear a marker from this flyout menu, too.

> **NOTE** You can also set Timeline markers in the Source view by selecting a frame in the Source with the frame marker line and clicking the marker icon to access the marker pop-up and flyout menus.

To Navigate TO A PARTICULAR MARKER:

1. Select Timeline | Go To Frame Marker.
2. From the pop-up menu, select the marker you want or use the shortcut keys indicated in this menu. For example, SHIFT-Q moves one marker forward, and SHIFT-W moves one marker backward. You can also use the content menu on the marker to do this.

To Delete A CLIP MARKER:

1. Right-click (Windows) or press CONTROL and click (Mac) a clip to access the context menu.
2. Select Clear Clip Marker.
3. Select the number you want to clear, or select Clear All Markers or Clear Current Marker.

You can also clear a marker from any of the pop-up menus that let you make a clip marker. And, you can clear In and Out points on a clip this way, too.

To Make COMMENTS ON A MARKER:

1. Select a marker in the Timeline.

2 **Right-click (Windows) or press CONTROL and click (Mac) on the top of the Timeline to access the context menu.**

3 **From the pop-up menu, select Edit Timeline Marker.**

4 **In the Marker dialog box, you can add comments.**

5 **Select Timeline | Edit Timeline Marker.**

6 **In the Marker Edit dialog box, you can include comments, add web links, target HTML frames, and delete markers.**

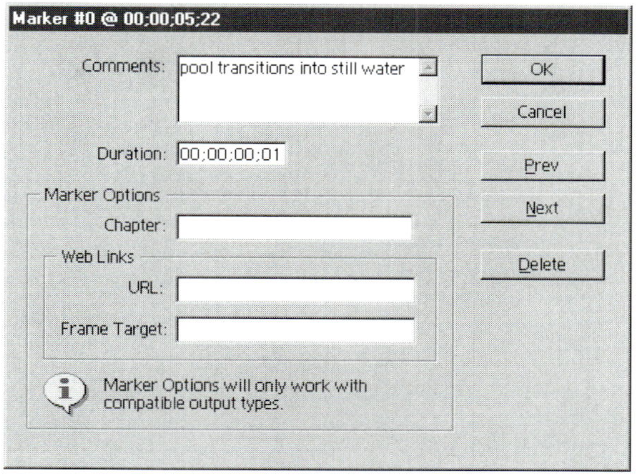

Markers are an easy way of customizing your navigation in Premiere, especially on large projects. Another aspect of controlling your movie in the Timeline is understanding how to control individual tracks. We cover this next.

CONTROLLING TRACKS IN THE TIMELINE

There are many ways you can control the way tracks look in Premiere. In Chapter 2, we learned about Single-Track versus A/B Editing. So far in this chapter, the file we've been manipulating (chapter05_begin2.ppj) uses Single-Track Editing. Shortly, we'll switch to A/B Editing to examine the difference between the two.

Let's look at some of the ways we can modify tracks.

Tracks, as discussed in Chapter 2, are a way of layering elements (Figure 5-6). This lets you blend together one or more elements that reside on different tracks to create some spectacular effects.

Although our movie is in an unfinished state, let's preview it. This way we can see how layers relate to one another.

To Preview THE MOVIE:

1 **Make sure the work area bar is over the entire Timeline. To set the work area so it spans all clips, with the bar selected, press ALT and click (Windows) or OPTION and click (Mac).**

FIGURE 5-6
Tracks in the Timeline

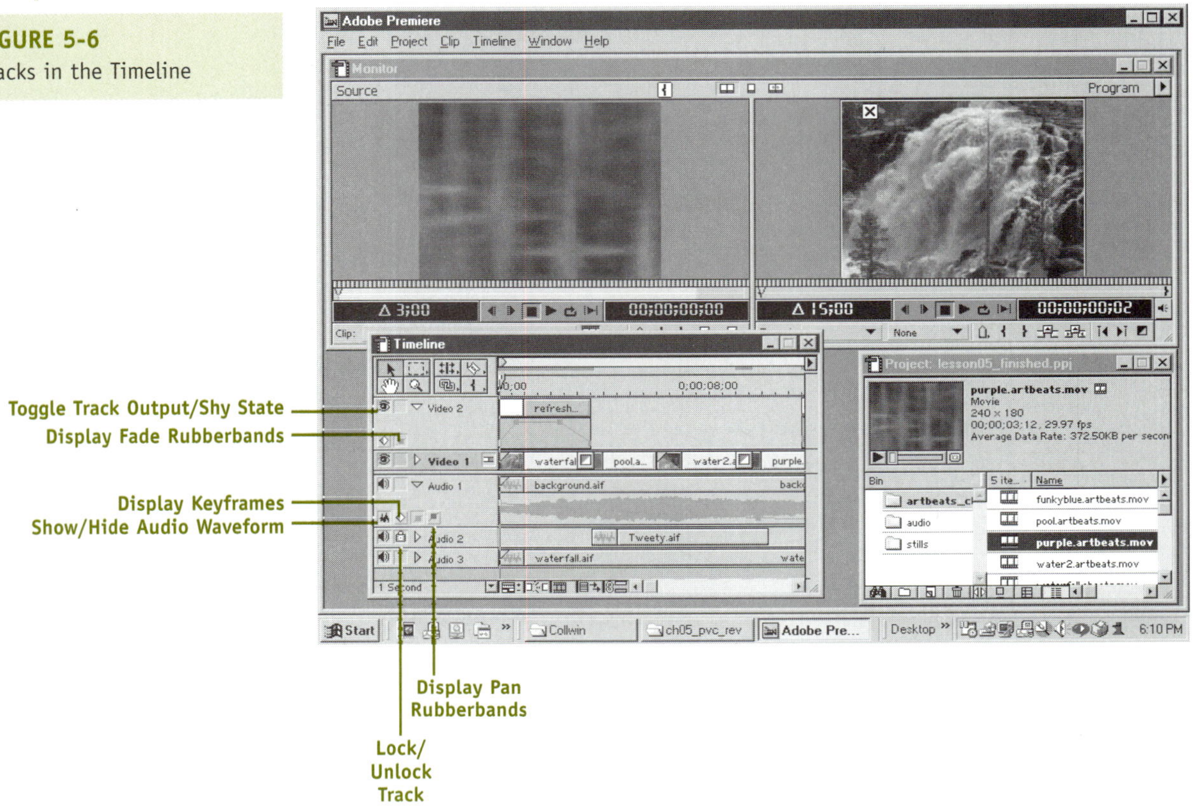

2 **Press ENTER (Windows) or RETURN (Mac) to render the Timeline.**

3 **When the preview is finished being rendered, it will appear in the Program view.**

Let's explore the various track features in the Timeline.

The main tracks are Video Track 1, where the main video clips reside, and Audio Track 1, where the main audio resides. Any subsequent video tracks will be layered on top of the main tracks in sequential stacking order.

You can expand and collapse tracks to view their contents.

To See THE CONTENTS OF VIDEO TRACK 1:

1 **Click on the RIGHT ARROW to expand.**

2 Click DOWN ARROW to collapse.

3 To expand the Track mode in Video Track 1, click the Track Mode button.

To Make tracks visible and invisible in the program:

1 Click the eye icon.

2 When the eye icon is not visible, the clip is *shy* (i.e., hidden from view until you click the eye icon again).

To Lock a track:

1 Click the box at the right of the eye icon in a track.

2 When a lock appears, a track is locked. Nothing can be moved on it.

To Add or delete a track:

▶ Click the Track Options icon button at the bottom left of the Timeline.

Editing Tools in the Timeline

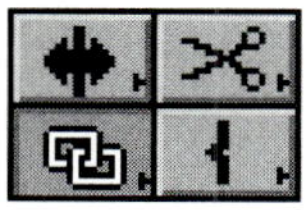

Now that you're feeling more comfortable with the Timeline, let's quickly explore the tools at the right side of the Timeline.

These tools are used to perform functions such as moving, editing, and cutting clips in the program.

Tools at the Right Side of the Toolbox

One tool immediately looks familiar: the In/Out point tool at the bottom right corner. You can actually click a clip in the Timeline with this tool and trim it. The four tools displayed in this part of the toolbox all have flyout menus offering different tool selections beyond what you see. When you select a tool from the flyout menus, the selected tool becomes the current tool. Let's start in the upper-left portion of the right side of the toolbox and examine these tools.

USING THE ROLLING EDIT TOOL

The Rolling Edit tool is located in the flyout menu in the toolbar with the Ripple Edit tool (Figure 5-7). With a *rolling edit,* the clips adjacent to the clip being trimmed (to the left and right) are adjusted to maintain the duration of the program. In other words, whatever is added or subtracted from the clip you're performing the rolling edit on, the altered duration of the clip will be figured into the adjacent clip. The program plays the same length of time as it did before you started trimming clips.

You'll notice that the Rolling Edit tool feels and works like the Trim In and Trim Out handles in the Timeline. Let's do a rolling edit in file chapter05_begin2, to help you get a feel for the tool.

To Use THE ROLLING EDIT TOOL:

1. **Select the Rolling Edit tool from the Timeline toolbar and mouse over the tail of the clip in the Timeline named pool.artbeats.mov.**

2. **When you do this, the pointer turns into the Rolling Edit icon, indicating the name of the clip in a tool tip pop-up box.**

3. **With the Navigator palette displayed, drag the clip to the right to lengthen its duration a few frames. You can display two adjacent clips in the Program view when Toggle Edge Viewing is on (Figure 5-8). To turn it on, click the Toggle Edge Viewing icon at the bottom left of the Timeline. This is a convenient feature because it lets you preview the results of this edit.**

FIGURE 5-7
The Rolling and Ripple Edit tools contain three other tools in their flyout menu

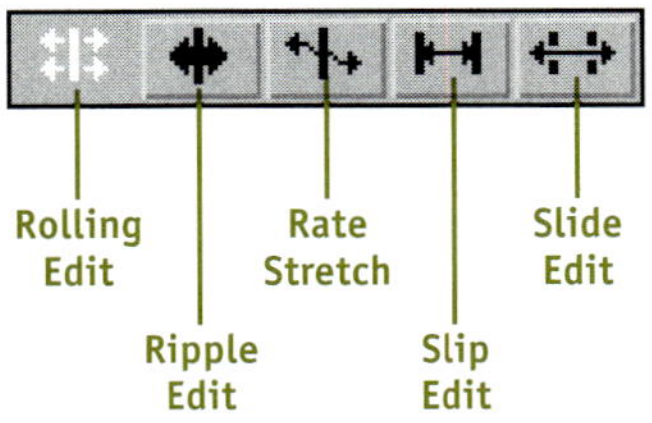

FIGURE 5-8
When you use the Rolling Edit tool, you can preview the results of the edit in the Program view when Toggle Edge Viewing is on

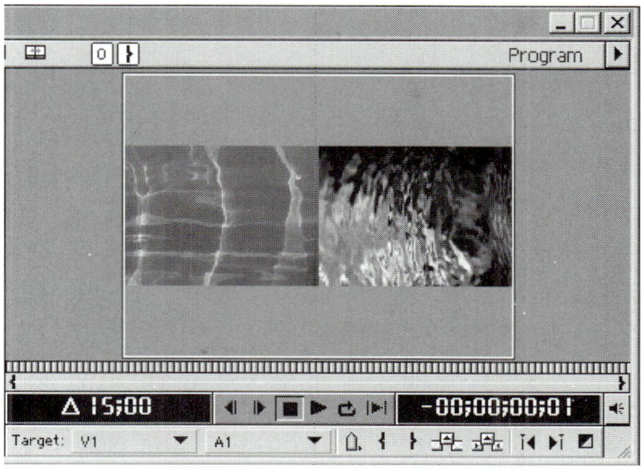

When you let go of the mouse, notice the clip to the right of the clip you trimmed is shorter, the clip you trimmed is longer, but the duration of the program is the same as before.

The Ripple Edit Tool

Performing a ripple edit changes the duration of a clip in the Timeline. The Ripple Edit tool is similar to trimming a clip with the Trim In and Out handles. It even works the same way in that you use it by dragging the end frame of a clip. The difference is that with the Ripple Edit tool, the clips adjacent to the clip being trimmed maintain their duration and sequential position when the trimmed clip is shortened or lengthened.

The result is the trimmed clip changes in length, the total program duration changes accordingly, and the other clips on the track clips still remain the same in sequence and duration. So the clips scoot over accordingly in a ripple edit to eliminate any gaps in the track that may have resulted. Let's undo our last edit so we can redo it with the Ripple Edit tool.

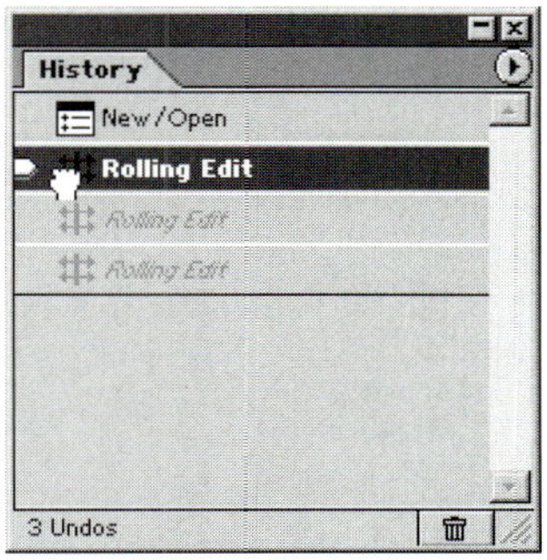

To undo the edit, we'll use the History palette. The History palette is similar to using an Edit | Undo from the menu. The difference is the number of undos is unlimited. The History palette records all your work in a particular project. Let's use the History palette to return to the project the way it was when we first opened it.

To Use the History palette:

1. **Select Window | History from the menu to display the palette.**
2. **Slide the arrow on the left slider up through the different edits you made with the Rolling Edit tool, back to the first entry (File | Open), when you first opened the file for this session.**
3. **You can now start fresh on this file.**

You can also redo your work by sliding the bar down again. Notice when you undo, the previous recorded information is dimmed.

Now that you've undone all the rolling edits, let's add a ripple edit to see how it affects the trimmed clips.

> **TIP** Another way to start from the beginning of a project is to select File | Revert to Saved from the menu. Then open the file in the state it was in when it was last saved.

To Use the Ripple Edit tool to trim a clip:

1. **In chapter05_begin2, display the Info palette from the Window menu (Window | Show Info). The Info palette will help you determine exactly where a clip begins and ends and where the Edit line marker is located. Notice it also indicates the name of the object you've selected and the type of object it is.**
2. **Select the Ripple Edit tool in the toolbox.**
3. **In the Timeline, click the head of the clip named water2.mov. Notice the Program window displays the adjacent clip, pool.artbeats.mov, because Toggle Edge Viewing is turned on (Figure 5-9). The Toggle Edge Viewing button is located at the bottom left of the Timeline.**
4. **Drag the clip to the right about an eighth of an inch to eliminate some frames. Notice when you eliminate these frames the total movie timecode changes in the Info palette, too.**

> **TIP** If you're having a problem trimming just a few frames from a clip, click the Toggle Snap to Edges button in the bottom left corner to turn the snap to function off in the Timeline.

FIGURE 5-9
The Program window displaying adjacent clips as the water2.artbeats.mov clip is being edited with the Ripple Edit tool (Toggle Edge Viewing is on)

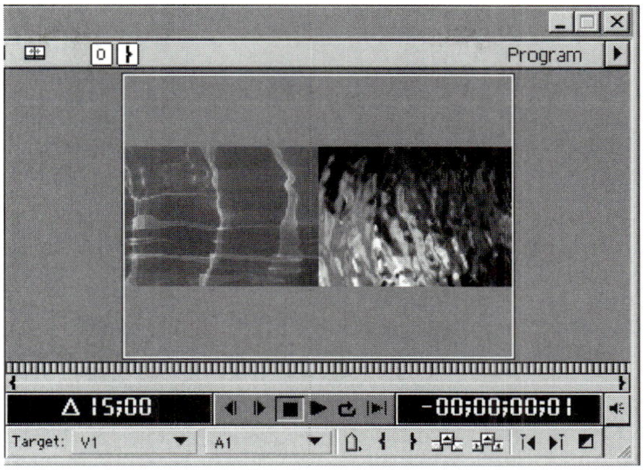

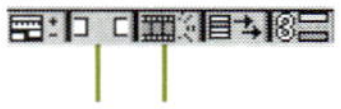

5 **Instead of leaving a blank space or adjusting the adjacent clip, the clips on this track move over, resulting in no gaps in the track and a shorter program duration.**

The remaining tools in this flyout menu are the Rate Stretch tool and the Slip and Slide tools. These three tools also provide you with additional ways of trimming in the Timeline.

USING THE RAZOR TOOL

The Razor tool is located to the right of the Ripple and Rolling Edit tools and resembles a razor (Figure 5-10). Use the Razor tool to split a clip into two pieces to apply effects you couldn't apply to only one clip. For example, if you wanted to change the frame rate twice on a clip, you might want to split it in two, set the frame rate on the first half to one rate and the second half to another. Splitting clips creates separate instances of the clip.

To Use THE RAZOR TOOL:

- **Select the Razor tool from the toolbox. In the Timeline, click the clip in the place where you want to split the clip. The clip is split in two.**

> **NOTE** **Clips that are locked can't be split with the Razor tool.**

FIGURE 5-10
The Razor tool has a flyout menu with additional tools.

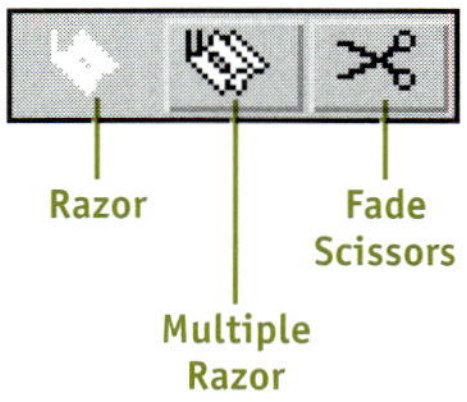

FADE SCISSORS TOOL The Fade Scissors tool appears as a scissors icon in the flyout menu with the Razor tool. This tool is used to adjust audio levels. Audio in Premiere is discussed in Chapter 11.

NOTE **The Multiple Razor tool appears as a double razor icon in the flyout menu with the Razor tool. It works the same way as the Razor tool, but it splits through all the clips on all tracks and creates separate instances of all clips.**

ADDITIONAL TOOLBOX TOOLS

Although the toolbox appears small at first, as you can see, it's filled with many tools hidden in flyout menus. Let's review the remaining tools in the toolbox.

SOFT LINK/UNLINK TOOL The Soft Link tool appears in the toolbox flyout menu with the Crossfade and Fade Adjustment tools (Figure 5-11). This tool is used to link together and unlink video and audio clips. When these clips are linked, they can be moved as one entity. Links are used for the syncing of audio and video in the Timeline.

To Link CLIPS TOGETHER:

1. **Select the link tool in the Timeline toolbox.**

FIGURE 5-11
The Soft Link tool is in a flyout menu with two other tools.

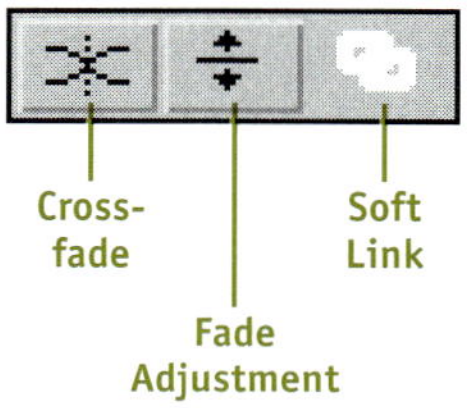

2 Click a video clip.

3 Click on an audio clip (see the illustration).

4 When the clips are linked together, they change into a light aqua color. You can move them now as one unit.

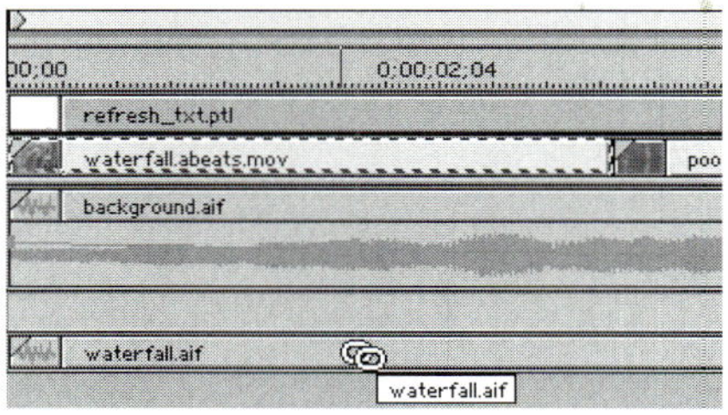

To Unlink clips:

1 Select the Soft Link tool in the Timeline toolbox.

2 Click on one clip of the linked clips.

3 Click on the other clip.

4 Now these two clips are unlinked and back in their original state.

> **TIP** When you turn off the Toggle Sync Mode button located at the bottom of the Timeline, you can edit linked clips independently. The Sync Mode button is a toggle button and is turned off when the lock icon disappears (see the illustration).

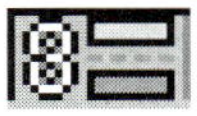

Soft links are also useful when you use DV clips with sound and you want to eliminate or move the audio to another place on the Timeline. Digital video that includes audio can then be imported with the video and audio linked together.

Crossfade and Fade Adjustment Tools The Crossfade and Fade Adjustment tools are used for editing audio. We'll experiment with these tools more in Chapter 11 on audio.

Shift Tracks Button

The Shift Tracks button is located at the bottom of the Timeline window (see Figure 5-12). This button is used in conjunction with editing in the Monitor window; specifically the Insert button in the Source view. The Shift Tracks button is a toggle button and has two states, the "Shift material on all unlocked tracks" state and the "Shift material only in target tracks" state.

When you perform an Insert edit (discussed in Chapter 4), clips move downward in time to accommodate the new clip. This makes the program duration longer. When we played with the Insert button in Chapter 4, we inserted only one clip in

FIGURE 5-12
Shift Tracks button

a single-track movie. But what happens when you use Insert edit on a track in a multitrack movie? The "Shift materials in all unlocked tracks" option lets you control the results of your insert. Clips on all unlocked tracks shift farther down the Timeline, so all the tracks are still in sync with one another.

The "Shift materials only in target tracks" option does just what the name implies. It shifts the clips in the Timeline only where the Insert edit was performed. So other tracks are unaffected by changes.

Finishing the Chapter Movie

At the beginning of this chapter, we started editing file chapter 05_begin.ppj. Let's return to that movie so it looks more like the finished version, chapter05_finished. To refresh your memory, take a look at the finished file. When you're ready, open the chapter05_begin.ppj file.

The final version of the movie has additional transitions in it that aren't in the chapter05_begin.ppj version. We discuss transitions at length in Chapter 7, but for this chapter, we'll just cover a few simple ones.

Transitions are effects you can add to clips to help one clip smoothly transition into another, as opposed to a simple cut.

To Add a default transition to a clip in a movie:

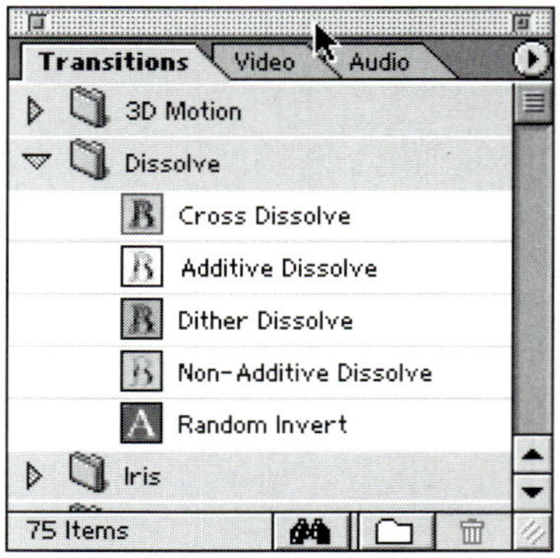

1. **Select Window | Show Transitions from the menu to display the Transitions palette.**

2. **Navigate through the various folders in this palette to find the folder called Dissolve. Notice you can scroll up and down on this palette just as in any other window.**

3 Double-click the Dissolve folder to view its contents. We'll add the transition called Cross Dissolve between the clips named pool.artbeats.mov and water2.artbeats.mov.

4 In the Transitions palette, click and drag the transition named Cross Dissolve between the clips named pool.artbeats.mov and water2.artbeats.mov in the Timeline.

5 The Fix Transition dialog box appears. This dialog box states there are not enough frames available to create this effect and offers a solution to the problem. We'll follow the suggestion of the dialog box, which is to make the duration of the transition 13 frames. The default duration setting for transitions in this project is 20 frames. Click OK.

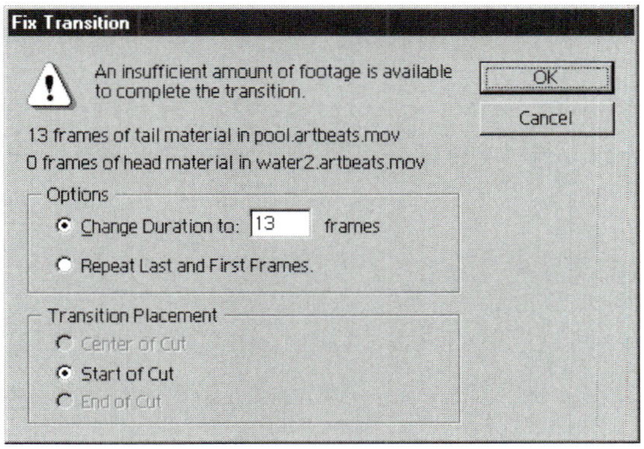

6 You'll now see the transition in the Timeline at the tail of the pool.artbeats.mov clip and the head of the water2.mov clip.

Now let's add a transition between the clips named water2.artbeats.mov and purple.artbeats.mov. We'll use the same method as before, but this time the transition will appear between two different clips.

To Add A TRANSITION BETWEEN THE CLIPS WATER2.ARTBEATS.MOV AND PURPLE.ARTBEATS.MOV:

1 From the Transitions palette, drag a Cross Dissolve transition (the same transition we used before) onto the clip named water2.artbeats.mov.

2 This time, the Fix Transition dialog box doesn't appear because there is sufficient footage for the transition to work.

To Add A ZOOM TRANSITION BETWEEN THE CLIPS PURPLE.ARTBEATS.MOV AND FUNKYBLUE.ARTBEATS.MOV:

1 From the Transitions palette, scroll to find the folder named Zoom and click it to open.

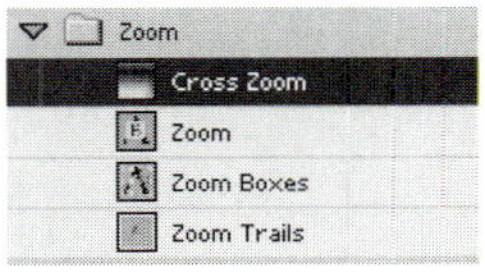

2 Select the transition named Cross Zoom and drag it to the tail of the purple.artbeats.mov clip in the Timeline.

3 **The Fix Transition dialog box will appear. Leave the settings as they are and click OK. The purple.artbeats clip is now transitioned into the funkyblue clip with a zoom transition.**

Let's play back the movie and view it in the Program view so we can see the transitions and other effects. In the Timeline, drag the edit line back to the first frame (or press the A key or UP ARROW). Select the Program view and click the L key to play.

Notice that you can't see any of the transitions you added. That's because transitions must be rendered before they can be seen. You can quickly preview your transitions by clicking the Timeline ruler while holding down ALT (Windows) or OPTION (Mac) key and scrubbing over the area, as shown in Figure 5-13. Or, you can preview the movie (or a portion of the movie).

To preview the entire movie, select Timeline | Preview from the menu, or press ENTER (Windows) or RETURN (Mac). When the project is finished being rendered, click the Program view in the Monitor window and play the movie. Use the Play button or press L. Now you can see all the effects that couldn't bee seen previously. We discuss previewing in more detail in Chapter 10.

FIGURE 5-13
To quickly view a transition, superimposed element, or effect, hold down ALT (Windows) or OPTION (Mac) while scrubbing over the Timeline ruler

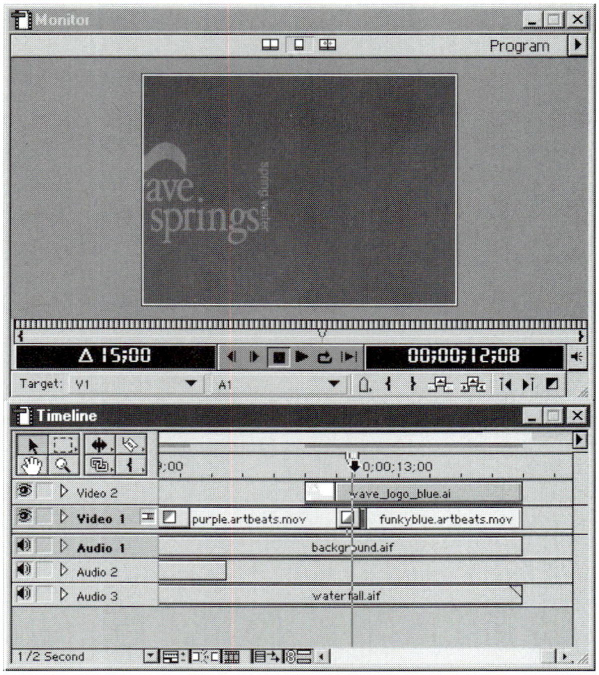

Previewing this file renders transitions, superimposed elements, or effects and saves them in a temporary folder that you've designated in the Edit | Preferences | Scratch Disks and Device Control dialog box.

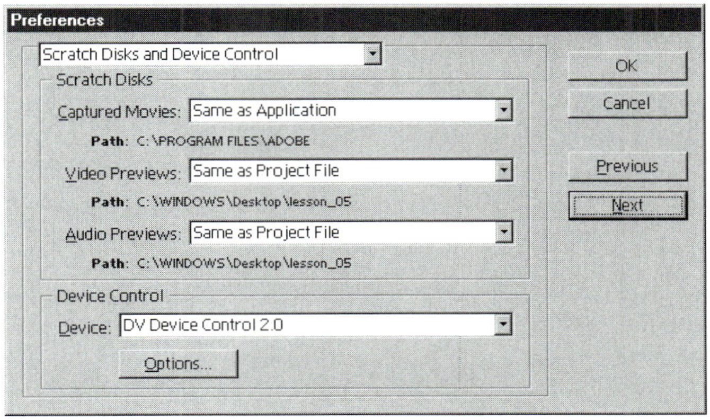

In the next chapter, we walk through the capture process with a DV camera. This process is essential for you to know if you'll be shooting and capturing your own digital video.

ON THE VIRTUAL CLASSROOM CD-ROM **The Timeline is where all your assets come together to form a production. In Lesson 3, "Manipulating Clips in the Timeline," learn how to navigate, manage, and edit clips in this window.**

6

Capturing Video in Premiere

If you plan to use your own footage to make a Premiere movie, you must capture the footage first. Capturing is simply the process of transferring your footage from a camera to your desktop in a digital format so you can assemble and edit clips to create a production.

Capturing in Premiere is simple, once you've set up the components correctly and understand how they work together. Because the success of your captures depends on these prerequisites, let's review the facts you need to know to ensure the process runs smoothly.

Because DV camcorders are growing in popularity and Premiere offers so many presets for DV and DV device control, we will briefly cover analog devices but focus in depth on the capturing process for DV camcorders.

Digital and Analog Media

In Premiere, you can capture both digital and analog video. If you're a beginner, it's helpful to understand the difference between digital and analog signals because in order to edit video on a computer, your video must be transformed into digital format, even if it originated as analog video.

Many older camcorders are analog devices, and you can still buy them. They are inexpensive because of the current surge in popularity of DV and mini DV formats.

Analog video signals comprise continuously fluctuating waveforms. These waveforms vary in their value at any given moment between a minimum and maximum range. When analog video is transmitted (as TV signals are transmitted live via airwaves), because of the varying nature of an analog transmission, extraneous noise is often introduced into the signal. Multiple duplications of analog video result in an accumulation of noise, making this a "lossy" format.

Analog video camcorders actually record video onto tape. Analog video doesn't become digitized until you capture it in Premiere via a video-capture card in your computer. So analog video goes through an extra process to become digital.

Digital signals on the other hand consist of discrete values that exist as precise points on a curve. Digital video such as is generated from a DV camcorder is already digitized before it gets to your computer. It's just a matter of getting the digitized video to your desktop from the camera, which is done with an IEEE 1394 connection. Digital video is "lossless" quality, meaning the quality remains the same with each generation no matter how many times it's duplicated.

Because analog and digital video are such different animals, you'll see how the capturing process for each format differs in the next section. Not only do they involve a different hardware configuration, but the Premiere settings are different for capturing digital and analog footage.

Working with Analog Video in Premiere

To capture analog video, an analog-to-digital video-capture card must be installed in your system. Computers don't come with video-capture cards as a standard feature unless you've purchased a customized configuration. These cards vary in price range and output quality. Some of the more expensive cards allow device control, which is the ability to run your device directly from the Premiere interface.

Connecting an Analog Video Camcorder to Your Computer

If your camcorder is analog, once your video-capture card is installed, you must connect the camcorder to the computer to capture the footage from tape.

There are three types of analog connections:

- Composite (typically found on VHS decks)
- S-Video (the standard for Hi-8 camcorders)
- Component (found on BetaSP decks)

The quality of these connections ranges from low to high, composite being the lowest. If the tape and video format are high quality, your digitized video will reflect this.

After your hardware is configured correctly, linking a device to your computer simply involves connecting a camcorder or tape deck from the S-video output jack (for example) to the S-video input jack on your computer's video-capture card. There will be separate cables for audio, too.

Many other issues are involved with analog video, such as additional cables for timecode and compression standards, that vary depending on your configuration. If this is your first time capturing analog video, you should acquire more knowledge about your hardware configuration before continuing in this chapter.

CAPTURING DIGITAL VIDEO IN PREMIERE

When you shoot footage with a DV camera, the footage is digitized and compressed right inside the camera. So, when you capture DV into Premiere, you're not capturing video as you are with an analog video-capture card. You're merely transferring it from tape to your computer.

If your configuration includes a DV camcorder, your hardware doesn't require a video-capture card. However, your system does require another card, known as an IEEE 1394 interface, FireWire (Mac), or iLink (Sony). The purpose of these cards is to enable the transfer of digital video from your DV camcorder to your computer's hard drive. Remember, the footage from the DV camcorder has already been digitized before it gets to your computer.

> **NOTE** **Before purchasing a FireWire/IEEE 1394 interface for your computer, it's a good idea to check on the Adobe web site just to make sure that the brand of card is approved by Adobe (www.adobe.com).**

Many of the newer Macs come configured with a FireWire interface. Because it's basically a connection, you can also use it for other FireWire peripherals such as hard drives and scanners.

Some PC configurations come equipped with IEEE 1394 interfaces, such as the Sony Viao, and some Dell and Compaq models. Most often, this card is an add-on that needs only to be installed in a PCI slot on your computer. Your IEEE 1394 needs to be OHCI (Open Host Controller Interface) compatible to work and, of course, you must have a slot available in your computer to accommodate the card. If this card is installed, the capture process is pretty much plug and play from there.

If you're not sure whether your system has a video-capture card or an IEEE 1394 interface or what format your camcorder is, ask a knowledgeable person to analyze all your hardware components. If your system is not configured for video capture in Premiere, you must configure it.

You have other hardware needs to address besides interface cards and cables. You want to make sure your configuration has sufficient RAM, a fast hard drive to capture and store your clips (using your internal hard drive is not recommended for a scratch disk), and the right size and kind of hard drive (Ultra SCSI, FireWire,

USB, or disk array). Covering configuration issues in detail is beyond the scope of this chapter. Before you reach the point where you can capture in Premiere, your system must be properly configured.

> **NOTE** For more information about configuring your system properly, go to the Help menu and select Adobe online, or go to www.adobe.com to search for Tech Notes on Premiere.

When you configure your system, make sure it's compatible with your objectives. For example, if you want to produce short, small video spots for the Web, your system doesn't need to be the powerhouse it should be if your output is lengthy broadcast quality footage.

CONNECTING YOUR DV CAMERA TO YOUR COMPUTER

Connecting a DV camera to your computer simply involves connecting an IEEE 1394/FireWire/iLink cable to the IEEE 1394 port on your computer (Figure 6-1). The connection method, cables, and port are essentially identical on Mac and Windows systems. The only variable is that the connectors come in different pin configurations (four and four, six and six, four and six), so you should make certain the pin configuration on the cable is compatible with your hardware.

FIGURE 6-1
Connecting your DV camera to the IEEE 1394 port on your computer

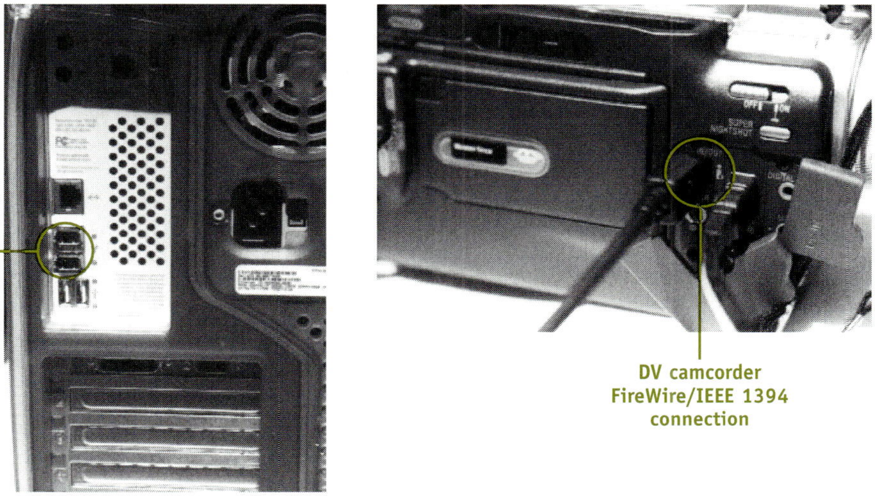

To Connect your DV camera for capture in Premiere:

1. Premiere should be launched *after* the DV camcorder is connected and turned on. Otherwise, Premiere can't recognize the device.
2. Make sure the camera is set to VTR/VCR mode.
3. Make certain the power cable is plugged into a wall outlet.

Preparing For DV Capture

After you've launched Premiere and connected your devices, check that your software settings are correct and in sync with your hardware and production objectives.

The capture process itself is generally the same on a Mac and PC, but some settings are different. Settings will also vary from project to project.

Let's examine a typical Windows-based setup using a DV camcorder. The Windows setup can be a little more complex than the Mac, but both processes are similar. It is assumed in this book that if you're capturing in Windows, your hardware is configured correctly and your IEEE 1394 connection uses the Microsoft driver. Although your card may have shipped with other drivers, Premiere recognizes only Microsoft drivers on the Windows platform.

> **TIP** Adobe has several tech documents available on its Premiere web site that show you how to identify and switch your IEEE 1394 drivers. The site even has some simple free utilities you can download that make it easy to switch the drivers back and forth, if necessary.

To verify your driver, display the properties on your hard drive (right-click) and select the Device Manager tab. Under Imaging Device, the Microsoft Video Camera driver should be listed. If it isn't there, you may be using another driver, and you must resolve this before you can move on. This driver issue applies only to a PC.

DV Settings

By now you're probably eager to get your footage into Premiere to create a production. Select File | New Project Settings. If it's the first time you've ever captured

DV in Premiere, you'll probably want to choose one of the preconfigured presets. After you've used the presets a few times, you may begin to develop and save your own custom settings relative to your production (Figure 6-2). If you're unsure what to select, use DV-NTSC, Standard 48 kHz or 32 kHz. 48 kHz is the audio sampling rate used by most DV camcorders, but check your DV camera to determine the rate the audio was recorded at, because with DV video you have to capture at the rate used to record the audio originally. Otherwise, your audio may be severely distorted or won't be captured at all.

From the Load Project Settings dialog box, you can access the new project settings by clicking the Custom button. Alternatively, if you're going straight to capture, you can customize settings in the Capture window. Premiere forces you to specify the settings before you can begin any new project.

Assuming we're capturing video in a Windows-based system, let's review a general selection of settings for an average capturing session.

To Preview THE SETTINGS FROM THE NEW PROJECT SETTINGS DIALOG BOX:

1. **Click the Custom button.**
2. **The first dialog box is the General Project Settings box (see the illustration on the following page.**

FIGURE 6-2
Choosing a DV-NTSC preset from the Load Project Settings dialog box

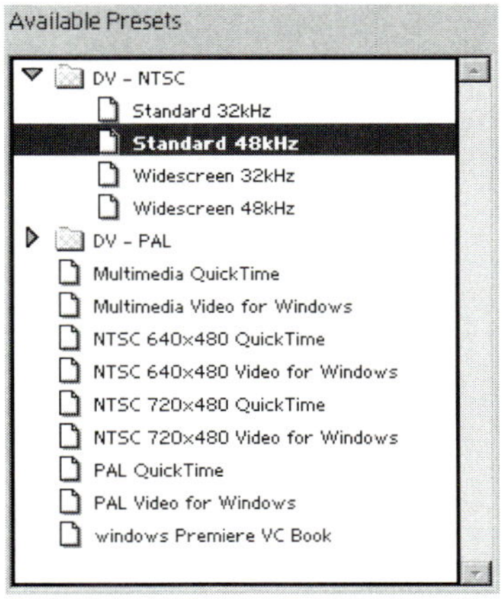

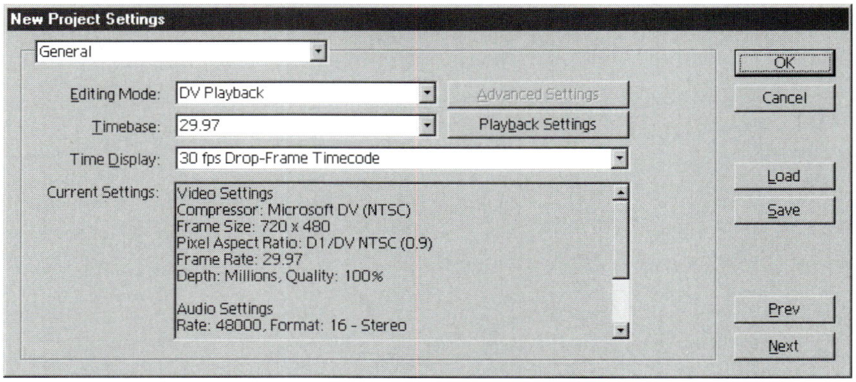

3 Because a preset was chosen, the correct settings are here; notably the Editing Mode is DV Playback, the Timebase is 29.97, and the timecode is 30 fps Drop-Frame. If you click the Playback Settings button, you can further customize your output and audio playback. Click Cancel to close this box. Back in General Project Settings, click the Next button to display the video settings.

> **NOTE** If you select the DV-PAL presets, the process is similar to that described here.

4 In the video settings, a default selection again is displayed because of the preset you chose.

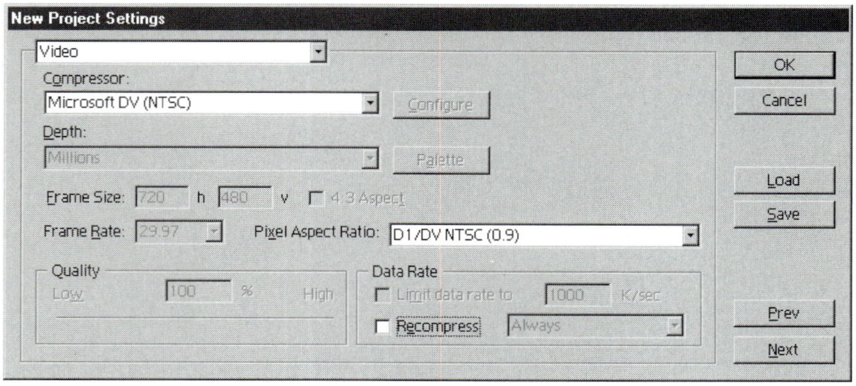

5 Because Windows uses a Microsoft-based DV editing mode and the Mac uses QuickTime, the settings are slightly different. For example, on a Mac, you can specify the size of the footage; in Windows you can't. The Pixel Aspect Ratio is 1:0.9 for DV. This refers to the relationship between the width and height of a pixel in an image. In DV, pixels are rectangular, not square. Recompress is deselected in both cases because DV doesn't need to be compressed again. Click the Next button several times until you see the Capture Settings dialog box.

6 The capture settings for DV differ in Windows and on the Mac. In Windows, the Capture Format is DV/IEEE 1394, and there is a DV Settings button that lets you further customize your preview options during preview and capture (see the illustration). On the Mac, your Capture Format is QuickTime and DV settings consist of three buttons: Video, Audio, and Advanced. Like the DV Settings button in Windows, these settings let you further customize your capture preview options. Click the Next button and go to the Keyframe and Rendering dialog box.

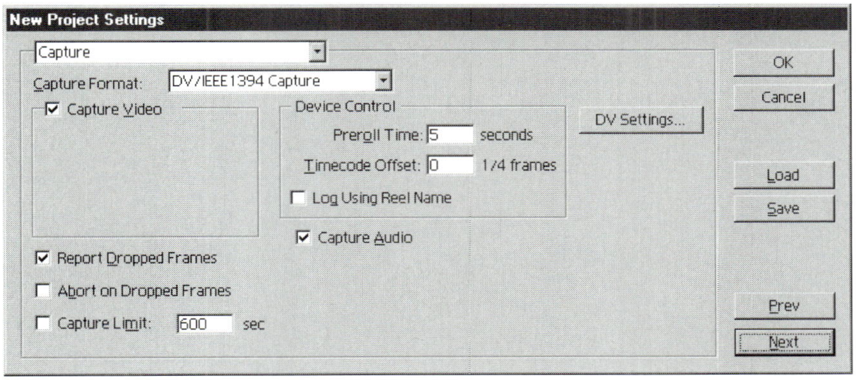

7 In Keyframe and Rendering, for Fields, select Lower Fields First. (DV is always Lower Fields First.) Fields relate to interlaced scan video, or the way the video frames are drawn as they display. Frames don't just suddenly appear as one whole image. Rather, each frame is created with a series of horizontal lines, known as "scan lines." "Fields" are alternating scan lines. "Interlacing" is dividing frames into two different fields. The first field, also called the "upper field," draws the odd-numbered horizontal scan lines from the top to the bottom of the frame. The second field, called the "lower field," fills in the even-numbered horizontal scan lines to complete the frame. The field you select in this Fields setting is the field that is drawn first. A "progressive scan" displays the horizontal scan lines in one field as opposed to two fields as with an interlaced scan. Camcorders record interlaced images, and video on a TV is interlaced. In contrast, computer monitors display in progressive scan. So if your final output is a computer screen, you would select No Fields. Selecting a field that's not consistent with your recording device will cause strange looking playback.

SELECTING A SCRATCH DISK AND CAPTURE DEVICE

Once you've determined your settings, you must select a scratch disk—the hard drive on which your capture files will be stored. Because your capture files will be large, you must make sure the disk you select is both your fastest and largest capacity. You can figure that four and a half minutes of DV video will use about 1 GB on your scratch disk. Again, for specs on the recommended speed of the disk you use for capture, refer to Adobe online.

To Select A SCRATCH DISK:

1 **Click Edit | Preferences | Scratch Disks and then Device Control in the menu to display the Scratch Disks and Device Control dialog box. In this dialog box, select a disk and a folder for your captures as well as your previews.**

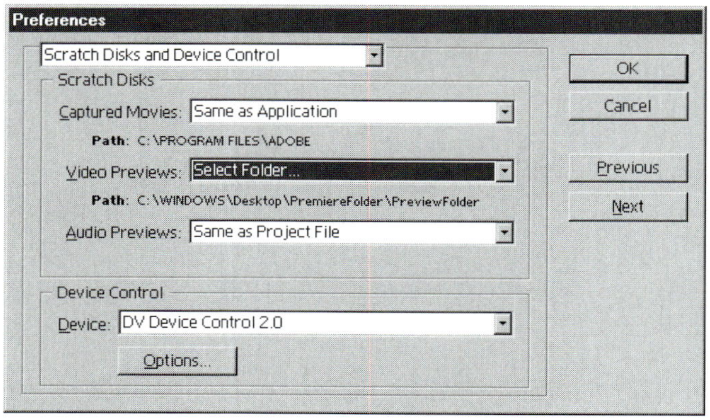

2 **You can also specify your DV device in this dialog box by clicking the Options button under Device Control. When you click this button, the DV Device Control Options dialog box lets you select your particular device, brand, and model from pop-up menus. Premiere offers a wide selection of different device drivers that were written specifically for these camcorders. If your DV camera is device-control enabled, Premiere can control it through the FireWire/IEEE 1394 connection with the DV Device Control plug-in.**

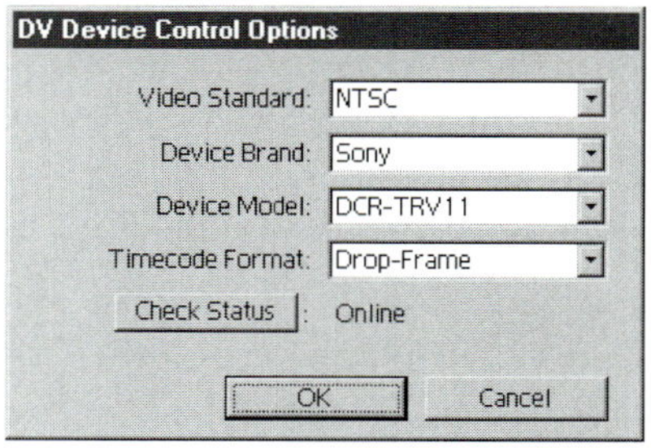

DEVICE CONTROL

Device control lets you regulate the tape in a video deck or DV camcorder in Premiere. You can control the device in Premiere as if you were playing the tape from the source itself. Device control also lets you use timecode to create *batch lists* (discussed later in this chapter), which let you record automatically in Premiere from a batch log.

For device control to work, your camera must support it. Then you must choose a corresponding control module for your particular device. DV device control varies from camera to camera, and drivers must exist for a specific device before it can be controlled from within Premiere. If your camcorder isn't listed in this menu, you can try choosing the closest or most similar model available in the list, but there are no guarantees that Premiere will be able to control it. In that case, check with Adobe to see whether any updates exist that support your camcorder.

Recording Timecode on Your Tape

If you want to take advantage of capturing with device control, a timecode track must be laid down on your tape. As discussed in Chapter 2, timecode keeps track of your footage by recording the hours, minutes, seconds, and frames. This ensures that all frames are accurate and consistent and each frame can be identified.

The timecode on your tape must be continuous and devoid of gaps to ensure it's recorded properly. If timecode is not present on your tape before you begin shooting, when you stop the camera, rewind, or switch tapes, your timecode becomes discontinuous. One way to prevent gaps in timecode is to continuously run your tape out and use the pause button if you have to stop.

Striping a Tape to Ensure Accurate Timecode

The other way to lay down timecode on your tape is to stripe a tape before recording. After the timecode is on the tape, you can record over it and the timecode still remains accurate. Thus, striping lets you stop, turn off, or switch tapes without worrying about maintaining the timecode.

To Stripe a tape:

1. **Insert a fresh tape into your camera.**
2. **With the lens cap on, plug the camera into a wall outlet. The timecode readout on your camera should be set at 0.**
3. **Press the Record button.**

4 **Play the tape through to the end. When it's done, the tape contains the proper timecode.**

5 **If the timecode is correct on the tape, the timecode in your capture window will match the timecode on your DV camcorder.**

The Movie Capture Window

To capture a clip, go to File | Capture | Movie Capture. In the Movie Capture window, among other things, you preview, control, and capture individual clips through your FireWire/IEEE 1394 interface (Figure 6-3).

The controls on the bottom of the capture preview control your camera or tape deck, assuming device control is set up correctly. Some of the controls will look familiar, like the Stop and Play buttons and the timecode readout. The other buttons control frames in different ways and are self-explanatory.

The Shuttle control slider lets you change the tape's speed based on the direction and distance you drag the slider from the center. The further you move it from the center, the faster the frames play.

FIGURE 6-3
Controls in the Movie Capture window

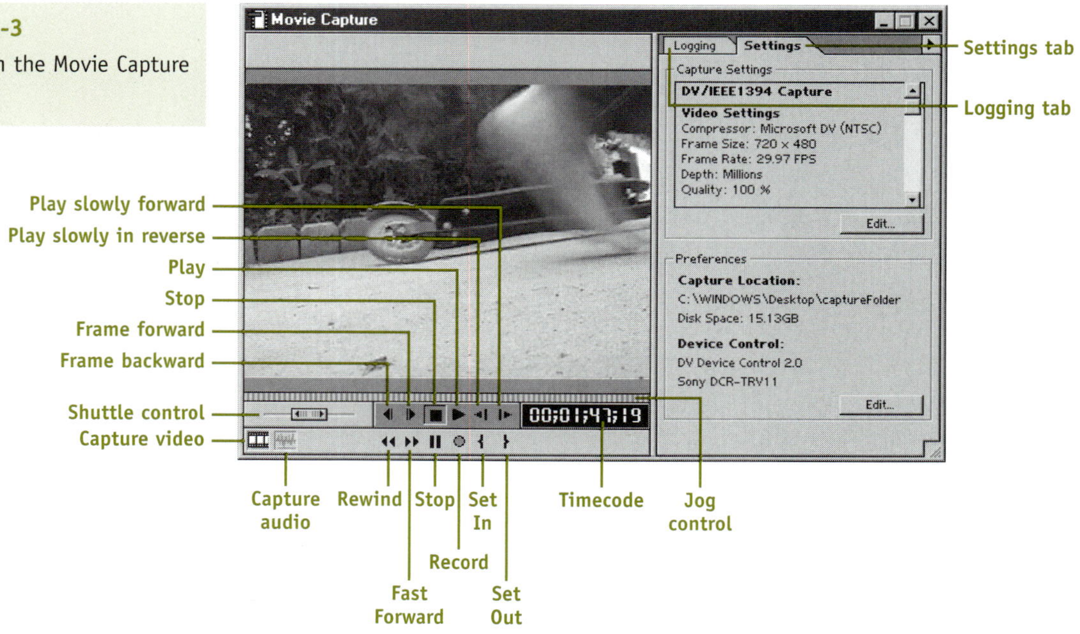

The Jog control, as in the Monitor window, lets you advance or reverse the tape one pixel at a time by dragging the control to the left or right.

The Capture video and Capture audio buttons let you record video or audio separately. To disable video or audio, click the appropriate icon to display a slash over it (Figure 6-4). For example, if you want video without the sound, click the audio and a slash will appear over the audio icon.

The Fast Forward and Rewind buttons work when the tape is playing or when it's stopped. When you fast forward or rewind while the tape is playing, the device moves the tape very quickly. When you fast forward or rewind when the tape is stopped, the tape moves even faster.

TIP **Some of the more common shortcut keys used in the Monitor window and Timeline also work in the Capture window. Remember the I and O keys for In and Out? You can use them here, too. The J (reverse), K (stop), and L (play) keys work as well. In addition, you can use the G key for Record. Familiarizing yourself with this set of keys (there are several more besides these), will help you move around the Capture window quickly.**

The Record button records the footage that's currently streaming. Clicking the Record button again is one way to turn off record.

You can change the Settings and Preferences directly in the Movie Capture window by clicking the Settings tab.

To Change THE SETTINGS:

1. **Click the Edit button under Settings. After you do this, the Project Settings window will display.**
2. **To change Preferences, click the Edit button under Preferences.**

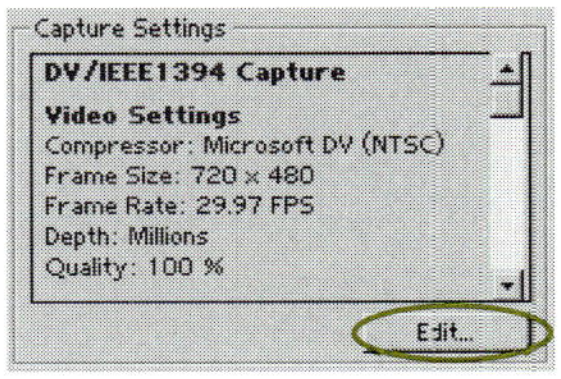

The Logging settings (under the Logging tab) are used to create a batch list, which is discussed in the section "Batch Capturing in Premiere."

FIGURE 6-4
To disable video or audio in a capture, click the appropriate Capture button, which displays a slash over the button, indicating audio or video is disabled

Capturing a Clip in the Movie Capture Window

Capturing a clip merely involves clicking two buttons and saving the clip. The hardest part of this process is deciding what portion of the tape you should capture.

To Capture a clip with device control in the Movie Capture window:

1. **Make sure the tape you want to capture from is in your device, the device is hooked up properly, and the proper settings have been selected.**
2. **Click the Play button or the L key to play the footage.**
3. **When you reach a segment you want to capture, click the Record button (G).**
4. **When you're done, press ESC or the Record button again to stop the recording.**
5. **In the File Name dialog box, name the clip. You can also add comments about the clip. The clip will appear in the Project window and be saved to the hard disk you selected in the Edit | Preferences | Scratch Disks and Device Control dialog box.**

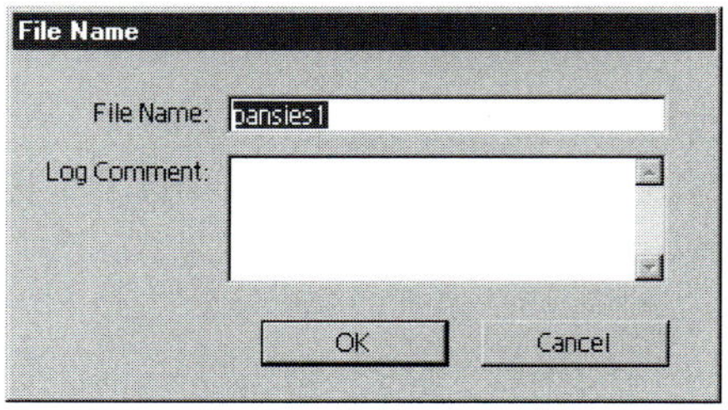

Capturing a Clip without Device Control

You don't have to use device control in Premiere, although it certainly makes the capture process much simpler because it involves using only the controls in Premiere. So if your camera is not device-control capable, you can still control the movie from the Movie Capture window.

To Capture footage from a device without device control:

1. **Display the Movie Capture window.**
2. **Play the tape from your camera's controls.**
3. **When you reach a segment on the tape you want to record, simply press the Record button (G).**
4. **Stop recording by pressing ESC or the Record button again.**

5 **Be sure to allow for additional footage on both ends for easy trimming in the Monitor window or Timeline.**

6 **Save the clip in the Save File dialog box.**

7 **The clip will appear in the Project window and be saved on your scratch disk.**

It's easy to capture a clip without device control. As you can see, it's similar to capturing with device control.

BATCH CAPTURING IN PREMIERE

Batch capturing helps automate the capturing process. If your settings are correct and your tape was recorded to timecode, you can use this automatic method to capture multiple clips in one session.

Batch capturing involves creating (logging) a list of segments of footage you want to capture. This list will appear in the Batch Capture window and can be created by either manually typing in timecode or visually using device control. Your DV camera or deck must support device control for batch capture to work.

To Create and Capture A BATCH LIST:

1 **Select File | Capture | Batch Capture to display the Batch Capture window (Figure 6-5).**

2 **Select File | Capture | Movie Capture to display the Movie Capture window.**

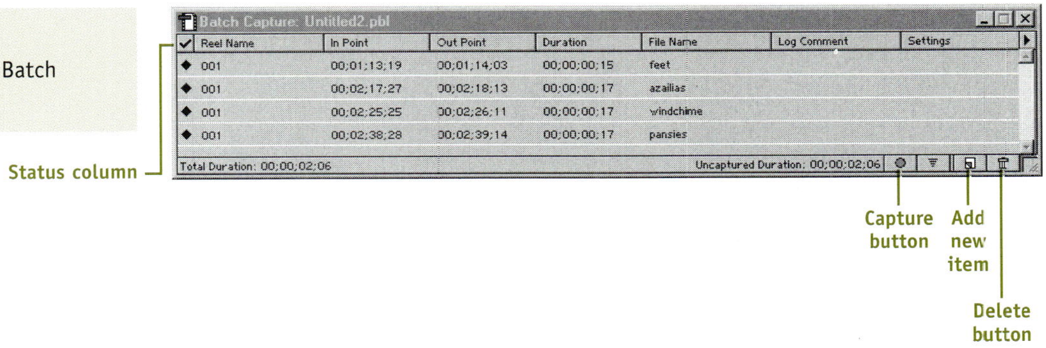

FIGURE 6-5
Batch list in the Batch Capture window

3. In the Movie Capture window, display the Logging settings panel.
4. You can either enter in a reel (tape) name or leave the default.
5. Play the tape.
6. When you reach the segment for which you want to start recording the timecode, and you've identified where you want a segment to end, click the Set In button under the Logging tab to enter an In point.

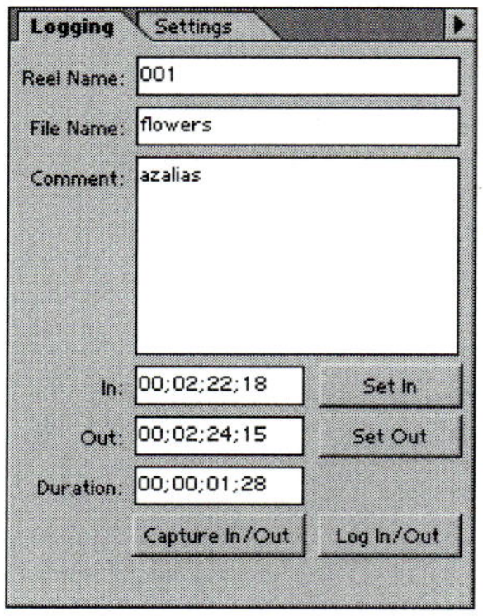

7. When you're done with the segment, click the Set Out button.
8. Click the Log In/Out button to log the new segment.
9. Name and save the logged clip.
10. The name with the timecode will now appear in the current batch list in the Batch Capture window.
11. Continue logging and naming your clips. If you will batch capture from multiple tapes, be sure to give each tape a different reel name, or Premiere won't be able to tell which tape a clip comes from.
12. Save the batch list (File | Save As). Notice that the batch is saved with a .pbl extension.

To Type in a Batch List Manually:

1. Display the Batch Capture window and click the Add New Item button at the bottom right corner of the Batch window.
2. In the Clip Capture Parameters dialog box, name the reel and file name and enter the timecode manually.
3. Click OK. The logged clip you input manually will now appear in the Batch window.

Understanding the Batch Capture Window

Once you've generated a list in the Batch Capture window, you'll notice in the status column that the icons in each row may include diamonds, checks, and an X.

- A diamond represents a clip that hasn't been captured yet.
- A check indicates a clip has been captured.
- An X indicates an error.

Once this batch is logged in, you can record it.

To Record YOUR BATCH LIST:

1. **Select a clip (or a group of clips).**
2. **Select Send In/Out to Movie Capture from the Batch Capture window pop-up menu.**
3. **Click the Record button at the bottom right corner of the Batch Capture list.**

> **NOTE** **When batch capturing, if your footage exists on more than one reel (tape), Premiere will notify you when to switch tapes in the batch-capturing process, provided you remembered to give each tape a unique reel name during logging.**

CREATING HANDLES

If you select Handles from the Batch Capture pop-up menu, you can add frames to the In and Out points to each clip. Select this to add a little extra footage to work with when you trim clips in your project. In this dialog box, you can specify the number of frames you want to add.

CAPTURE USING THE STOP MOTION WINDOW

You can use the stop-motion feature to capture multiple frames, single frames, or time-lapse frames. Stop motion is useful for capturing a single frame as a still image. It's also useful when you want to create the feeling of time passing in your video by eliminating frames. It's much easier to use a stop motion to do this than to edit the clip afterward. You can also indicate the number of frames you want dropped from the time-lapse motion.

You can select from three different stop-motion options:

- **Still Image** Recording a single frame
- **Manual Capture** Controlling the stop motion manually
- **Time Lapse** Selecting time intervals as in time-lapse motion

Although there are three different ways to capture stop motion, we'll experiment with capturing a single frame. The settings may vary on different platforms and with different hardware, but the technique is basically the same.

To Capture a stop-motion clip still image:

1. **Select File | Capture | Stop Motion.**
2. **Right-click (in Windows) or press CONTROL and click (on a Mac) on the preview window to display the context menu.**
3. **Select Capture Options from the window to display the Capture Options dialog box. (On a Mac, select Recording Settings.)**
4. **In the Capture Options (Recording Settings) window, from the pop-up menu select either Still Image, Manual Capture, or Time Lapse. In Figure 6-6, Still Image is selected. Different settings are available depending on your selection.**
5. **Click OK.**
6. **Play the tape. Depending on your configuration, the way you do this will vary.**
7. **When you find a frame you want, click the Capture button at the top of the Stop Motion dialog box (Figure 6-7).**
8. **Save the new frame.**

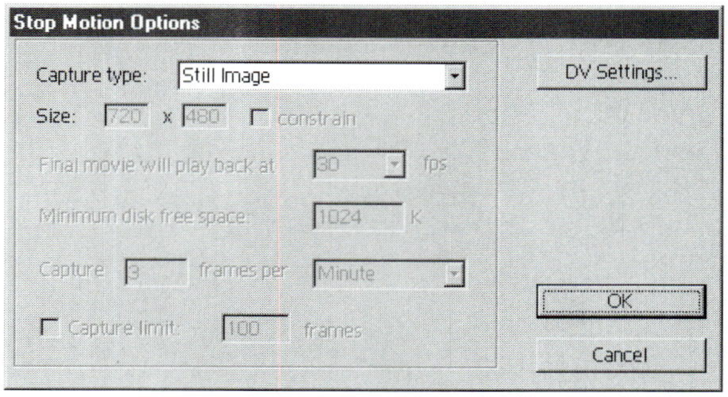

FIGURE 6-6
Selecting the Still Image stop-motion capture option

FIGURE 6-7
Capturing a single frame in the Stop Motion window

9 **Export the single frame using the File | Export Clip | Frame dialog box. Click the Settings button to select a file format. Formats include TIF, GIF, Targa, BMP (Windows), and PICT (Mac).**

Shooting your own footage and seeing it come to life in Premiere is an exciting process. Once you become comfortable with capturing and some of the shortcut keys associated with it, you can start creating truly unique productions.

> **ON THE VIRTUAL CLASSROOM CD-ROM** **In Lesson 4, "Capturing Footage in Premiere." the instructor walks you through the process of capturing footage in Premiere using DV device control.**

7

Using Transitions in Your Premiere Movie

When you roughly arrange clips sequentially in a Timeline, you're creating a *simple* cut. A simple cut is a transition in its most natural form. Transitions are merely the process of one clip transforming into another in time. They're found in the Transitions panel and range from simple to intricate. You can customize existing transitions to create an unlimited number of different effects. Premiere offers 75 different default transitions to choose from. In Chapter 5, we added some transitions to the video in our lesson using a drag-and-drop method. In this chapter, we take a closer look at transitions to better understand how to use them.

You've probably seen transitions used in all sorts of media without being aware of them. Transitions show up in many places, such as self-running slide presentations, animation, and multimedia. They are also often used in video and movies, when one scene cuts to another to create a certain mood. The interesting aspect about transitions is that if they're done with careful thought, they can assist you in subliminally setting the tone of your video.

With this in mind, let's examine the essentials of transitions in Premiere.

Working with Transitions in Single-Track Editing Mode

In Chapter 5, when we added a transition between two clips, we were working in Single-Track Editing mode. In this mode, the Timeline displays the clips and transitions on Video Track 1. In Single-Track Editing mode, clips (and transitions) appear butted up against each other. In reality, clips that transition into one another have to overlap on tracks, which remain hidden in Single-Track mode.

> **NOTE** **As we will discuss in the next section, in A/B Editing mode, transitions can work only when they overlap on tracks.**

Remember when we added a transition in the last lesson, we dragged it from the Transitions panel into the Timeline. This was a simple process, which involved selecting a clip and dragging the transition between two clips. Sometimes, it's hard to imagine the results of adding a transition when you're working in Single-Track Editing mode, especially if you're a beginner. This is because you're viewing the overlays on a single track. Occasionally, beginners prefer A/B Editing mode for transitions as you'll discover in the section "Adding Transitions in A/B Editing Mode."

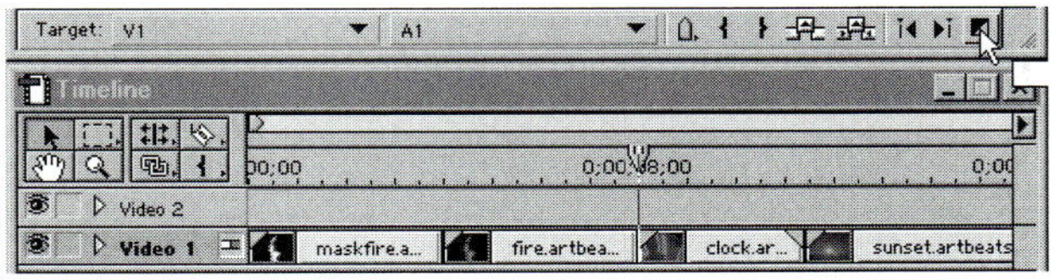

There are other ways to add transitions to the Timeline in Single-Track Editing mode. You can add a transition by dragging the Timeline Edit line to a place where you want a transition to appear and selecting Edit | Apply Default Transition or pressing CONTROL-D (Windows) or COMMAND-D (Mac). Or, after the Edit line is positioned where you want the transition to appear on the Timeline, you can click the Apply Default Transition button in the Program view (see the illustration).

The default transition is the Cross Dissolve, located in the Transitions folder. You can change the default transition, which we'll discuss later in the section, "Changing the Default Transition."

Preview Clips Using the Split-Track Button

In Single-Track Editing mode, clips and transitions appear butted up against one another in Video Track 1. For a transition to work in this mode, there must be sufficient overlapping footage (trimmed-out footage) existing within the clip. For example, if the duration of your transition were 20 frames, ideally you would have an extra 10 frames (or more) on the tail of the first clip and an extra 10 frames (or more) on the head of the next clip. Because the transition is 20 frames long, this would provide sufficient additional footage to make the transition work well.

When you add a transition, if there isn't enough footage on either clip to support the transition, a Fix Transition dialog box will appear. This box lets you make adjustments to the frames to enable the transition to occur. Because the overlap remains hidden in Single-Track Editing mode, it becomes more difficult to visualize the overlap. Refer to Chapter 5 for more information about this editing mode.

You can take a quick glance at a hidden overlap in the Single-Track Editing mode by clicking the split-track mode button on Video Track 1. When in split-track mode, Video Track 1 resembles A/B Editing mode but still maintains its differences, which we'll cover in the next section (see the illustration).

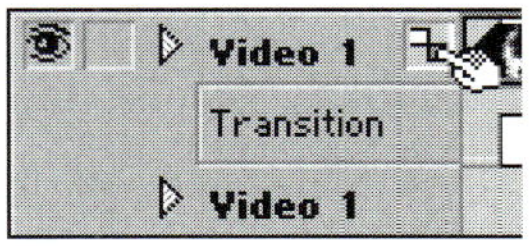

If you're following along with the chapter, open the file named chapter07.ppj. If not, you can gather your own clips on a Video Track 1 timeline or refer to the figures in the chapter. We will review the process of adding a default transition, fixing it, and viewing it in Single-Track Editing mode with a split-track.

Adding a Transition in Single-Track Editing Mode

In chapter07.ppj, the clips are already arranged for you on the Timeline.

To Add a transition in Single-Track Editing mode:

1. **Drag the Edit line where the clip named maskfire.artbeats.mov ends and the clip fire.artbeats.mov begins.**

2 We'll apply a default transition between these two clips. To do so, press CONTROL-D (Windows) or COMMAND-D (Mac), or use any of the methods outlined above to add a default transition.

3 The transition appears between these two clips with no problem. This is because the default transition was set to last through 20 frames and there are enough extra frames at the beginning of the first clip and the end of the second to accommodate the transition.

NOTE You don't have to place the edit line between two clips. You can put the transition anywhere. However, you may have to adjust the transition in the Fix Transition dialog box.

Let's say there isn't enough footage to accommodate the transition. Let's create this scenario to see what would happen.

To Create the Scenario:

1 Let's place the edit line in the middle of the clip fire.artbeats.mov. Let's also change a couple of the default settings on a transition.

2 Display the Transitions palette by selecting Window | Transitions from the menu. In the Transitions palette, click the Dissolve folder to preview its contents. Notice the transition called Cross Dissolve in this folder. You'll know this is the default transition because it's outlined in red. Click the Cross Dissolve transition. From the pop-up Transitions menu at the upper-right of the palette, select Set Selected as Default. The Default Effect dialog box will appear (see the illustration).

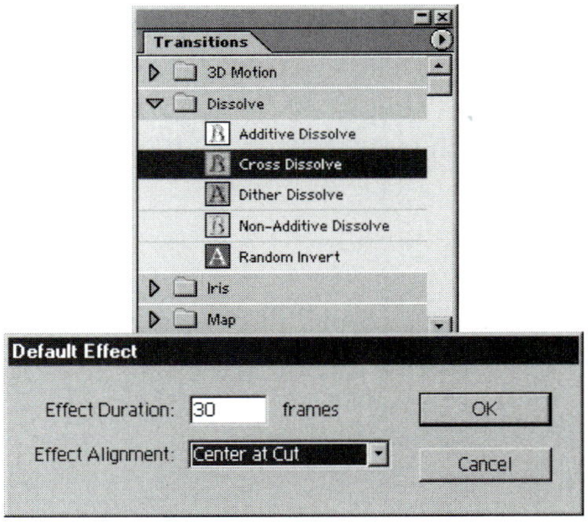

3 Set the Effect Duration to 30 seconds and the Effect Alignment to Center at Cut. When the Cross Dissolve (default transition) is now applied, it will span 30 frames and the transition will align in the center of where the clips butt, instead of at the start of the second clip or the end of the first clip.

4 Close the box and press CONTROL-D (Windows) or COMMAND-D (Mac) to apply the transition to the place where your Edit line is located.

5 The Fix Transition dialog box will appear, indicating there is insufficient footage to complete the request. Now that the default settings have been changed and we moved the Edit line, there's not enough additional footage to create a sufficient overlap for both clips. The dialog box also indicates the exact amount of head and tail footage available. In this box, you can adjust the transition by changing the clip duration, repeat the first and last frames to create additional footage for the transition, or modify the alignment of the transition between clips.

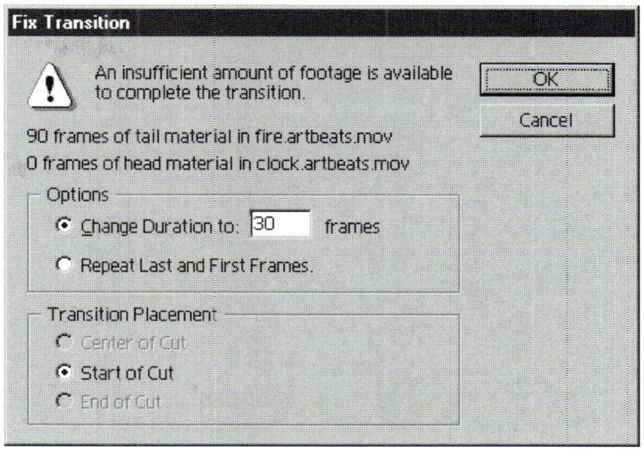

6 Under the Options choices, leave all the suggested settings intact. Notice it recommends that your transition placement begin at the start of the cut instead of where we set it when we changed the default, that is, at the center. Notice your other alignment selections are dimmed.

7 Click OK and look at the Timeline.

8 If you right-click (Windows) or press CONTROL and click (Mac) the new transition and in the context menu select Duration, you'll notice in the Clip Duration dialog box that the duration of the transition is 1 second, which translates to 30 frames. This is another way you can check the duration of a clip.

> **NOTE** The duration and frames per second are based on the project settings. In this case, it's NTSC-based timecode, 30 fps. If you're working in PAL, timecode will be different.

9 From this context menu, you can also adjust your transition by selecting Transition Settings. Doing this displays the Transition Settings dialog box for the transition you've selected, which we'll discuss in the section "The Transitions Palette."

10 To quickly preview the transition, while holding down ALT (Windows) or OPTION (Mac), click the Edit line and scrub the area of the Timeline where the transition is. You'll see the result of the transition in the Program view.

11 It's a little hard to visualize the transition we just made in Single-Track Editing mode, so let's click on the split-track mode. When you do this, you'll notice how the clips overlap for a duration of 30 frames.

12 **To quickly preview the transition, while holding down ALT (Windows) or OPTION (Mac), click the Edit line and scrub the area of the Timeline where the transition is. You'll see the result of the transition in the Program view.**

In the Fix Transition dialog box, had you selected Repeat Last and First Frames for Options, you could have then selected Center of Cut, Start of Cut, or End of Cut for Transition Placement. This is because Premiere would repeat frames to make up for the lost footage to create this effect.

Undo the last transition using either Edit | Undo from the menu or CTRL-Z (Windows) or COMMAND-Z (Mac). Return to the place you were before you applied this transition. You can also use the History palette as we did in Chapter 5 to undo your last few moves.

> **NOTE** When transitions are moved or deleted, the In and Out points of your clips return to their original settings.

Adding Transitions in A/B Editing Mode

To some, adding a transition in A/B Editing mode may seem a little easier than working with transitions in Single-Track Editing mode.

In the file named chapter07.ppj, let's view the Timeline in A/B Editing mode. To do so, click the pop-up menu in the upper right of the Timeline and select A/B Editing. Remember, make sure the last transition was undone.

Let's move to the second (fire.artbeats.mov) and third (clock.artbeats.mov) clips again. If you move the Edit line between these two clips and try to add a default transition as we did in the last section, it won't work. Why? Because, unlike Single-Track Editing mode, A/B Editing mode works only when clips overlap. To remedy this, all you need to do is overlap the clips.

> **TIP** In A/B Editing mode, transitions are always sitting on the Transitions track.

To Overlap CLIPS:

1. **Select the clip named clock.artbeats.mov with the Track Select tool from the toolbox. Doing this also selects all the clips to the right of clock.artbeats.mov. Move the clip over to the left, so it overlaps about a quarter of the previous clip on Video Track 1B.**

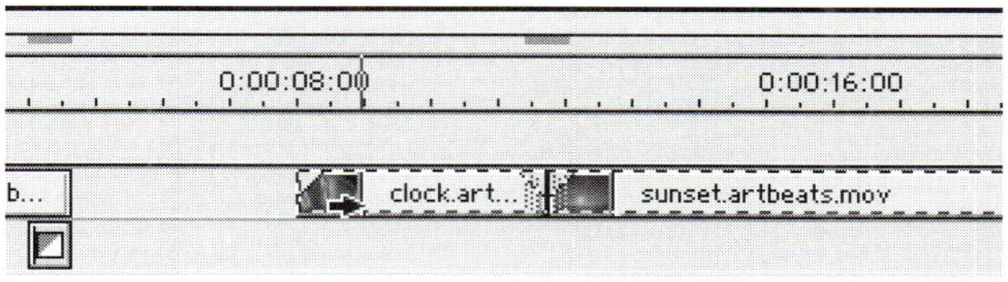

2. **Move the Edit line to the head of the clock.artbeats.mov clip and apply a default transition by pressing CONTROL-D (Windows) or COMMAND-D (Mac). The transition automatically appears (see the illustration).**

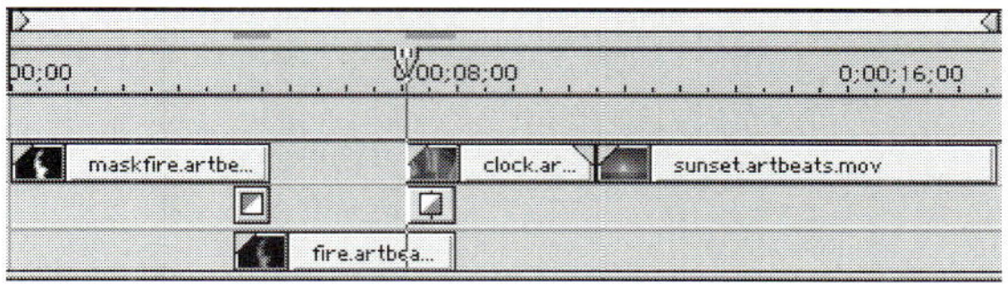

3. **In the Timeline, scrub over the new transition with the Edit line. Don't forget to hold down ALT (Windows) or COMMAND (Mac) before you scrub to preview the transition in the Program view.**

In A/B Editing mode, transitions are a little easier to visually manipulate in the Timeline if you're a beginner. You can move them by clicking and dragging the transition. You can also extend or shorten the handles of a transition to span clips virtually any way you want. In Single-Track Editing mode, you can drag handles also, but in a limited way. Transitions are locked to the heads and tails of overlapping clips, so if you move them, the clips move also. If you edit the handles, the clips are edited accordingly.

You trim the duration of a transition in the Timeline just as you would if you were dragging the track handles on a clip to trim footage in the Timeline.

> **TIP** You can also apply a transition by clicking and dragging it right from the Transitions panel to the Transition track, as we did in Chapter 5.

To do this, simply click and drag the transition in the Timeline. Extending the handles lengthens the duration of the transition, and vice versa (see the illustration).

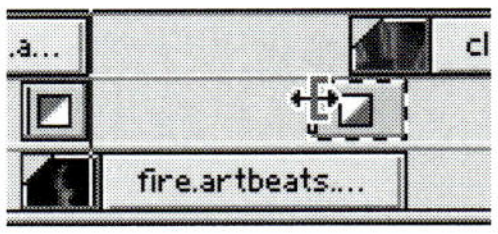

Transitions, so far, probably seem easy to apply. For the most part, they are. Once you've adapted to your favorite method of applying a transition, the remainder of the work is browsing through the 75 or so choices, deciding which one is right for you, and further customizing the transition, if necessary. It's time to explore the actual transitions palette.

THE TRANSITIONS PALETTE

We've played with applying default transitions and dragging and dropping a transition. At this point, you most likely have the feel for how and where to apply a transition. Now let's shop around and see what transitions might be right for your projects.

If it's not already displayed, access the Transitions palette from the Windows menu. This palette, like any other, is nested in a group. The expanding and collapsing folders (Figure 7-1), organized by category, contain all the transitions. The names of the transition folders are indicative of their contents. For example, the Page Peel folder contains transitions that resemble a page peeling to a page underneath it.

You can also scroll up and down in this palette to view its contents as in any other window.

FIGURE 7-1
Expand and collapse folders in the Transitions palette by clicking the folder's arrow

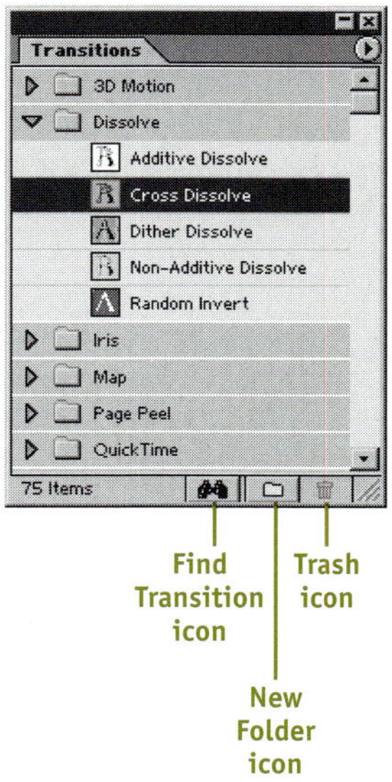

If you're following along with the lesson, open the file named chapter07_2.ppj. Now let's browse around the palette and examine its contents.

Premiere offers a simple way to test and preview what a transition looks like. The simplest way (although you have to have really good eyesight to see this) is to select Animate from the Transitions pop-up menu. This animates all the icons in the Transitions panel. The animated icons appear very small in this view so it's very difficult to determine how each transition animates from this source.

CHANGE SETTINGS ON A TRANSITION IN THE TRANSITIONS PALETTE

To Preview and Change THE SETTINGS ON A TRANSITION STYLE:

- **Double-click a transition in the Transitions palette. The dialog box corresponding to that transition will appear. Figure 7-2 shows the dialog box for the Center Peel transition. You can also access a dialog box by double-clicking a transition in the Timeline.**

In each dialog box are properties that can be adjusted for that particular transition. In other words, you can customize a transition to suit your projects needs. Because of this, you can actually create an unlimited number of customized transitions by simply messing around with the settings. There's also a good chance you'll invent some combination no one else has ever devised.

Let's examine the Stretch In transition. Go to the Stretch folder and expand it. Double-click the transition called Stretch In (Figure 7-3). The transition's name gives you an idea of what the "stretch" will look like. This transition naming

FIGURE 7-2
The Center Peel Settings dialog box

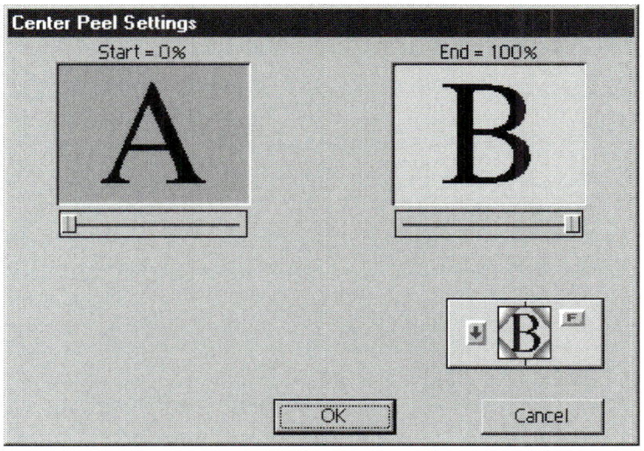

FIGURE 7-3
The transition called Stretch In is located in the Transitions palette Stretch folder

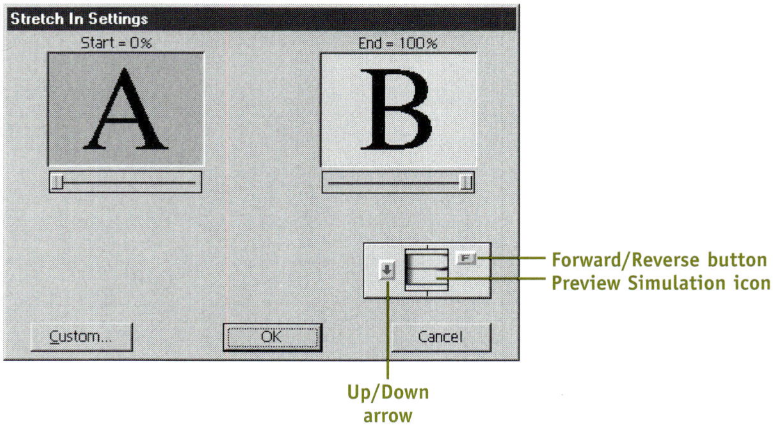

convention is a convenient feature. If the transitions were identified with alphanumeric names instead of names relating to their function, you'd have to spend a lot of time browsing through these folders to find what you wanted.

Let's examine some of the settings you can change in the Stretch In Settings dialog box.

This dialog box is fairly typical of many of the settings dialog boxes associated with transitions. At the bottom right of the box, you can see an animation preview of the transition. You can also customize the animation here. By clicking the Up/Down arrow, you can change the start and end position of the transition. This position is reflected in the above Start and End preview thumbnails. As you can see in the thumbnail previews, Start is set at 0 percent, and End is set at 100 percent.

You can also change the direction of the transition to forward or reverse by clicking the F/R button.

By clicking the sliding bars under the Start and End thumbnail previews, you can change the position where the transition starts and ends in its duration. You can also use the sliding bar under the Start or End thumbnail to preview an entire effect. Do this by changing the settings and then dragging the sliding arrow from left to right then back again.

Notice the Custom button at the bottom left of this dialog box. Click this button, and the Stretch In Settings dialog box appears. In this box, you can change the number of bands used to create the stretch effect. To do this, just type in a new

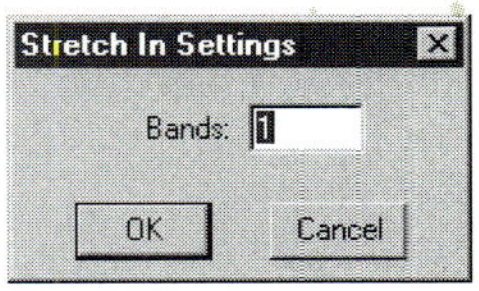

number. You might want to test it to see what effect your new setting would have if you used a larger number of bands. Do this by typing a new number, clicking OK, and then dragging the slider under the Start box to test it. When you're done, click Cancel to exit the dialog box.

The Stretch In Settings dialog box is indicative of the many customized settings that are available in other transition settings dialog boxes. In many cases, the settings are similar and fairly intuitive. And even if they're not, it takes only a moment to double-click a transition, play with the settings, and preview your results.

Customize a Transition

Let's apply a transition to clips in A/B Editing mode and customize the transition. We'll continue to use the file named chaper07_2.ppj as our example for this section.

As you can see, the Timeline in this movie is similar to the last movie we worked on. We're in A/B Editing mode, and some clips are overlapped in the Timeline.

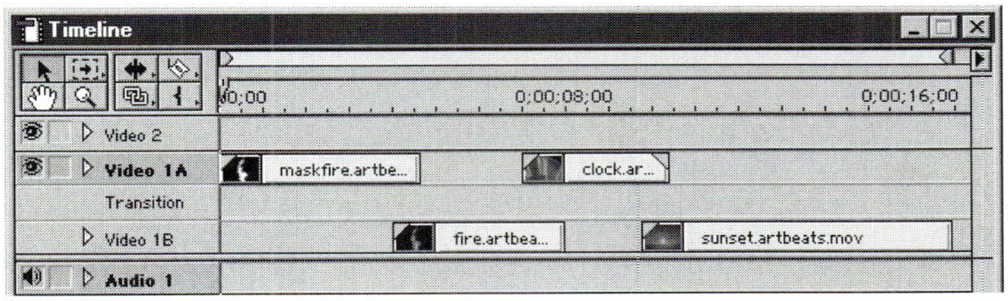

To Customize a Transition:

1. Make sure the Transitions palette is displayed (Window | Show Transitions). Expand the Stretch folder and navigate to the transition Stretch In, the same transition whose dialog box we've been studying.
2. Click and drag the Stretch In transition onto the Transition track to transition fire.artbeats.mov into clock.artbeats.mov. Position the transition so it aligns with the head of clock.artbeats.mov (Figure 7-4).
3. Double-click the transition in the Timeline.
4. This displays the Stretch In Settings dialog box just as before. Use the dialog box to customize the transition as you like.

FIGURE 7-4
Align the Stretch In transition with the head of file clock.artbeats.mov.

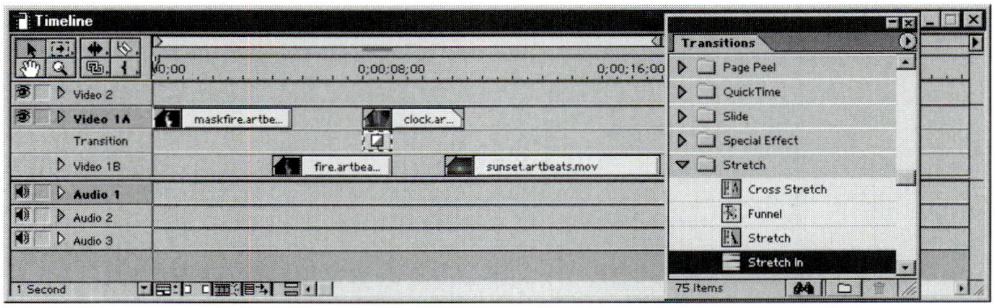

5 **In the dialog box, when you click the button Show Actual Sources, you can preview how the transition looks on the transitioning clips in both the Start and End boxes. A miniature preview of the clips appears. By dragging the sliding bars under the Start and End boxes, you can see how your transition settings will affect the clip.**

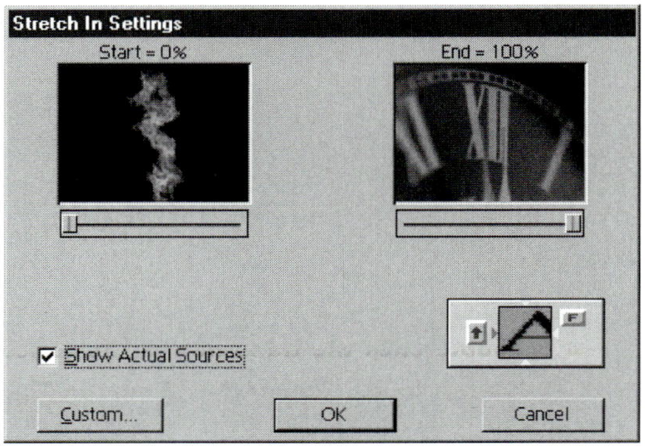

Now let's add another transition between the clips clock.artbeats.mov and sunset.artbeats.mov.

To Add A TRANSITION BETWEEN THESE TWO CLIPS:

1 **In the Transitions palette, click and expand the Wipe folder. Navigate to the Gradient Wipe transition.**

2 **Click and drag it into the Transitions track in the Timeline so it aligns with the head of the clip named sunset.artbeats.mov.**

3 **After you drop the transition, a Gradient Wipe Settings dialog box appears. In this box you can change the degree of softness of an image by dragging the slider to the right. Leave the setting as is and click OK.**

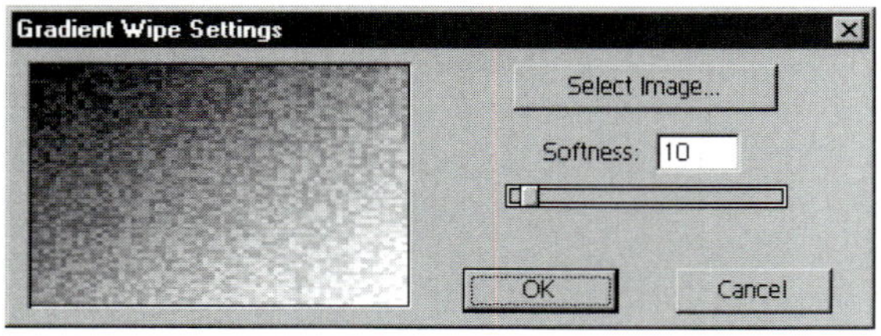

4 Hold down ALT (Windows) or OPTION (Mac) and scrub over the area of the Timeline where you applied the transition so you can preview it in the Program view.

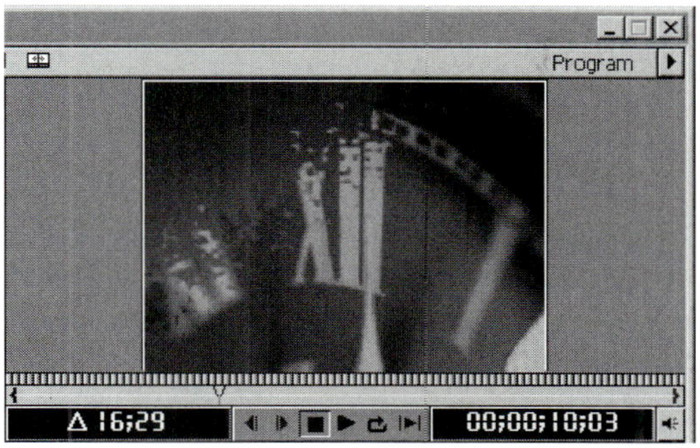

To Further Customize GRADIENT WIPE SETTINGS:

1 Double-click the transition in the Timeline to display the Gradient Wipe Settings dialog box, and click Show Actual Sources. This causes the actual footage to preview in the Start and End boxes. In the slider bar under the Start box, slide the controller to the right to preview how the transition plays.

2 Click the Custom Settings box and, in the new dialog box, click the Select Image button. This button lets you import a bitmap image from another source and use it to create the texture of your gradient wipe. You can create numerous custom effects using your own bitmaps. Let's try it and see what happens.

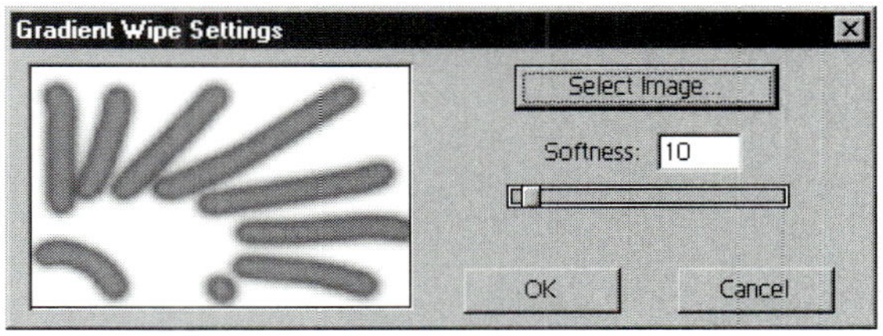

3 When you click the Select Image button, you can navigate to an image. There is a bitmap image named sun.psd in the chapter 07 folder. Select this image. Notice that a preview of the image appears in a thumbnail to the left in the Settings box. Click OK. Make sure Show Actual Sources is checked, and test the results in the Start (see illustration) or End box by using the slider under the box.

4 Click OK in the Gradient Wipe Settings dialog box. Now test the results by scrubbing over the transition in the Timeline. In Figure 7-5 you can see the results in the Program.

To refresh your memory, the presence of red bars under the work area bar in the Timeline indicate areas of the Timeline that must be rendered to be previewed. You can render, or preview, by pressing ENTER (Windows) or RETURN (Mac). You can also isolate the rendering of a specific area by moving the work area bar only over the area where your transitions exist (see the Timeline in Figure 7-5). Do this by dragging the handles and adjusting the length of the bar over this area.

> **NOTE** **You can also render a work area by right-clicking (Windows) or pressing CONTROL and clicking (Mac) the work area bar. Then, in the context menu, select Render Work Area (see the illustration).**

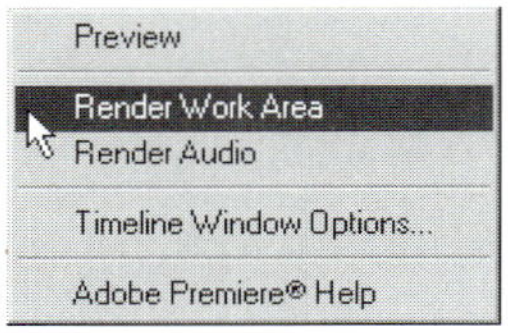

Now that you have a feel for transitions, return to the first set of clips in the Timeline in the file named chapter07_2.ppj that we didn't add a transition to. Go wild and experiment with any transition you like. Apply it and modify the settings. Don't forget to save the file.

CHANGING THE DEFAULT TRANSITION

As mentioned in the section, "Working with Transitions in Single-Track Editing Mode," you can change the default transition. Premiere assigns a Cross Dissolve

FIGURE 7-5
A bitmap image is used with a Gradient Wipe transition

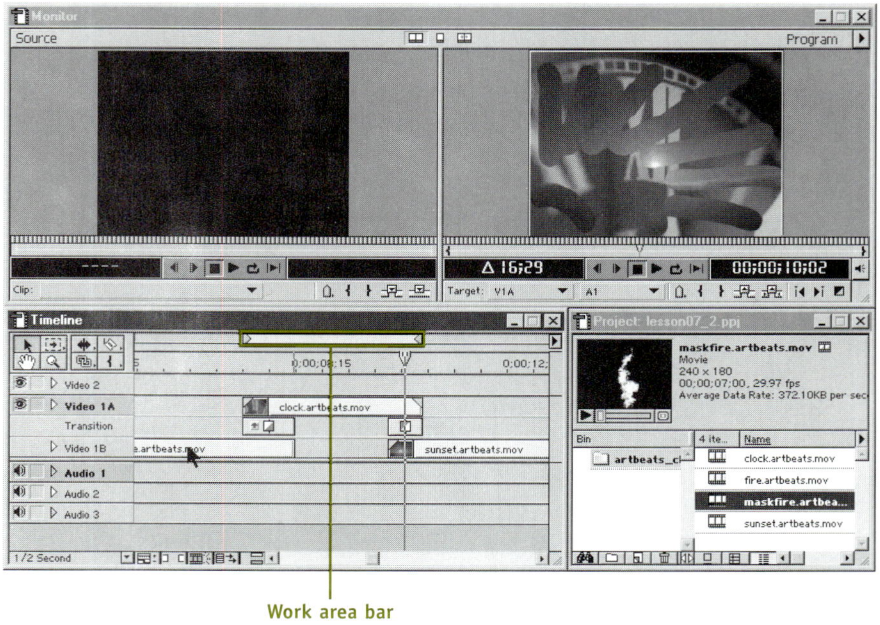

as the default transition, but you can easily change this. Let's say, for example, you were working on a large project using many of the same Page Peel transitions, and they all had to have the same settings. You could assign a Page Peel transition as the new default.

To Change THE DEFAULT TRANSITION:

1. **Select a transition of your choice from the Transitions panel.**

2. **From the pop-up Transitions menu, select Set Selected as Default.**

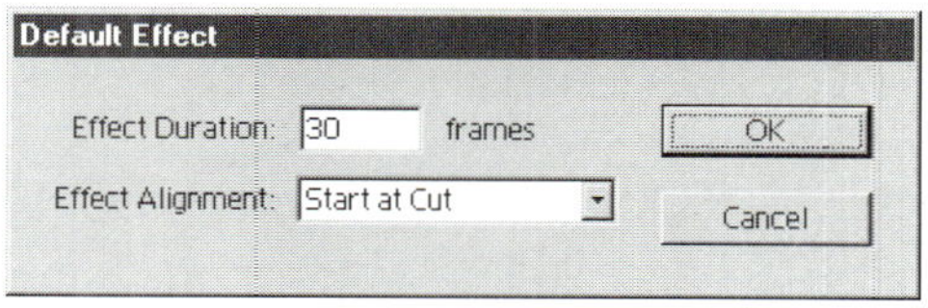

3. **In the Default Effect dialog box that appears, you can set the new duration and alignment of the transition (see illustration).**

4. **That's all there is to it. Now you have a new default transition. Try to apply the new default transition and see what happens.**

As you can see, you could easily spend hours getting lost in these transitions because there are so many different types of effects. Because of their visual nature, you will probably find it more fun to experiment with them and see for yourself what they do rather than read more explanation.

In Chapter 10, we'll experiment with effects in Premiere. Effects offer many other methods for transforming your clips in ways you can't even begin to imagine.

> **ON THE VIRTUAL CLASSROOM CD-ROM** **In Lesson 5, "Adding Transitions in Between Clips," the instructor shows you the Transitions palette and how to apply transitions in Single-Track Editing Mode.**

8

Creating Titles in Premiere

Titles in Premiere provide an easy way to add quick text, rolling titles, and simple graphics to your video. You can add movement to text as well as change the size and rotation over time. Although it's easy to create and modify text and graphics in other programs and import these elements into Premiere, if you want to create text that's quick, simple, and high quality, the Title window delivers the goods.

In Chapter 2, we examined a movie, spring.ppj, which used simple titles generated in the Title window. Titles in Premiere are saved as separate files and, as such, are stored on your hard drive. They have a file extension of .ptl and become available in the Project window of the current movie.

Titles in Premiere are easy to create. You'll find the learning curve for titles and graphics is rapid. This lets you get down to the business of being creative with titles in a short time.

THE TITLE WINDOW

You create titles and graphics in the Title window. You display the Title window by selecting File | New | Title from the menu.

> **TIP** You can also create a new title by clicking the Create Item button at the bottom of the Project window.

When you select New Title, the Title window appears (Figure 8-1).

The Title window is actually a simple graphics application within Premiere. In this window, you can create vector-based objects and text. This means the objects you

FIGURE 8-1
The Title window in Premiere

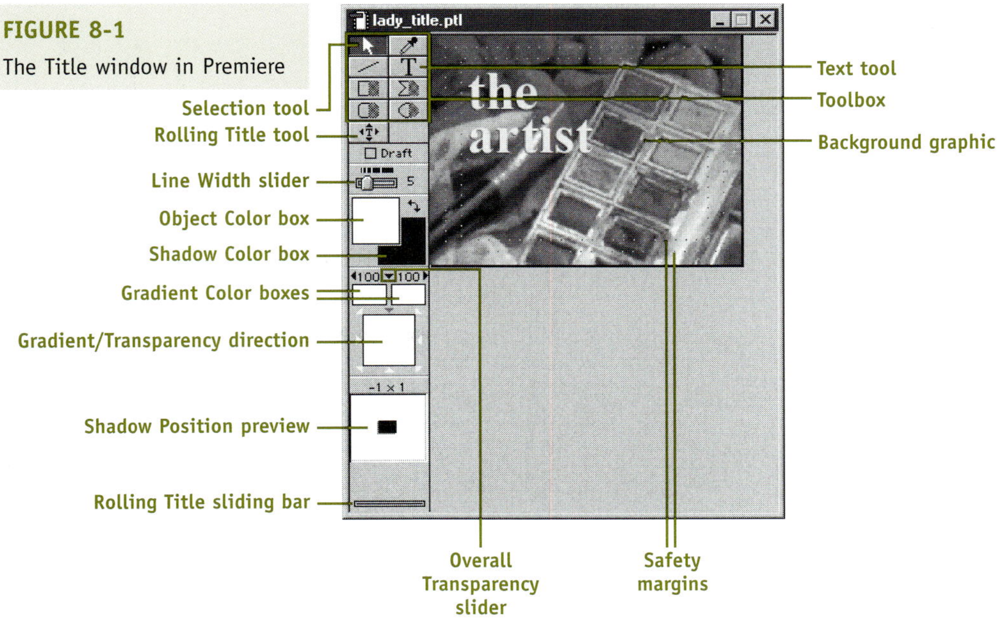

create will always appear crisp and legible and can be scaled to any size without compromising their quality.

Note that the safety margins in the window are depicted as dotted rectangles. Just like the margins in the Monitor window, the outer margin is the action safety margin and the inner margin is the title safe margin. Remember, use safety margins to ensure your titles or clips will be displayed properly and won't be cut off if you're outputting to a format that may be viewed on a TV. The casing around TV picture tubes, called the bezel, could obscure part of your production when objects are placed too close to the edge. To ensure that layers in motion remain visible, keep them within the action safe area. To ensure that the text you create isn't cut off by a TV's bezel, keep the text fully within the title safe area.

MAKING TEXT IN THE TITLE WINDOW

Let's play with some of the Title tools. We'll start with the Text tool, learn to make basic text, and then change the properties of this text.

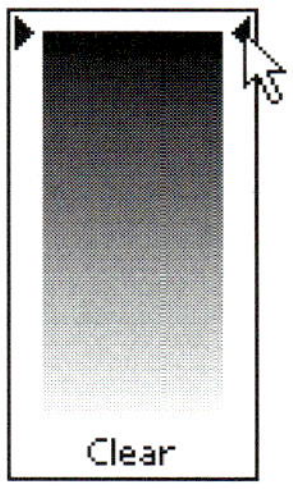

Before we begin, you should understand that the transparency of objects created in the Title window defaults to 50 percent unless you change the default. To change the transparency of an object you're about to create, click on the Overall Transparency slider in the Title window (the little arrow in between the Gradient Color boxes) and slide it up to create an object at 100 percent opacity. Slide down the Transparency slider to create various levels of transparency. As you slide the bar, the current transparency is indicated at the top of the slider. You can use this method to change the transparency of text and objects.

To create basic text, select the Text tool in the toolbar of the Title window. Click anywhere within the title area and start to type. If you've used this tool previously, the text you type will maintain the same properties (e.g., font, size, color) from the last time it was used.

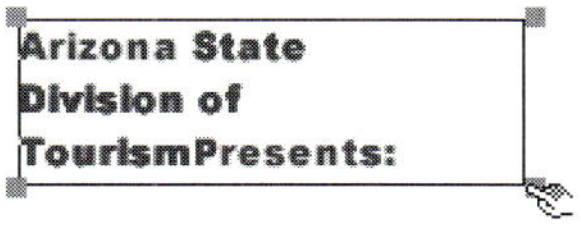

You can type as many lines as you want. Press ENTER (or RETURN on a Mac) to enter text on another line. When you're done, click anywhere in the title area. When you do this, four selection handles appear around the text, as shown.

If you click and drag the selection handles, the size and kerning/tracking won't change as it does in some other video-editing programs. Dragging the handles changes only the width of the text box itself. You can scale the text horizontally and/or vertically by using the following key combination: CONTROL-drag (Windows) or OPTION-drag (Mac), as shown.

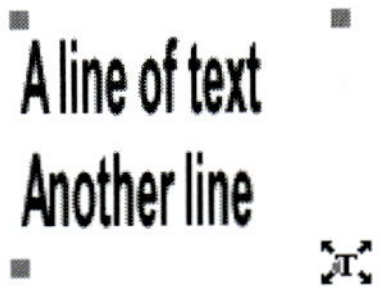

Modifying Text Attributes in the Title Window

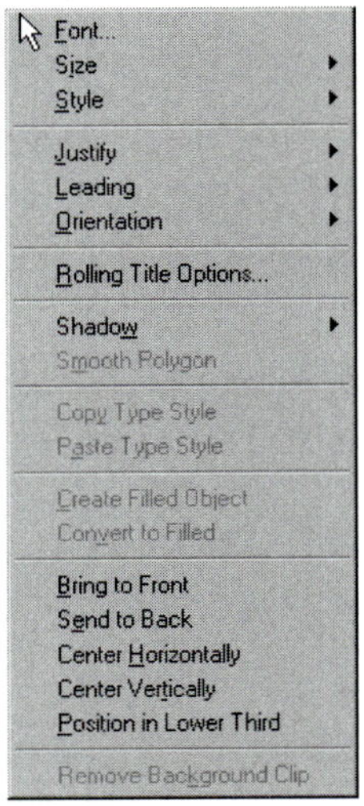

After you create text in the Title window, you can fine-tune it. Among other things, the Title window offers the ability to kern/track text and change font, size, style, justification, and leading for text with multiple lines. If you've used even the simplest drawing or desktop publishing program, all these features in the Title window will seem familiar to you.

You can modify a font by clicking the Selection tool in the Title toolbar and selecting a text block. To modify only a portion of the text in the text box, select that text with the Text tool. You can change the attributes of the text such as font, size, and style by choosing the specific attribute in the Title window's pop-up menu.

To Change the kerning/tracking on text:

1. **Select the Text tool.**
2. **Double-click on the area where you want to adjust the kerning/tracking.**
3. **Use ALT-LEFT ARROW and ALT-RIGHT ARROW in Windows or OPTION-LEFT ARROW and OPTION-RIGHT ARROW on the Mac to kern or track text.**

You can also change the leading on a text block by selecting the text with the Text tool and by using ALT-UP ARROW and ALT-DOWN ARROW (Windows) or OPTION-UP ARROW and OPTION-DOWN ARROW (Mac).

Creating Basic Objects in the Title Window

The toolbox in the Title window offers an array of basic geometric shapes that you can draw with. These shapes include a rectangle, polygon, rounded rectangle, and oval. The drawing tools aren't the most exciting element in the Title window because they're limited. This limitation shouldn't hamper you, though, because it's so easy to import complex vector graphics, such as logos, into Premiere from other applications. The tools work well for simple shapes such as a rectangle here and there. Let's look at how to use them.

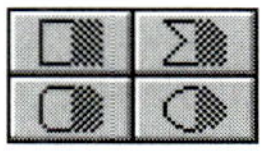

Notice the drawing tools in the toolbar appear split in two. The left half represents an outline shape, and the right half indicates a filled shape.

A *fill* is an object filled with color. A *frame* is an object that has only an outline, sometimes referred to as a *stroke*.

Interestingly, unlike other drawing programs in which you can assign a fill and an outline or stroke to the same object, in Premiere you can select only one or the other. Objects with a fill color are referred to as "filled," and objects with an outline, or stroke with no fill, are referred to as "framed."

Let's play around with the basic shapes. The rectangle, rounded rectangle, and oval work the same way, so choose any one of the three.

Drawing a Filled and Framed Object

To Make a basic filled object:

1. **Click the right half of the Rectangle, Rounded Rectangle, or Oval Tool.**
2. **Select an object color from the Object Color box.**
3. **In the title area, click and drag from the upper left to the bottom right to create a shape.**

> **TIP** You can convert a filled object into a framed object in the Title menu by selecting Convert to Framed.

To make a framed object, simply click the left half of the tool and repeat the process you would use for a filled object.

You can specify the line width of a frame by dragging the Line Width slider on the toolbar left or right to control the frame weight. Here, you can select a weight from 1 to 16.

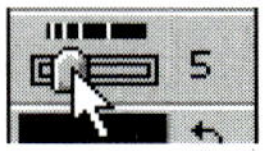

Shadows on Text

Shadows work the same way with shapes as they do with text. Clicking the Shadow Position preview reflects the type of object you're currently working with. For

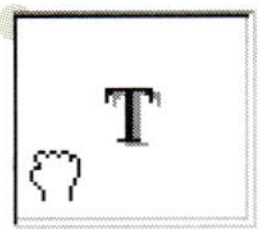

example, in the illustration, the drop shadow preview shows a text character. If you were making a line, the box would show a preview of a line. Drop shadows for text and objects are discussed in detail in the later section, "Modify the Properties of Text and Graphics."

Changing the Size of Objects

You can easily resize shapes in the Title window.

To Modify the size of a rectangle, a rounded rectangle, or an oval:

1. **Click and drag one of the four surrounding handles to change the shape.**
2. **Hold down the SHIFT key to constrain the shape to a perfect square or circle.**

Creating Lines and Polygons in the Title Window

Creating lines and polygons is a little different from creating other basic geometric shapes. Polygons either can be opened and appear as a continuous line that connects the points, or it can be closed to complete an entire polygon shape.

Creating a Line Creating lines is self-explanatory.

To Create a Line:

1. **Select the Line tool.**
2. **Select a line color from the Object Color box.**
3. **Change the line width from the Line Width slider. You can select a width from 1 to 16.**
4. **Click and drag on the stage to complete the line.**

5. **Hold down SHIFT to constrain the line to a 45-degree angle.**

> **NOTE** If you will view your final movie on a TV monitor, avoid creating lines only one pixel thick, because single-pixel lines will flicker terribly on NTSC or PAL monitors.

CREATING POLYGONS Polygons are more difficult to create than lines. Again, even if you've worked in the simplest graphics program, you probably don't need much of an explanation to create polygons. If you're used to using a bezier curve tool, the Polygon tool may annoy you, unless you're looking for a point-to-point effect. You'll find you don't have the bezier tool precision you have in programs such as Adobe Illustrator or Macromedia FreeHand.

To Create A POLYGON:

1. **Click on the left side of the Polygon tool to create a framed object or the right side to create a filled polygon.**

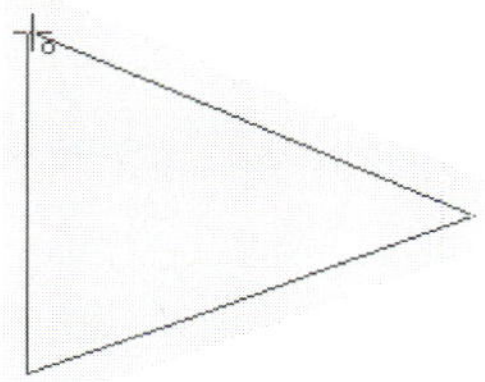

2. **Select any other attributes you want to assign your polygon, such as color or shadow.**
3. **In the title area, click from point to point to create a polygon. As in most drawing programs, to create a closed polygon, click the last point to the first point.**

When you position the pointer over the last point of a polygon (the first and last point), the cross hair will have a ring in the bottom right corner.

To create an open polygon, just double-click on the last point.

> **TIP** **Creating a framed, point-to-point polygon path is done the same way as creating a framed polygon. Just select the Frame side of the tool in the toolbar.**

To Change A POLYGON TO A CURVED PATH:

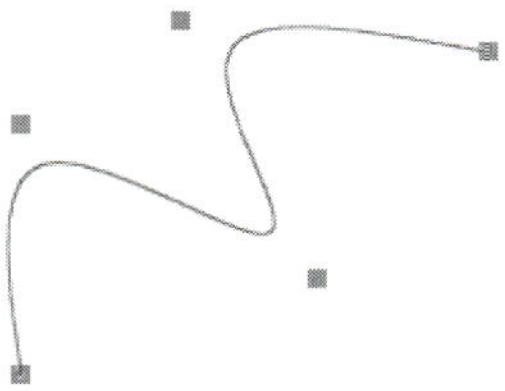

1. **Click the object.**
2. **Select Title | Smooth Polygon from the menu.**
3. **The connecting points smooth out, as shown.**
4. **Click any of the handles and drag to change the polygon's shape.**

Modify the Properties of Text and Graphics

You can change the color, size, position, drop shadow, and other properties of objects, just as you can with text. Although the number of properties you can change is limited, all the basic properties are available, making the Title window a well-rounded alternative for creating a quick graphic element.

Add Color to Text and Graphics

It's easy to modify the color of text and graphics in the Title window. All you do is select the object and click a color in the Object Color box.

Gradient color is easy to make, too. Gradient color is the gradual transition of one color to another in an object.

To Apply gradient color to text or graphics:

1. **Select an object.**
2. **Click the Gradient Start Color box to access the Color Picker. Select the first color you want in your gradient, and click OK to close the window (Figure 8-2).**
3. **Click the Gradient End Color box to select the last color.**

The object will now reflect your choice of gradient, and the Gradient Start Color box will display a preview of the gradient on the selected object.

The numbers at the top of the two gradient boxes indicate the percentage of opacity/transparency that's applied to an object. The default is 100 percent, which is solid

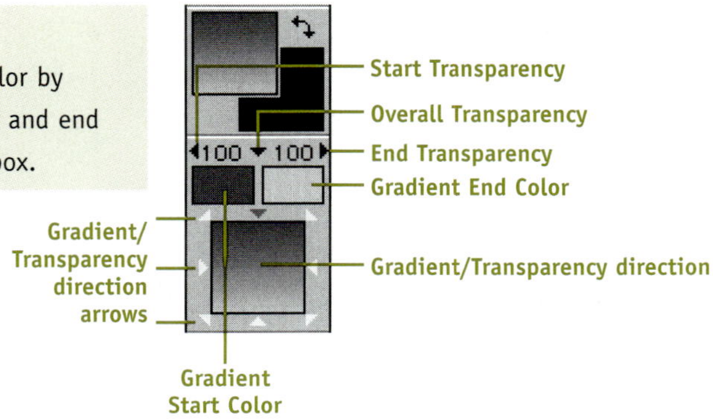

FIGURE 8-2
Create gradient color by selecting the start and end colors in the toolbox.

color; 1 percent is almost devoid of color. You can change the opacity on the beginning and end color on both text and graphics. This lets clips on Video Track 1 be seen through the text or graphic.

When a text or an object is less than 100 percent opaque and has been superimposed over video in a lower track, the video will show through the text or object to some degree. The lower the percentage of the opacity, the more transparent the object appears; the higher the number, the more obscured clips are on lower video tracks.

TIP You can easily change the direction of a gradient or transparency by selecting an object and clicking the Gradient/Transparency direction arrows.

To Change THE TRANSPARENCY ON A GRADIENT COLOR AT A BEGINNING OR END OF A GRADIENT:

1. **Select the object.**
2. **Click the arrow at the left of the Start Transparency number (or the left of the End Transparency number) to access the pop-up opacity slider.**
3. **Select an opacity percentage.**

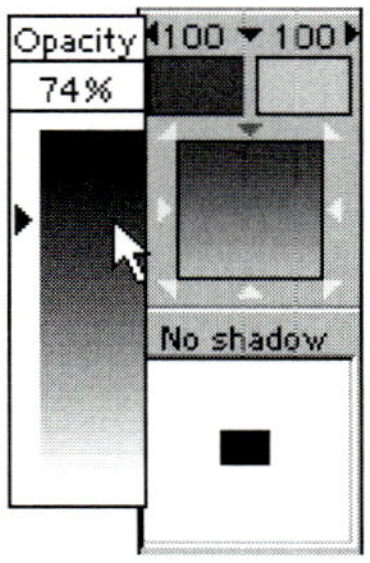

CREATE A SHADOW ON TEXT OR GRAPHICS

The text and graphics you create in the Title window can also have shadows. Shadows can sometimes help text or an object stand out from the clip on which it's superimposed. If you want to create a drop shadow, select an object in the Title window. Then,

To Create A DROP SHADOW:

1. **Click and drag the icon within the Shadow Position box located at the bottom of the toolbar. If you're adding a shadow to text, the box displays the letter "T" as a reference so you can position the shadow to the text. If you've created another object, that type of object will appear in the Shadow Position box.**
2. **Not only do you see what the shadow looks like in the Shadow Position box and the title area, but Premiere also displays, in pixels, the numerical offset position of the shadow at the top of the preview box (Figure 8-3).**

FIGURE 8-3
To modify a shadow in the Title window, click and drag on the object in the Shadow Position box

3 If the shadow is positioned dead center in the Shadow Position box, the shadow is turned off as is indicated in the box. You can also disable the shadow for text or an object by selecting it, clicking in the Shadow Position box, and dragging the shadow right out of the box.

> **TIP** You can change the color of a shadow by clicking the Shadow Box after you've selected the object and selecting a color in the Shadow Color box, next to the Object Color box.

Place a Background Clip in the Title Window

If you're creating text or a graphic that is superimposed over a clip, you'll probably want to see what it looks like beforehand. In Premiere, you can place a background clip in the Title window to help you position a title or graphic (Figure 8-4). This makes it easier to position the object and choose a color that makes it stand out.

To Place a background graphic in the title area:

1 Click on a clip in the Project window or the Source window.

2 Drag it to the Title window. You now have a background to help you position your title.

> **TIP** Use the slider and the Poster Frame button in the Project window to select a particular frame in a clip for a background.

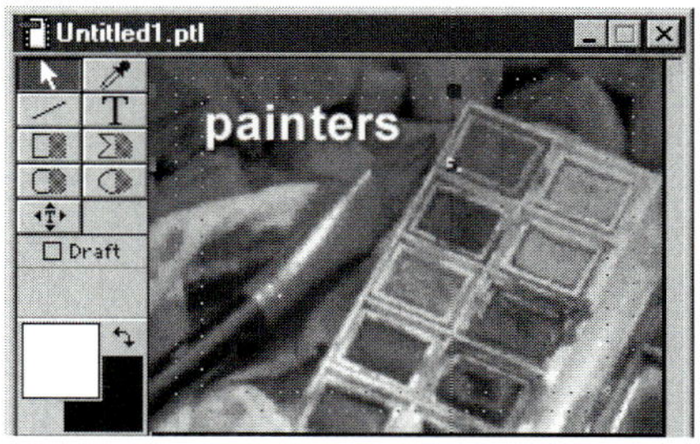

FIGURE 8-4 Using a background clip in the Title window can help you position your text or graphic in the frame

When you're done using the clip as a guide, you can remove it from the title area by selecting Title | Remove Background Clip from the menu.

TIP You can change the color of the Title window background by selecting Title Window Options from the context menu. Here, you can select a color swatch for the background color. This is useful when you want to create white text but can't see it against the default white background. Note that this background color will only appear in the Timeline if the opaque option is checked in the Title Window Options dialog box.

Saving a Title or Graphic

Once you've created and tweaked your title or graphic, you must save it. As mentioned at the beginning of this chapter, elements you create in the Title window are saved as individual files and have the extension .ptl. You save a title just as you save a Premiere file: by selecting File | Save from the menu.

You can also save a title by dragging the contents of the Title window right into the Timeline. When you do this, the Save File dialog box asks you whether you want to save the file. Click Save and, in the dialog box that follows, name the file and save it to your hard drive.

Creating Moving Titles

Now that you have a solid idea of how most elements work in the Title window, we can take a look at rolling and crawling titles.

Rolling titles are titles that move vertically in the video frame, usually from bottom to top. You've seen rolling titles many times on film and video. They're often used at the end of a movie for credits. Once you know how to make and modify basic text, making a rolling title is very simple (Figure 8-5).

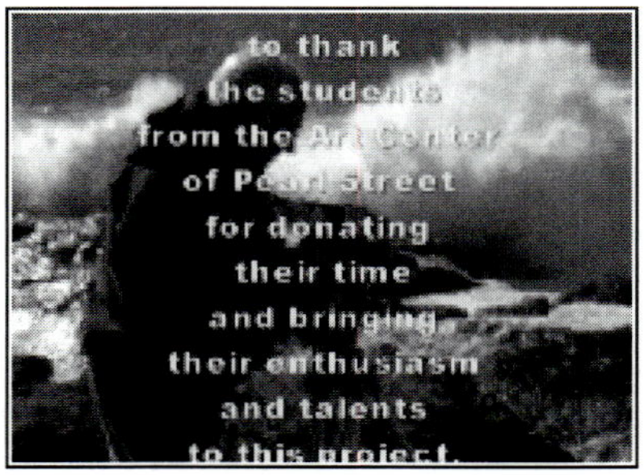

FIGURE 8-5
Rolling title in the Program window

Crawling titles are similar to rolling titles, but they move horizontally in the frame, usually from right to left. In the film and video business, the terms "rolling titles" and "crawling titles" are frequently shortened to just "rolls" and "crawls."

Let's examine in more detail how to create rolling and crawling titles.

Rolling Titles

As with everything else in the Title window, rolling titles are easy to create.

To Create a rolling title in the Title window:

1. **Select File | New | Title from the menu.**
2. **Click the Rolling Title tool and drag the crosshair onto the title area.**
3. **Click in the upper-left corner of the frame and drag to the bottom-right to create a rolling title text box.**
4. **You can now format the rolling text by selecting font properties from the Title window.**

When the text is selected with the Type tool, you can scroll up and down on this text. Rolling title text can roll in an up or a down direction. The direction the text rolls in depends on the nature of your title. In our example, the text must roll from the bottom up. Otherwise, it won't be read correctly when it rolls. Rolling credits, on the other hand, would probably roll from the top to the bottom.

To Change the direction of a roll:

1. Select the rolling text.
2. From the menu, select Title | Rolling Title Options.
3. In the Rolling Title Options dialog box, select the direction you want the text to roll in (Move Up or Move Down).
4. Click OK.

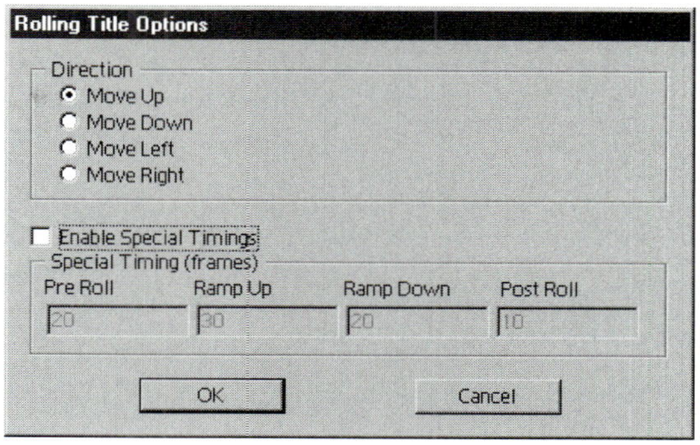

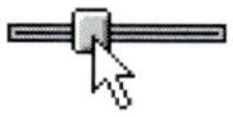

You can get an idea of how the text will roll by dragging the slider in the Title window.

You can also change the timing of the roll in the Rolling Title Options dialog box. Specify the number of frames on four states: Pre Roll, Ramp Up, Ramp Down, and Post Roll. By doing this, you give the illusion of the text entering the movie very slowly, gradually accelerating, gradually decelerating, and then slowing to a stop. You may need to control the speed differently, but this option helps pace the roll over time. You change the timing by checking the Enable Special Timings box. This lets you select from these settings. Let's look at what each one does:

- **Pre Roll** Indicates how many frames you want the title to remain motionless before it begins moving.
- **Ramp Up** Indicates how many frames you want to use to accelerate the speed of the clip to normal. Typing in a zero immediately brings the clip to normal speed.
- **Ramp Down** Indicates the number of frames that will be used to decelerate the clip. Typing a zero would stop the clip.
- **Post Roll** Indicates for how many frames you want the clip to appear motionless after it stops moving.

> **NOTE** Changing the length of the rolling or crawling title alters overall duration and playback of the title by adding more frames in time.

To Change THE POSITION OF ROLLING TEXT IN THE FRAME:

1. **Double-click the clip in the Timeline to open the rolling text in the Title window.**
2. **Double-click the rolling text and place your cursor at the top left of the text box.**
3. **Press ENTER to add empty lines until the position of the text is vertically centered (Figure 8-6).**

After adding any type of title to the Timeline, you probably want to preview it. To preview the title, press ENTER. Titles, like video effects and transitions, must be rendered.

Preview files are stored in the place you designated in the Scratch Disks and Device Control dialog box.

To delete preview files, select the clips in the work area that have been previewed and press CONTROL-BACKSPACE (Windows) or COMMAND-DELETE (Mac). The green preview bar at the top of the Timeline will be gone. The preview files stored on your hard drive must still be trashed because deleting those files merely eliminates their reference in the Premiere file from which they're deleted.

CRAWLING TITLES

Crawling titles are another type of moving title. They are similar to rolling titles in the way they are modified and created but differ in that they run horizontally across frames. Crawling titles are sometimes used for special news bulletins or special messages that run along the bottom third of the frame (Figure 8-7). You can see a sample of a crawling title in chapter 08_finished.ppg. It's over the clip on frame marker 1, cave.mov. Press ALT and drag (Windows) or OPTION and drag (Mac) to scrub over this clip in the Timeline if you want to see a sample of a crawling title.

FIGURE 8-6
You can alter the vertical spacing on a rolling clip by adding line spaces before and/or after the title

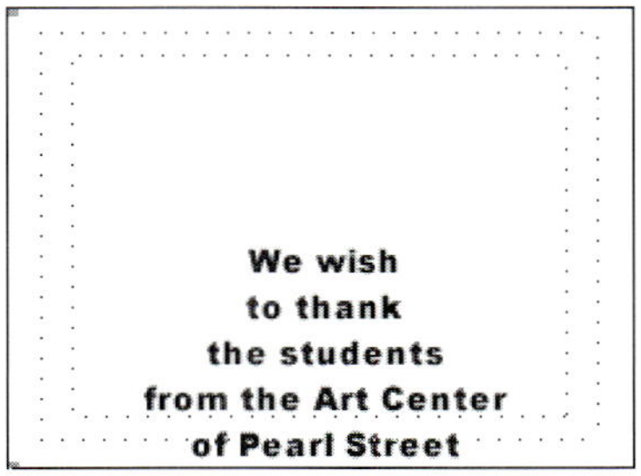

FIGURE 8-7
Crawling text in the Program view

A crawling title is different only because it runs horizontally across frames as opposed to a rolling title, which runs up and down.

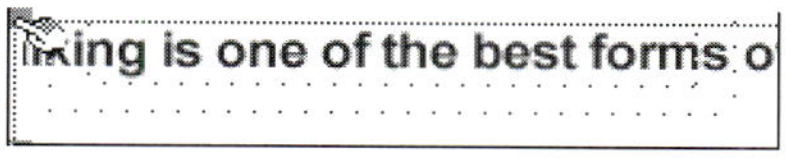

In the Rolling Title Options dialog box, for Direction, choose Move Left or Move Right.

Depending on what type of title effect you want, both rolling and crawling titles should address any scenario where you need a substantial amount of information to be read by your viewer.

ADDING MOTION TO TITLES

Rolling and crawling titles enable text to move in time. Although you can change some of the settings, for the most part, you can't get too creative with this technique.

Premiere offers another way to add motion to a frame, with Motion Settings.

Motion Settings not only let you move and change the size of an object, they also let you zoom and distort elements (Figure 8-8).

> **TIP** **Open the file named chapter_08_finished.ppj and scrub the Timeline (ALT and drag in Windows or OPTION and drag on a Mac) over the last clip on the Timeline (SHIFT-3 to get to frame marker 3). Notice that the title, "focus_title," changes in size and moves over time. This is an ordinary title with a rectangle background. The name of this clip is focus_title.ptl. Motion Settings were applied to this clip to create movement.**

Although the Motion Settings dialog box may look complex, it's a simple matter to add motion to a clip. Doing so involves adding keyframes to a clip and modifying the properties of the clip in this dialog box. Keyframes are frames on which one or more properties of a clip change. To display movement, you must have at least two keyframes: a beginning and an end. However, you can create keyframes between these two points.

FIGURE 8-8

The Motion Settings dialog box

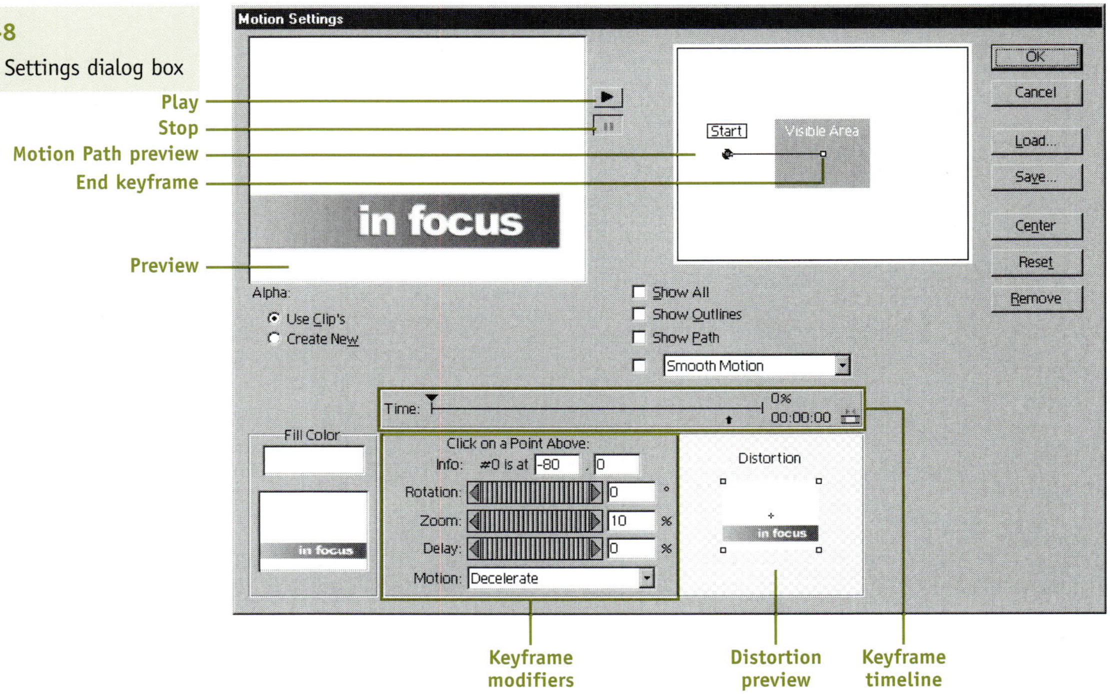

On keyframes, you can change more than the position of an object. You can also change the zoom, rotation and distortion of a clip. A static title might be a typical application for Motion Settings.

Here's How TO ADD MOVEMENT TO A CLIP:

1. **Select the clip in the Timeline and choose Clip | Video Options | Motion from the menu.**
2. **In the Motion Path preview, you can change the position of a clip in time and see a preview of the clip in this box. You can also see the start and end keyframe depicted in this preview. In Figure 8-9, the keyframes on this title have been positioned so the start keyframe begins outside of the frame and moves into the center of the frame in time (end keyframe). You can see the way the motion will occur by looking at the preview on the left and also following the motion path line. To move the keyframes, simply drag the keyframe handles and drop them to their new position.**

In the Motion Path preview, you can also click a keyframe to select it, then go to the bottom of the dialog box and select a new rotation or zoom for that keyframe.

FIGURE 8-9
Click and drag keyframes in the Motion Path preview box to reposition

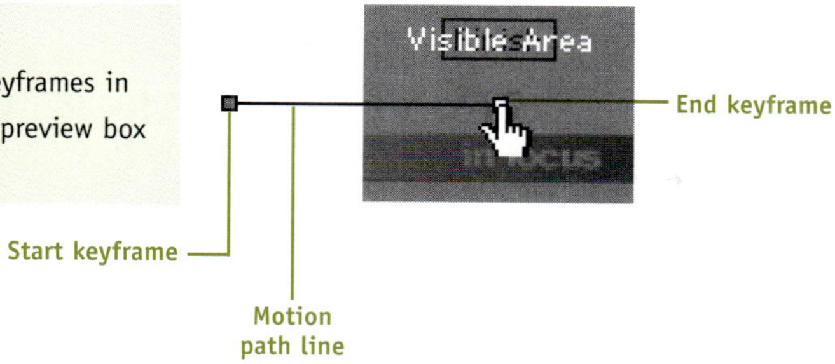

You can either type in a number for the zoom and rotation, or you can drag the zoom and rotation slider to set the percentage. Changing the rotation on two or more keyframes gives the clip the illusion of spinning in time. Changing the zoom on one or move keyframes gives the clip the illusion of changing size in time.

At the bottom center of the Motion Settings dialog box in the Keyframe modifiers section, you can also select Decelerate. With a Decelerate motion setting, a clip or the title in the clip will appear to come in fast and then slow down before it stops. To see the animated results of your settings in the Motion window, click the Play button in the motion preview area. To stop the movement, click the Stop button.

To Add ADDITIONAL KEYFRAMES TO THE MOTION PATH IN THE MOTION SETTINGS WINDOW:

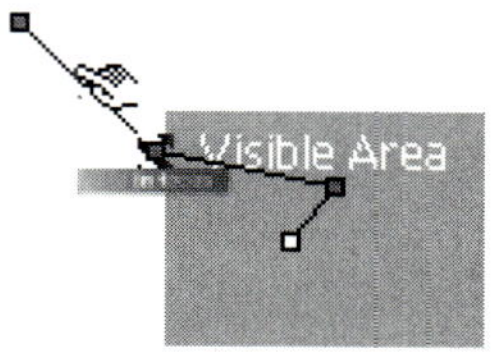

1. **Click anywhere on the motion path, in between the Start and End keyframes.**
2. **New keyframes appear as handles and are represented on the motion timeline with a tick mark. The motion timeline represents the clip over time. You can alter the motion over time by dragging keyframes and positioning them in different places in the motion timeline, or you can move them in the path preview.**
3. **Once you've moved keyframes and/or created new keyframes and changed the properties of the clip on keyframes, click OK and preview the clip by ALT-scrubbing in the Timeline in Windows or pressing OPTION and scrubbing on a Mac or pressing ENTER or RETURN.**

NOTE When you mouse over the motion path to add a keyframe, the cursor turns into an index finger. This finger is the Add Keyframe icon. Delete a keyframe by selecting the keyframe and pressing BACKSPACE (Windows) or DELETE (Mac).

There are tons of fun things to do with titles in Premiere—so many that it's hard to control the urge to overdress titles. The Motion Settings window is filled with many other features. After you become comfortable with the basics, you'll be able to build on that and add to the many new tricks you've learned in Premiere.

> **ON THE VIRTUAL CLASSROOM CD-ROM** **In Lesson 6, "Adding Titles to Movies," the instructor demonstrates the process of creating, testing, and applying a rolling title over a movie clip.**

9

Superimpose in Premiere with Transparency Settings

Superimposing in Premiere is when a clip or image is positioned on a superimpose track (Video Tracks 2 and higher) over another clip. By default, the clip on Video Track 2 obscures the clip on the underlying track. In Premiere, you can change the opacity of superimposed clips so the underlying clip or image can peek through. Premiere also offers a plethora of transparency settings that let you remove parts of a superimposed clip or still image based on the particular settings you choose. The transparency settings offer many impressive effects that can be achieved by using keys, or selective transparency.

In Premiere, you have a great deal of control over the way a superimposed clip blends into an underlying clip. First, we'll look at the simplest way to control the opacity of a superimposed object. This method is to use the rubberband line, or the *fade line* as it's sometimes called, right in the Timeline to alter the clip's (or object's) level of transparency.

Control Fading in the Timeline

> **NOTE** **If you don't see the fade handles, click the Display Opacity Rubberbands icon in the expanded portion of the superimposed track. Check the icon at the left (see the illustration) to view effect keyframes.**

When you expand tracks above Video Track 1, you can modify the opacity of clips and graphics right on the tracks. You've probably noticed and maybe even played around with the fade controls (Figure 9-1). The fade controls consist of a red line with rubberband handles on the head and tail of the clip. As with other handles, you can drag them in the Timeline.

The fade controls are easy to use. If you want to refer to the Premiere source files, copy the Chapter 09 folder and the artbeats_clips folder to your hard drive and open the file in this folder named rubberband.ppj.

This file consists of a few clips on Video Track 1. In this section, we'll adjust the transparency of the clips on the superimpose track to see how they blend in with the clips on Video Track 1. You'll remember from Chapter 8 that text or objects in the Title window, with empty or semitransparent areas, are converted into alpha channels. "Alpha channels" are transparent or semitransparent areas of a video clip. This means the clip on Video Track 1 will show through the background of a clip in Video Track 2 if it's a title. Let's test this by altering the transparency of the title on Video Track 2, named lady_title.ptl.

FIGURE 9-1
Expand superimpose tracks to use the fade controls

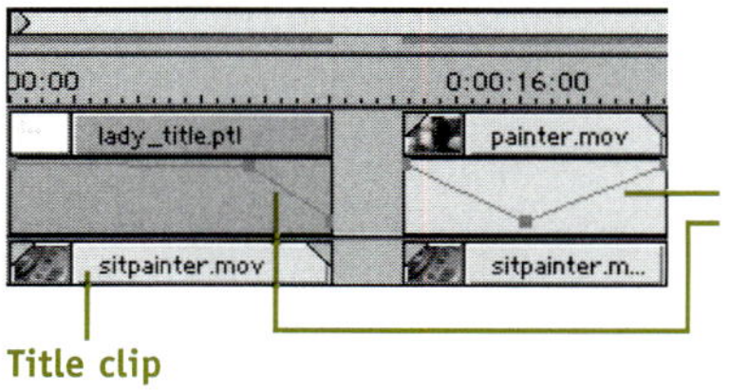

To Change THE OPACITY OF A TITLE:

1. Expand Video Track 2 by clicking on the expand arrow. By manipulating the red fade line in the expanded area of the panel, you can control the transparency of the title on this track.

2. When you position the pointer over the fade control line, it turns into a white pointing finger with a plus and minus sign. Use this pointing finger (see the illustration) to create new handles and manipulate the fade line. You'll notice that, by default, there are fade handles at the beginning and end of the fade line.

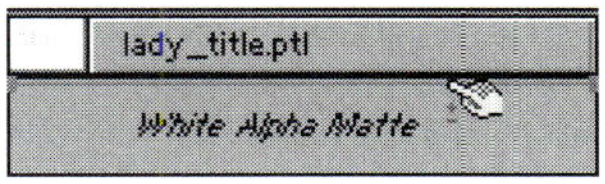

On the title clip, click the fade line about three-quarters into the clip to create a third handle. Drag the handle down vertically a few pixels from the top to create a slight transparency on the title at this point.

Position the pointer over the last handle and drag the handle vertically to the bottom of the track panel. Notice the finger turns gray when positioned over an existing handle (see the illustration). Doing this makes the clip gradually become transparent.

Scrub over the clip in the Timeline (ALT-drag in Windows or OPTION-drag on a Mac) and notice at the point where you created the handle, the title gradually becomes transparent, as you can see here.

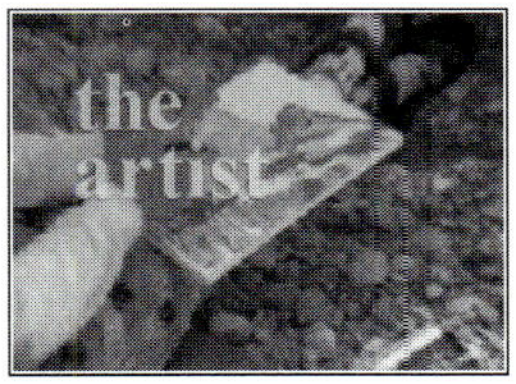

To Delete A HANDLE:

- Click and drag upward on the handle you just created up and out of the rubberband area to remove it. The handle now disappears, and the fade line on this title gradually changes from opaque to transparent in its duration.

Now let's see what happens when we superimpose one video clip over another.

1. Double-click the artbeats_clips folder in the Project window to preview its contents. Drag the clip named painter.mov to Video Track 2, above the second instance of the sitpainter.mov clip. Shorten the length of the superimposed clip by dragging the clip's handle and flushing it with the clip on Track 1 (see the illustration).

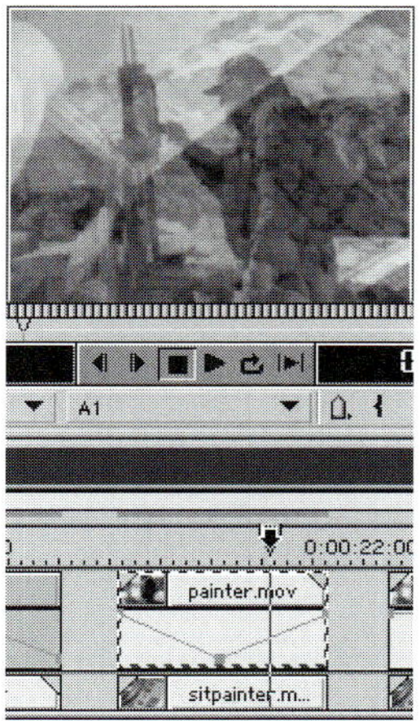

2 Scrub over this area of the Timeline and preview the clips in the Monitor window. As you would expect, the clip on the superimpose track obscures the clip on Track 1.

3 With Track 2 expanded, position the pointer over the middle of the painter.mov clip and click to create another handle.

4 Drag the middle fade handle to the bottom of the panel and now scrub over the clip's Timeline. The top clip appears to blend into the underlying clip toward the middle of the clip, then returns to opaque at the tail of the clip, as in the illustration. Play with the handles on the head and tail of the fade line to see the different types of effects you can create by altering a clip's transparency in this way.

Hold down SHIFT while you drag to move in one-percent increments. When you use this method, a pop-up label appears next to the clip, indicating the exact fade percentage as you drag.

> **TIP** To preview the numeric percentage by which you are moving a handle, you can also display the Info palette from the menu (Window | Show Info). As you drag a handle, the Info palette displays the exact percentage of the opacity of that handle.

Using the Fade Tools in the Toolbox

If you recall from Chapter 5, there are a couple of tools in the Timeline toolbox that are used in conjunction with the fade line. You might not have fully understood what they were used for back then. Now that we're studying the fade line, it's time to address these tools. The Fade Adjustment and Fade Scissors tools give you more ways to fade a clip.

Fade Adjustment Tool

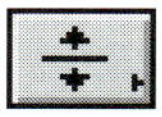

The Fade Adjustment tool is located at the right side of the toolbox in a flyout menu with the Link tool and Cross Fade tool (see the illustration). With this tool, you can move a segment of the fade line in between two handles. This way, you can maintain the position ratio between two handles when you move them.

To Use the Fade Adjustment tool:

1. Select the tool from the toolbox (or press the U key) and position the pointer over a fade line segment, in between two handles.
2. The pointer turns into the Fade Adjustment tool, a vertical, double-headed arrow with a red line in between the arrow heads.
3. Drag the segment to change its position. Notice the segment moves as a unit and maintains the angle of the segment, but the opacity percentage changes.

Fade Scissors Tool

The Fade Scissors tool is located at the right side of the toolbox in the same flyout menu with the Razor tool, as shown here.

This tool creates two adjacent handles on your rubberband fade line. In other words, it's simply a quick way to add an additional segment to your rubberband fade line.

To Use the Fade Scissors tool:

1. Select the Fade Scissors tool (or type the letter C) from the toolbox.
2. Place the pointer over a fade line, in between two handles. Remember, you can delete handles by clicking them and dragging them outside in the panel. The pointer turns into a scissors icon.
3. Click the fade line to create two handles.

TIP You can create up to 99 video tracks in Premiere. You probably won't need that many, but you can superimpose more than two clips at a time by creating an additional track or two and achieve some interesting effects. The easiest way is to create another video track is to right-click (Windows) or CONTROL-click (Mac) in the Timeline and select Add Video Track.

As you can see, the fade control tools are easy to use and provide you a storehouse of different effects you can achieve by making a clip or graphic transparent. Let's now move on to transparency settings to see how we can further change the appearance of a movie by blending clips or parts of clips together with different key effects.

TRANSPARENCY SETTINGS

The other way you can superimpose clips in Premiere is by using the key effects in the Transparency Settings dialog box. When you "key out" a portion of an image, it becomes hidden, or transparent, when it is superimposed over another image.

There are 14 different key types you can choose from this dialog box. Although some are very similar, each key type gives clips a different effect. Depending on which key type you select, additional controls become available in the dialog box. As you will see, the controls that are unavailable for a key are dimmed.

The keys are basically divided into four types:

- **Chroma (color) keys** These include Chroma, RGB Difference, Blue Screen, Green Screen and Non-Red. Chroma keys let you superimpose clips by making certain colors in the clip transparent.
- **Luminance (brightness) keys** These keys include Luminance, Multiply, and Screen. Luminance keys use levels of brightness to define a transparent area.
- **Alpha keys** These keys include Alpha and Black and White Alpha mattes. Alpha keys use the alpha channel of a clip to define a transparent area. The alpha channel of a clip defines the levels of transparency of a clip. Alpha channels are either straight or premultiplied. Straight alpha channels contain transparency information only on the alpha channel of the clip or image. When an alpha channel is premultiplied, transparency information is contained on all the channels (Red, Green, Blue, and Alpha), causing the background to blend in with the edges the image when superimposed. Premiere titles use premultiplied alpha channels.
- **Matte keys** The matte keys include Image Matte, Track Matte, and Difference Matte. Matte keys use a specific image or clip as a matte to define transparent areas. The matte can be a different image from the foreground or background clips.

USING THE TRANSPARENCY SETTINGS DIALOG BOX

Now that you have a basic idea of what the transparency settings do, let's open the dialog box and look around. Before you access the Transparency Settings dialog box, you must select a clip on a superimposed track where you want to key out an element.

There are several ways to display the Transparency Settings dialog box:

- Select Clip | Video Options | Transparency or CONTROL-G (Windows) or COMMAND-G (Mac).
- Right-click (Windows) or CONTROL-click (Mac) a clip on the superimpose track and select Video Options | Transparency from the pop-up menu.
- Select Window | Show Effect Controls. In the Effect Controls palette, click Transparency Setup (see the illustration), which displays the Transparency Settings dialog box.

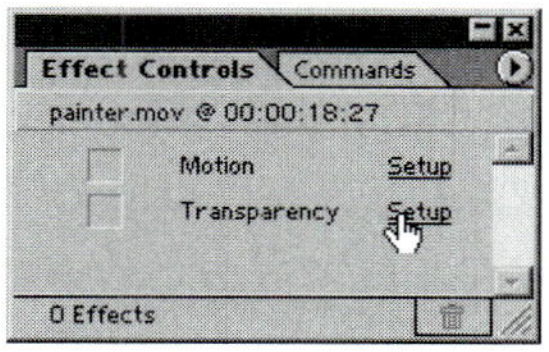

Although the slider controls change depending on which key is selected, some elements remain the same. For example, the preview controls under the Sample thumbnail at the top right of the Transparency Settings dialog box are available for every key type (Figure 9-2). Here you can preview an animated version of the key you've selected and test your control settings by dragging the slider under the Sample thumbnail. Unfortunately, Tool Tips don't work in this dialog box, so if you forget what an icon does in this box, you have to rely on the clarity of the picture to figure it out.

Under the sample, there are five preview options. The following settings are available for you to customize the sample:

- **Black/White Transparency** This is viewed in the sample area as black or white when this icon is selected. Click to toggle between black and white.
- **Checkerboard** When the checkerboard icon is selected, transparent areas are previewed in the sample as a checked pattern.

FIGURE 9-2 The Transparency Settings dialog box

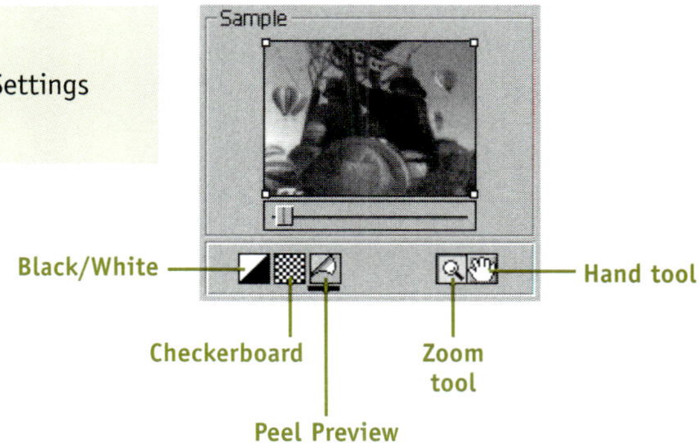

- **Peel Preview** This icon uses the underlying clip on Track 1 to fill in transparent areas.
- **Zoom** Use the Zoom tool to zoom in and out of the preview to refine areas of the clip. To use this tool, click the Zoom icon. Then position the magnifier with the plus sign over the preview sample and click to zoom in. To zoom out, OPTION-click (Windows) or ALT-click (Mac).
- **Hand** Use the Hand tool to scroll the preview sample.
- **Collapse** This tool is available on the Mac only. Use this tool to toggle between previewing the key in the Monitor window and the preview sample in the Transparency Settings dialog box.

The rest of the settings in this dialog box will become available as you select different key types. Let's explore some of the key types and how they work.

Chroma Key

Chroma-based keys are often used as composites. For example, a film with a boat might be shot indoors against a color background. Then in production, the color could be keyed out and superimposed over an underlying film of the sea. Of course, making this effect look real would take a lot of work, but the concept here is always the same—that is, using color to key out, or define, transparent areas. Chroma-keying is also how the weather person on TV is superimposed over the weather map, an effect you've probably seen many times.

You access the Chroma key in the Key Type pop-up menu in the Transparency Settings dialog box (Figure 9-3). To use the Chroma key, select a color in a clip that you want to be transparent.

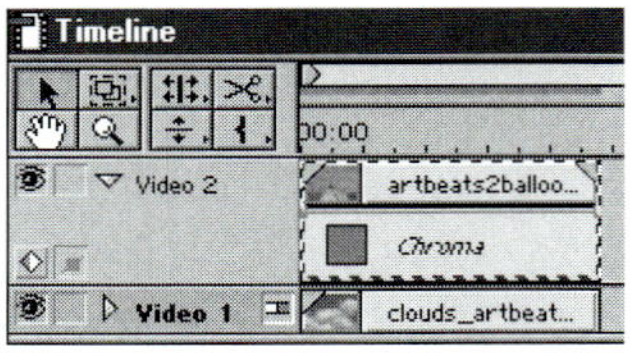

Let's look at the file named chroma.ppj in the Chapter 09 folder. The first clip on Video Track 2 in the Timeline is a clip named artbeats2ballons.mov. This clip has a Chroma key applied to it. It is superimposed over another clip on Video Track 1 named clouds_artbeats.mov (see the illustration). If you're following along with the chapter lesson, you can scrub the Timeline (ALT [Windows] or OPTION [Mac]) over the first clips to see how the Chroma key blends these clips.

To Set a Chroma key on a clip:

1. **Select a clip on the superimpose track.**

FIGURE 9-3 The Chroma key in the Transparency Settings Key Type pop-up menu

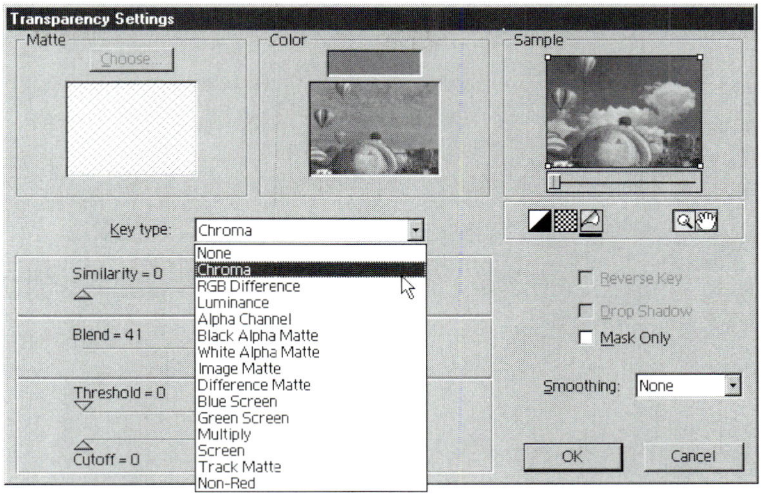

2 **Access the Transparency Settings dialog box using one of the methods outlined at the beginning of this section (Clip | Video Options | Transparency).**

3 **In the Transparency Settings dialog box, select Chroma from the pop-up menu; adjust the settings and click OK. When Chroma is selected, the following settings with sliding arrow bars controls become available to further refine the key:**

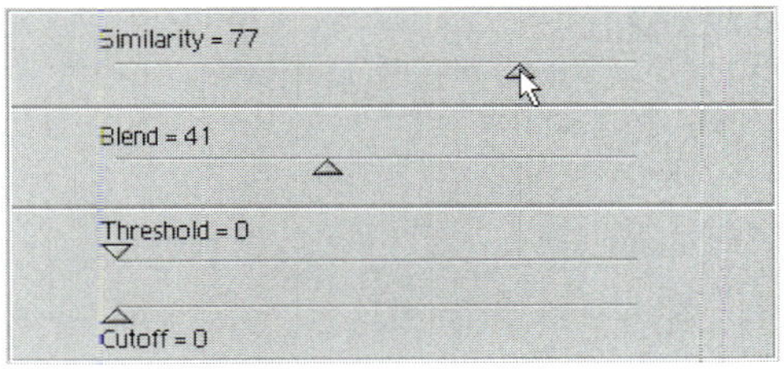

- **Similarity** Slide the arrow bar to the right to increase the range of colors to be keyed out. As you drag the bar to the right, the range of keyed-out colors gradually is decreased.
  - **Blend** Slide the Blend arrow to the right to eliminate fringe pixels that create a halo effect between clips.
  - **Threshold** This slider controls shadow areas. The farther to the right the slider is dragged, the more shadow areas are visible.
  - **Cutoff** This slider darkens and lightens shadows. The farther to the right the slider is dragged, the lighter the shadows.

In the Transparency Settings dialog box for the clip named artbeats2ballons.mov, the color swatch above the thumbnail color preview matches some of the sky blue tones in the preview. If the cursor is positioned over the thumbnail preview, it turns into an eyedropper (see the illustration). You can select any color in the thumbnail preview as the key color by clicking a color with the eyedropper.

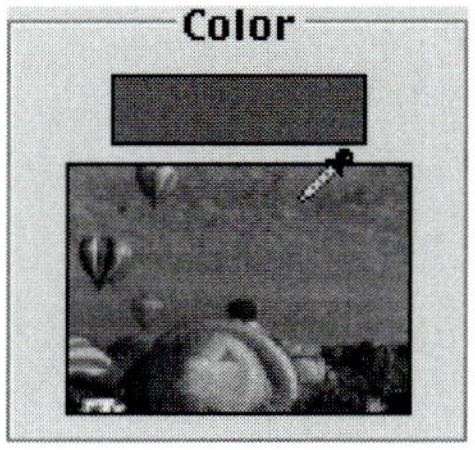

You can also click the color swatch above the Color preview thumbnail and select a key color from the Color Picker. Click OK to close it.

Let's examine some of the other settings in this dialog box. When you test the results of applying a Chroma key by dragging the slider under the Sample thumbnail, you'll notice that with the current settings in this file, certain objects still some have visible halos. Although these two clips will never be superimposed perfectly over one another in their present state in Premiere, you can achieve an acceptable balance between the halo, or fringe, effect around objects and parts of the clip becoming transparent that aren't intended to be there. This balance is achieved by dragging the Similarity and Blend sliders.

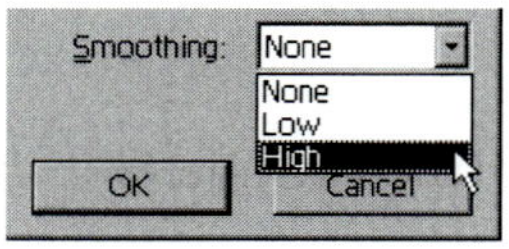

Smoothing has been turned on in the dialog box, as shown in the illustration. Smoothing can help an object blend into a background by more gradually dispersing the pixels in between the object and background. The result of the settings on these particular clips is a sort of surreal feeling where parts of some objects appear translucent.

The other Chroma-based keys, Non-Red, RGB Difference, and Blue and Green Screen, work in a similar manner but key out different colors in different ways.

NON-RED KEY The second clip on Video Track 2 (which is identical to the first set of clips) has a Non-Red key applied to it (see the illustration). The Non-Red key is similar to the Chroma key but yields slightly different results. If you select Non-Red from the Transparency Settings dialog box, you can change the Blend, Threshold, and Cutoff, but you can't change the Similarity as you can in the Chroma key type.

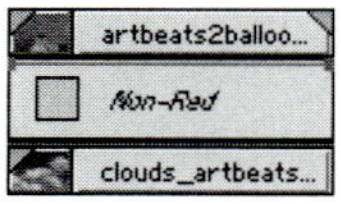

You can see a slight difference between the two keys when you ALT (Windows/OPTION (Mac) scrub over the second set of clips in the Timeline and compare the results with the first set of clips. The Non-Red key simultaneously keys out green and blue areas while providing a blending slider so you can control the blend between the two clips.

The RGB Difference key is a simpler version of the Chroma key, offering only the ability to adjust the Similarity between clips. Last, the Green and Blue Screen keys hide the colors green and blue respectively to show the underlying image in these areas.

LUMINANCE KEY

The Luminance key and keys that perform a similar function (Multiply and Screen) use brightness levels to define transparent areas. This keys out dark areas of a clip and makes them transparent. The more contrast your clip contains, the more sharply defined the transparency will appear.

Open the file named luminance.ppj (in the Chapter 09 folder you copied from the CD to your hard drive). Notice that the first clip on the superimpose track, named artbeatsGlide.mov, has a Luminance key assigned to it (Figure 9-4).

As you can see from the Transparency Settings dialog box on this clip, when Luminance is selected from the Key Type pop-up menu, only the Threshold and

FIGURE 9-4
Transparency Settings for the clip named artbeatsGlide.mov

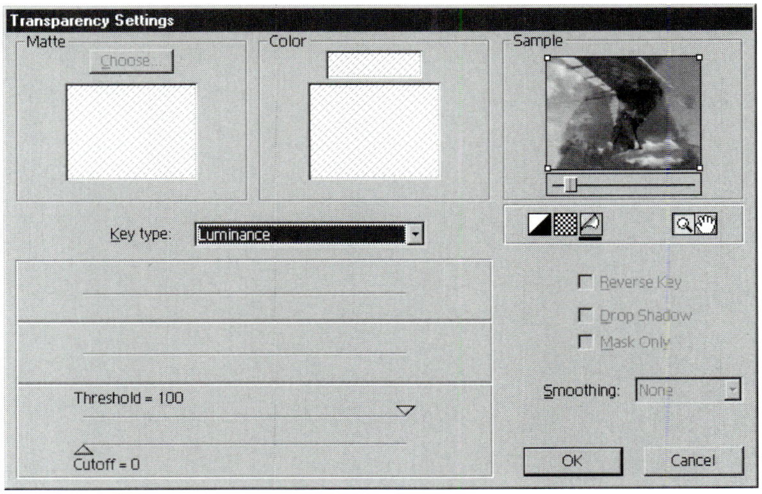

Cutoff sliders are available. The Threshold on this clip is set to 100 percent. Increasing the Threshold on this clip creates a wider range of transparency. The Cutoff sets the opacity of areas that have been defined by the Threshold setting.

SCREEN AND MULTIPLY KEYS The second clip on the superimpose track in file luminance.ppj has a Screen key applied to it. Both the Screen and Multiply keys use the tonal values of the underlying clip to determine the transparency of the superimposed clips. With the Screen key, the parts of the clip that become transparent are the dark areas that correspond to the clip underneath. The Multiply key, on the other hand, creates transparency in the bright areas that correspond to bright areas of the clip underneath.

If you ALT (Windows)/OPTION (Mac) scrub the Timeline over the second clip that has the Screen key applied to it, you'll notice that the transparency creates a subtle blend between the two clips (Figure 9-5).

In the Transparency Settings dialog box for this clip, you can use the Cutoff slider to increase the clip transparency by sliding it to the right, as shown in the illustration.

USING THE ALPHA CHANNEL KEY

The Alpha Channel key and other keys in the alpha category use alpha channels to determine transparency. Alpha channels are most universally known in programs such as Adobe Photoshop, although you can create alpha channels in some other programs as well. In video, the three channels (red, green, and blue) are used to create RGB images, and the fourth channel is for transparent (or semitransparent)

> **TIP** Hold down the SHIFT key when you drag the rubber band line down to see the exact opacity percentage.

FIGURE 9-5
A clip with a Screen key applied to it

areas of these images. Alpha channels in Photoshop are "straight" alpha channels. A "straight" alpha channel is a channel that holds all the transparency information on an image. A "premultiplied" alpha channel on the other hand blends the transparent background with the edges of the image. The Alpha Channel key is used in conjunction with images generated from programs like Photoshop, Illustrator, and After Effects, or other programs that contain straight alpha channels.

In the file named alpha.ppj (in the Chapter 09 folder), the first element on Track 2 is a still image named pray2.psd. This Photoshop file contains an alpha channel. The alpha channel on this image (on Track 2) defines the curves of a man's body. The body is transparent, so the underlying clip, smoke_artbeats.mov, is visible through the alpha channel, creating a mask effect, as shown in the illustration.

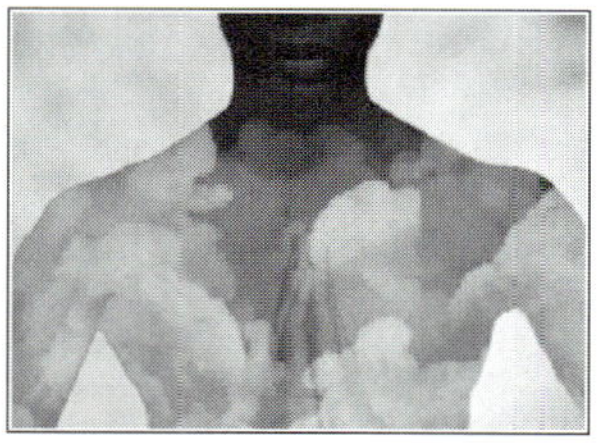

There is a duplicate instance of pray2.psd on Video Track 3. On this clip, the fade controls have been adjusted with the Fade Adjustment tool, so the rubberband is a third of its opacity, or approximately 30 percent. This makes the figure in the still picture partially visible in the alpha channel area, as the illustration shows. Scrub through the clips on the Timeline to see how the Alpha Channel key affects images and clips on other tracks.

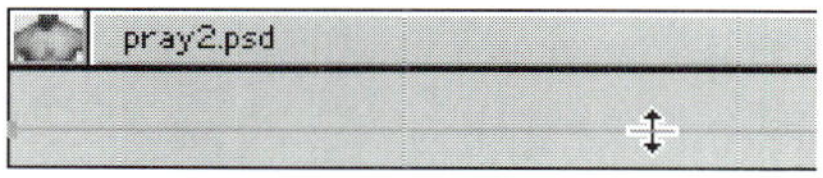

To Add an Alpha Channel key to a clip:

1. **Select a clip on a superimpose track. The clip must contain a straight alpha channel.**
2. **Display the Transparency Settings dialog box (Clip | Video Options | Transparency).**
3. **From the Key Type pop-up menu, select Alpha Channel. Two things to note: No slider controls are available for this option, and you can check the Reverse box to invert the key. Doing this reverses the transparent/opaque areas of the clip.**

BLACK AND WHITE ALPHA MATTES As mentioned in the earlier section, "Control Fading in the Timeline," when you create a title or simple graphic in the Premiere Title window, you create an alpha channel. Alpha channels in Premiere titles or graphics are premultiplied, so the transparent background color of these images also becomes blended into the edges of the image. For black alpha mattes, the background must be premultiplied with black; for white alpha mattes, the background must be premultiplied with white.

The second clip on Track 2 of the alpha.ppj file (DEsun.ai) has a white alpha matte applied to it. The logo is yellow on a white background. If you scrub over this clip, you'll notice the yellow logo is opaque and the white background is transparent, as shown in the illustration.

Black and white alpha mattes are commonly used for line art logos and text.

IMAGE MATTE KEY

The Image Matte key lets you use a still image to define transparent areas of a clip. High-contrast grayscale images work the best for this purpose. With a grayscale image, black areas are transparent and white areas are opaque. In-between areas are semi-opaque.

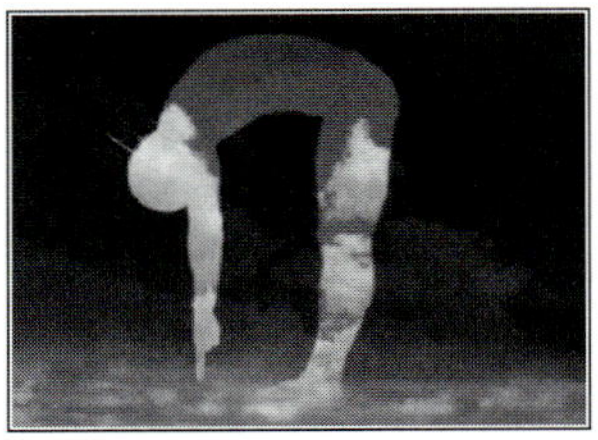

In file matte.ppj in the Chapter 09 folder, the first clip on the superimpose track (clouds_artbeats.mov) has an Image Matte key applied to it (see the illustration). If you want, ALT (Windows/OPTION (Mac) scrub over the clip in the Timeline to see what type of effect this key creates.

To Apply AN IMAGE MATTE:

1. **Select a clip on the superimpose track and display the Transparency Settings dialog box (Clip | Video Options | Transparency).**

2. **In the dialog box, for Key Type select Image Matte.**

3. **When you select Image Matte, the Choose button under the Matte thumbnail preview becomes active. Click this button to display the Load Matte dialog box and navigate to the file you want to use as the image matte. In file matte.ppj, a Photoshop grayscale image, yoga_invert.psd, was selected as the Image Matte key (see the following illustration).**

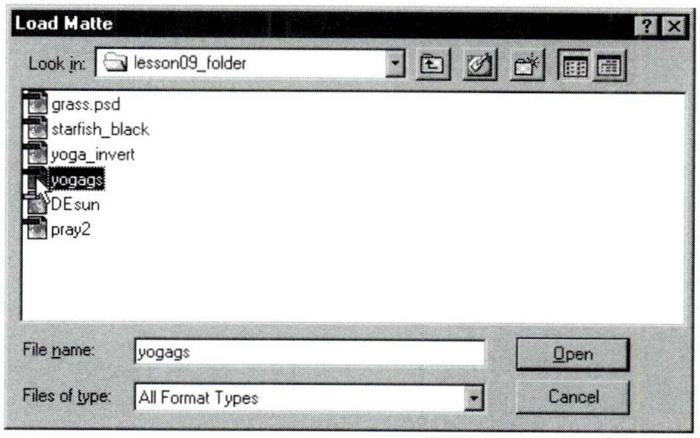

Control sliders aren't available when Image Matte is selected as a key, but you can test the results in the thumbnail preview. You can modify the Image Matte key effect on an image by going back to the program in which it was created and adjusting the image's contrast.

TIP **Click the Reverse key button to reverse the transparency and opacity levels in the foreground image.**

Difference and Track Matte Keys The Difference key is most often used for clips with moving objects on static backgrounds. For example, if your clip was a plane flying against a solid blue sky, you could use the Difference key to eliminate the blue sky and replace it with another image. To key out a static background, check the Reverse key. This key works by comparing the still images with the clip, then removing the areas in the clip that match the still image. The Difference key compares the pixels in the clip with the moving object to the pixels in the image without the object, and wherever the pixels match, makes them transparent. Only pixels that are different are kept, hence the name Difference key.

The Track Matte key is used to create a traveling matte that moves across the screen, masking out one clip while another clip acts as a backdrop. Thus, this key actually involves three tracks. The background clip is on Video Track 1, the superimposed clip is on Video Track 2, and the clip or still image that integrates these two clips by creating a matte resides on Video Track 3. Where a matte is white, areas of the underlying clip on Track 1 are opaque. Where a matte is black, areas of this underlying clip are transparent, and levels of gray, as you'd expect, produce semi-opaque areas.

You can create some cool effects using a Track Matte key. Let's look at a simple application of a Track Matte key used on matte.ppj from the Chapter 09 folder, the file we looked at previously. The Track Matte key has been applied to the second set of clips in this file.

To Create a track matte:

1. **Place a clip or still image on Video Track 1, which will serve as the background to the track matte. In this file, the clip is sunset_artbeats.mov.**
2. **Place a clip on Video Track 2 directly above the first clip. The clip in this file is artbeatsGlide.mov.**
3. **Create a Video Track 3 (in the Timeline, right-click in Windows or CONTROL-click on a Mac).**
4. **Place a white or grayscale image on a black background on Video Track 3. Make sure all the clips are the same duration and flush with one another. In the matte.ppj file, a still grayscale image of a starfish imported from Photoshop was used (starfish_black.psd).**
5. **Click the clip on Video Track 2 and display the Transparency Settings dialog box. In this box, for Key type, select Track Matte from the pop-up window (see the illustration) and click OK.**

6. **When you scrub over the clips in the Timeline, you'll see that the track matte masks the other superimposed clip and the clip on Video Track 1 serves as the background, as shown in the illustration.**

To make the track matte move and change as the underlying clips play, you simply need to apply motion settings to the image that acts as the track matte (in this case, the starfish on Video Track 3).

To Add motion to a Track Matte key:

1. **Click the clip or image that serves as the Track Matte key in Video Track 3 and display the Motion Settings dialog box (Clip | Video Options | Motion). In the sample file, the clip is named starfish_black.psd (Figure 9-6).**

FIGURE 9-6
The Motion Settings dialog box for the clip named starfish_black.psd

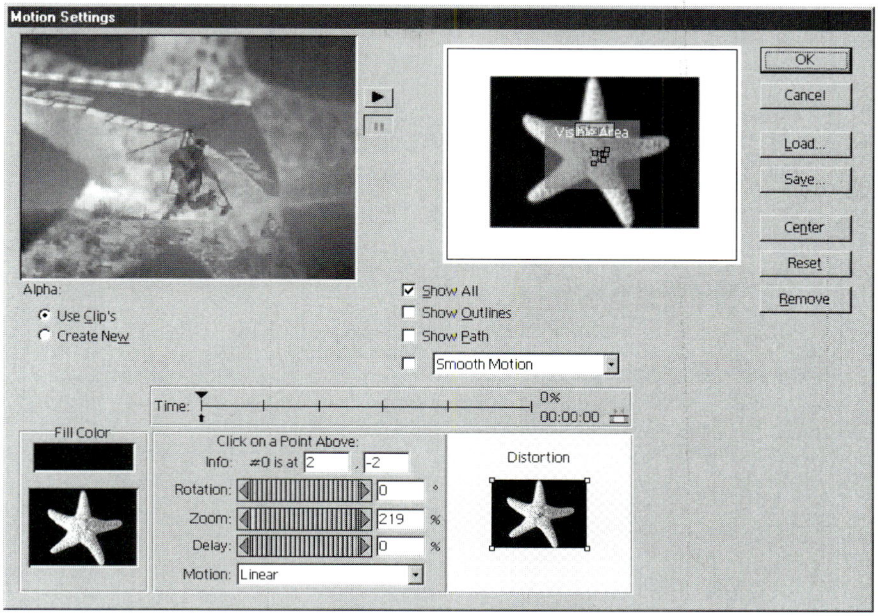

2 In this box, you can change the position, rotation, zoom, and other properties of the matte in time. Make sure that the fill color preview swatch is black to match the background of the matte. Otherwise, the edges of the clip on Video Track 2 may periodically show through when the matte changes properties.

3 On starfish_black.psd, the position, zoom, and rotation were changed at various intervals on keyframes in the motion Timeline. These properties follow the movement of the glider clip on Video Track 2.

4 To change these attributes in time, click the motion Timeline to create a new keyframe, as shown in the illustration. In the lesson file are four additional keyframes on the Timeline that were added this way. They are all spaced out evenly in the motion Timeline.

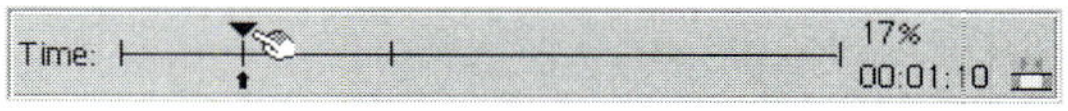

5 Click each keyframe in the motion Timeline and adjust the properties you want to change. If you want the matte to follow a movie object, move the matte over the traveling object on each keyframe. To move the matte, use all the arrow keys to move up, down, back, and forward. To rotate or zoom, use the slider controls at the bottom of the box. Because your new information will be based on what you see, you probably won't be inputting exact coordinates in these boxes.

6 When you're finished adjusting the matte on each keyframe, click OK.

TIP If you import a still image with a dimension that differs from the project, the image will appear distorted when previewed. To fix it, try selecting Clip | Video Options | Maintain Aspect Ratio from the menu.

Track mattes work particularly well when you use text as the matte. Try creating a single word in the Title window. Make the letters solid black, and use a heavy font and a font size that make the letters fill the frame. Save it into your project. Add video clips to Tracks 1 and 2, and put the title in Track 3. Apply the Track Matte key to the clip in Video 2, click the Reverse key switch in the Transparency dialog box, and the video in Track 2 will appear in the shape of the letters in the title, while the video in Track 1 fills the background.

It's quite simple to add any of the matte effects. The hardest part is planning it out and selecting the clips you will use to create just the right effect.

Garbage Mattes

Garbage mattes have a simple and specific purpose: Use them to mask out unwanted areas or objects in a clip.

You can also use garbage mattes to split a screen between tracks.

To Apply a garbage matte or split a screen:

1 Select a clip on a superimpose track that has an underlying clip.

2 Display the Transparency Settings dialog box (Clip | Video Options | Transparency).

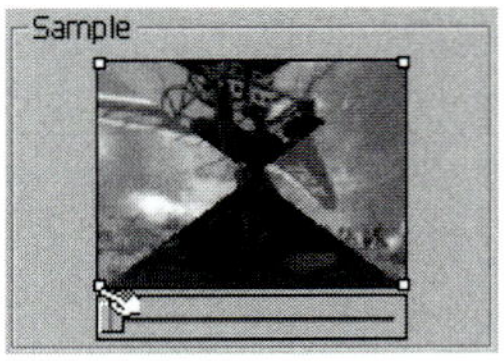

3 For a garbage matte, in the Sample thumbnail, drag the white handles in the four corners of the sample to obscure the element you want to eliminate, as shown in the illustration.

4 **Apply your key effect.**

5 **For a split screen, drag any of the four handles in the four corners of the sample to hide an area of the underlying clip, as in the illustration.**

There are many different ways to use superimposing techniques and keys and combine them with other techniques. Once you understand the basic concept behind superimposing and how to use keys, you can go wild creating new and unique effects in Premiere.

ON THE VIRTUAL CLASSROOM CD-ROM **Follow along with the instructor on Lesson 7, "Using the Fade Tools in the Timeline." Learn how to apply different types of keys to remove a background so parts of underlying clips can show through.**

10

Creating Video Effects in Premiere

If there's one thing about Premiere everyone can agree on, it's that video effects are fun to experiment with. Effects were called "filters" in older versions of Premiere and some users still refer to effects as filters. In Premiere 6, many new effects have been added, including some After Effects filters.

You're probably familiar with the concept of filters from cameras. Camera *filters* are attachments that screw on to a camera lens and alter the appearance of your photos. Common camera filters create such effects as blurring the edges of a picture or altering the color. Like filters on a camera lens, Effects in Premiere perform a similar function in that they alter the appearance of video clips. Unlike photographic still images, though, *effects* can alter the appearance of video clips over time, by animating effects. Also, Premiere Effects are much more extensive than a filter on a camera lens.

> **TIP** If you become hooked on effects, you can purchase plug-ins from third-party manufacturers. Different plug-ins perform different tricks. For example, Boris FX, among other plug-ins, creates 3-D digital effects on text and graphics. For a more complete listing of various plug-ins available for Premiere, see Appendix B. If you need something a little more industrial strength than just a lone plug-in here and there, by all means try Adobe After Effects. After Effects works wonderfully with Premiere and can add incredible depth to your effects. To download a free After Effects tryout, go to www.adobe.com.

In this chapter, you learn all about organizing and applying single and multiple video effects, and how to modify these effects. In addition, you also look at several different effects, see how they're used, and learn what kind of results you can expect from them. In no time, you'll identify your own set of favorite effects that you'll use frequently on your own productions.

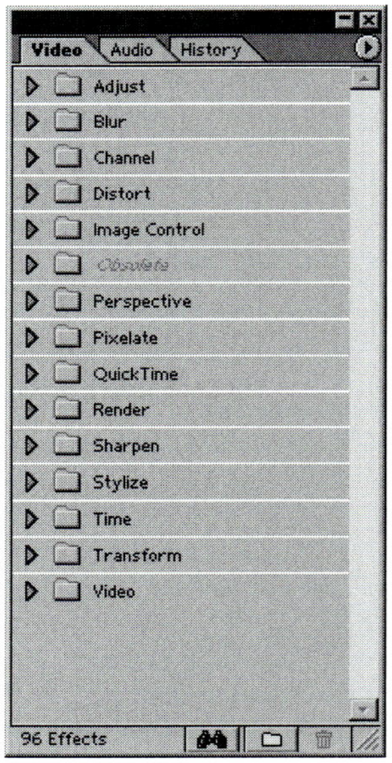

Effects in Premiere can be found in the Video Effects palette. You can display this palette by selecting Window | Show Video Effects from the menu. The Video Effects palette is chock full of effects. In fact, almost a hundred different effects can be found in this palette (see the illlustration).

To Follow ALONG WITH THIS CHAPTER IN A CLASSROOM-LIKE FASHION:

1. **Create a new file in Premiere.**
2. **Use a Multimedia QuickTime preset from the New Settings dialog box.**
3. **Click the Custom button and navigate to the Video Settings panel.**

4 **Change the Frame Size to 240x180*.**

5 **Click OK.**

6 **In the Project Window, import video files from the artbeats_clips folder located on the CD. As always, copy this folder to your hard drive before using it.**

7 **Add a clip or two to the timeline.**

8 **Save the Premiere file.**

Because it's important to familiarize yourself with the Video Effects palette to find just the right effect for your needs, let's discuss navigating through this palette.

> **NOTE** The standard multimedia frame size is 320x240. The lesson clips we're using have a frame size of 240x180. They're small and compact because they're being used for learning purposes.

> **NOTE** If you want to review the effects discussed in this chapter, project examples are stored in the Chapter 10 folder on the CD. To use these examples, copy the Chapter 10 folder and the artbeats_clips folder over to your hard drive.

THE EFFECTS PALETTE

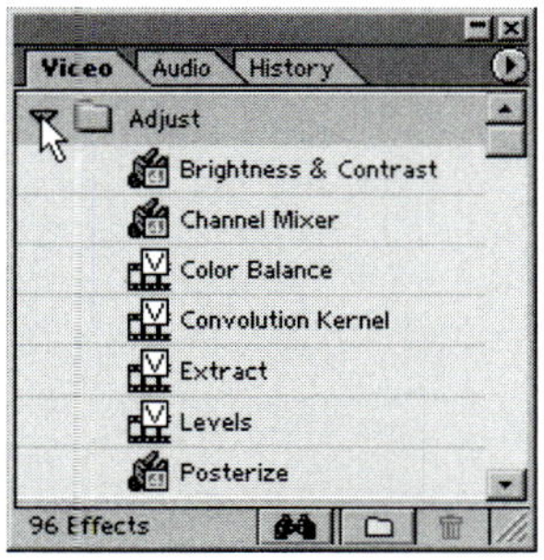

The *Effects palette* is where you select, organize, and manage your effects. Just like the Transitions palette, effects reside in expandable folders.

To Expand a folder in the Effects palette:

1 **Select the folder and click the left arrow.**

2 **Close an open folder by clicking the left arrow.**

If you look at the contents of the folders, you'll notice the effects are depicted as icons. As you'll notice in this palette, some icons appear as a filmstrip with the letter *V* on them. Others appear as a camcorder with a number 4. The filmstrip icon represents native Premiere effects and the camera icon represents plug-ins that have been imported from After Effects.

Apply an Effect to a Clip

Applying an effect to a clip in Premiere couldn't be easier. The hardest part is deciding which one to use.

NOTE When you apply an effect to a clip, a blue/green bar appears above the clip in the timeline, reminding you the clip has an effect associated with it. In addition, the familiar red render bar appears below the Work Area bar, which means the effect needs to be rendered before you can see it in the Program.

To Apply an effect in Premiere:

1. **Display the Effects palette.**
2. **Navigate to an effect you want to apply.**
3. **Click-and-drag the effect to a clip.**
4. **The Effect Controls palette for that effect pops up (see Figure 10-1). In this palette, you can further customize the effect for that clip with the various control sliders that become available to you. This panel and how it works are discussed in the next section.**

That's all there is to it. Effects are powerful and you can do a lot more than just apply them to a clip. As this chapter unfolds, you discover the incredible power of Effects as a creative tool.

The Obsolete Folder in the Effects Palette

If you look at the Effects palette, you'll notice one of the folders named Obsolete is dimmed out, meaning you can't apply it like the others. You can see this clearly in the first figure in this chapter. If you expand the Obsolete folder, even though

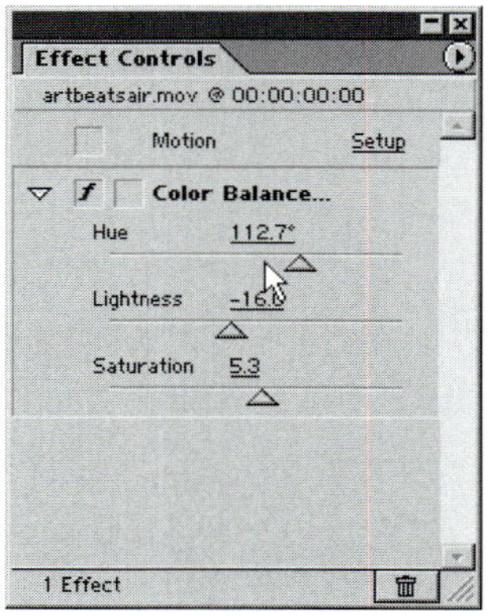

FIGURE 10-1
The Effect Controls palette for an effect on a video clip

it's dimmed, you'll see it's full of a long list of filters. These filters are from an older version of Premiere and are obsolete in version 6. So why are they here? If you need to open a file from the previous version of Premiere that used an obsolete filter, you could do so. In fact, you can even apply an old filter to a new clip.

TIP If you can't see the Obsolete folder in the Effects palette, from the Video Effects pop-up menu, select the Show Hidden option.

To Apply AN OBSOLETE FILTER TO A VIDEO CLIP:

1. Select a filter in the Obsolete folder in the Video Effects palette.
2. From the pop-up menu in the palette, select Show Selected. This will enable you to see and apply the selected filter, as shown in the illustration.

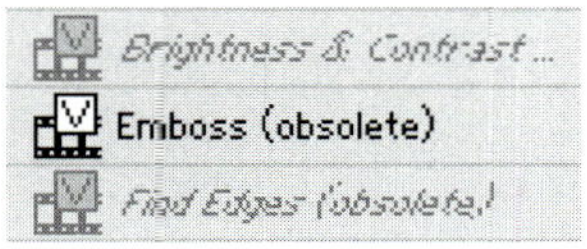

DRAG THE FILTER ON TO A CLIP IN THE TIMELINE.

Although you could apply one of these old filters, there would probably be little need to do so. The new filters, including After Effects plug-ins, have replacement effects, which, for the most part, perform better than the old filters.

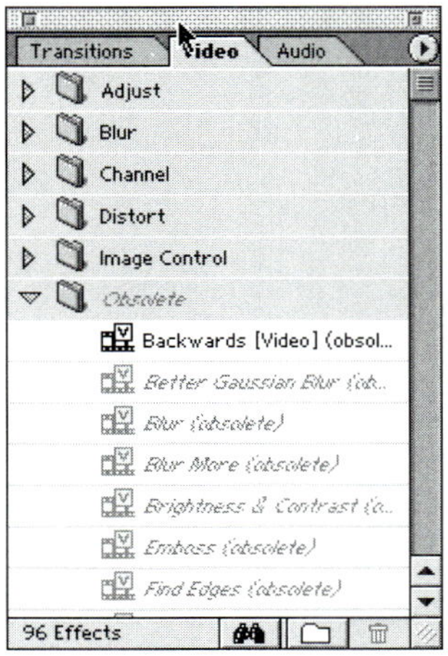

TIP The pop-up Video Effects palette contains various ways to help customize the management of your effects. For example, you can expand and collapse all folders from the Video Effects pop-up menu (see the illustration), as well as make new folders, delete old folders, and rename folders.

THE EFFECT CONTROLS PALETTE

Earlier, when we discussed how easy it is to apply an effect to a clip, you'll recall the Effect Controls palette being mentioned. The *Effect Controls palette* not only keeps a running list of the effects applied to a clip, but it also enables you (in some cases) to control the way effects look on a clip from this palette. Each time an effect is applied, the parameters for that particular clip (if any exist) will display in this palette.

NOTE **To see an effect in the Program view, it must be previewed (Timeline | Preview or press Return to render) or scrub the timeline while pressing ALT (Windows)/OPTION (Mac).**

In Figure 10-2, a Posterize effect from the Adjust folder has been applied to the artbeatsGlide.mov clip in the timeline. When the clip is applied, the Effect control panel displays with the name of the clip and an adjustment slider. This particular effect adjusts the number of tonal values on the RGB channels (that range from 2 to 255) of a clip. At a level 4 setting, you get four levels of red, four levels of blue, and four levels of green, creating a flatter color effect.

If you happen to close the Effect Control palette and need to access it again, select Window | Show Effect Controls. To see the effects on a particular clip, select the clip and the effects will display in that palette.

You also probably noticed the letter *f* is to the left of the effect name in the Effect Controls palette (see Figure 10-3). You can click this letter *f* to enable or disable an

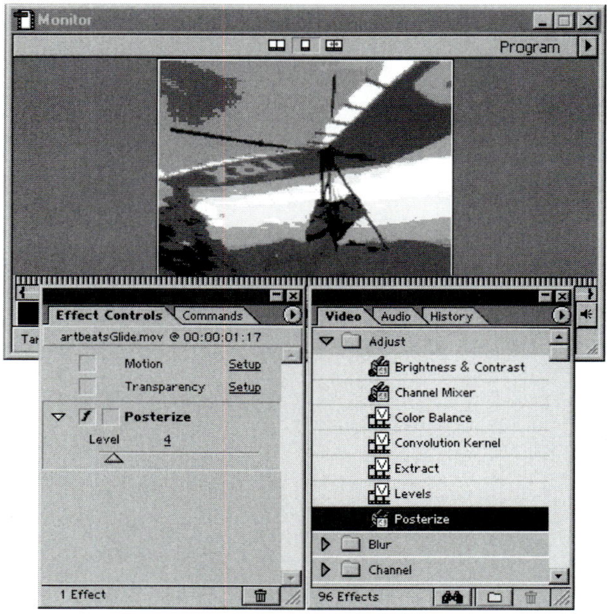

FIGURE 10-2
The Posterize effect is applied to the artbeatsGlide.mov video clip

FIGURE 10-3
The Enable Effect button in the Effect Controls palette

Enable Effect

effect. If the *f* is visible, the effect is enabled. If you click the *f* again, it disappears and disables the effect. When an effect is disabled, it doesn't display in the preview and it also won't display in the Program, even if you if you scrub the timeline while pressing Alt (Windows)/Option (Mac).

To Remove an effect from a clip:

1. **Click a clip that has an effect applied to it.**
2. **Select the effect in the Effect Controls palette.**
3. **Click the Trash can in the bottom right of the Effect Controls palette.**
4. **The effect is now removed from the clip.**

Effects can also be removed from a clip by selecting the effect in the palette and clicking Remove Selected Effect from the pop-up menu. All effects can be removed by selecting Remove All Effects in the Effect pop-up menu.

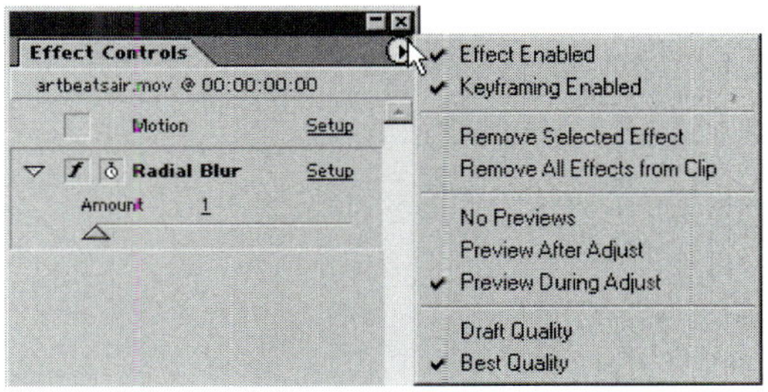

You can also customize the Effect Controls palette with options in the corresponding pop-up menu (see illustration). The Preview selections include No Previews and Previews After and During Adjust. The default setting is Preview During Adjust. This setting enables you to see how an effect is going to look when it's applied to the clip and generally is the easiest way to preview an effect on a clip. Preview After Adjust enables you to see a preview of the effect on a clip after you finish adjusting the settings.

In the pop-up menu, you can also opt to display the clip in Best Quality or Draft Quality. Selecting the Best Quality setting is a better choice because this will display the effect more accurately. Some effects yield subtle changes that wouldn't be visible if you chose Draft Quality. However, selecting Best Quality as a setting will probably cause the video to preview at a slower speed, depending on your system's configuration.

Adding Multiple Effects to a Clip

Let's say you want to add more than one effect to a clip. Adding multiple effects is as simple as adding a single effect and you can accomplish this in two different ways. In Figure 10-4, the artbeatsGlide.mov clip has a Posterize effect applied to it, in addition to a Wind effect from the Stylize folder. As you can see, the clip takes on the attributes of both the effects and their settings. Also, both effects are listed in the Effect Controls palette.

The *Posterize effect* reduces tonal levels in the RGB channels. It also reduces the number of colors or shades of gray in your clip, "flattening out" the tonality. By dragging the Levels slider to the right, you increase the number of colors or shades of gray. Dragging the slider to the left decreases the number of colors or shades of gray.

The *Wind effect* smears the pixels in the clip across the frame and yields an outcome that looks like a heavy wind is blowing on the clip.

FIGURE 10-4
The clip named artbeatsGlide.mov has two effects applied to it

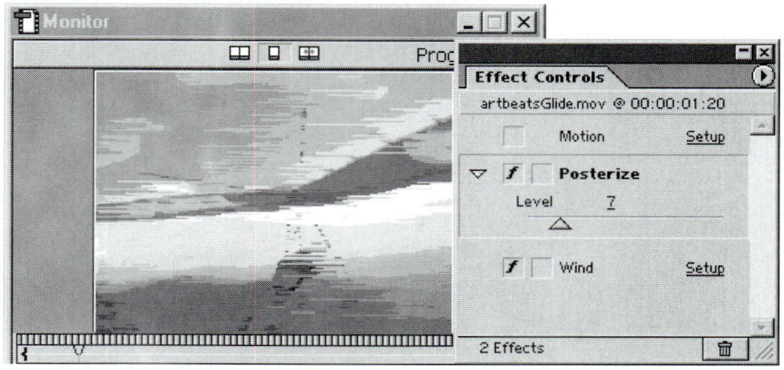

To Add multiple effects to a clip:

1. Select a clip with an effect.
2. From the Effects palette, drag another effect on to the selected clip or in to the Effect Controls palette.
3. With some effects, such as the Wind effect, a settings dialog box will give you the option of setting additional parameters on the effect. Figure 10-5 displays the dialog box that appears when the Wind effect is added to a clip. The look and feel of the wind effect can be customized by selecting the Wind, Blast, or Stagger options. On this clip, the Blast option, which creates sharp, hard vertical lines resembling a wind of tornado-like force, was selected.
4. The new effect name will appear underneath the previously added effect.
5. Click the name of an effect in the Effect Controls palette to modify the controls on a particular effect.

TIP If you decide to change the parameters of an effect after you apply it, select the clip and go to the Effect Controls palette. If it's an effect that has slider controls right in the palette, adjust the sliders. Other effects like the Wind effect, have setup buttons you can click to get back to that effect's settings dialog box. Still other effects, like the Horizontal or Vertical Flip in the Transform folder, or Black and White in the Image Control folder, don't have any adjustable settings. So effects are all unique because of the variety of customized parameters that can be adjusted.

When you use multiple effects on a clip, the manner in which they're stacked in the Effect Controls palette determines the way the clip will look. So, in some

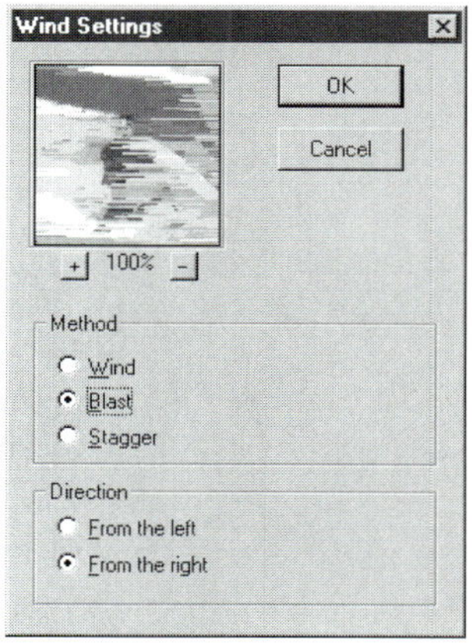

FIGURE 10-5
The Wind Settings dialog box from the Wind effect in the Effects palette

cases, depending on the position of effects in the palette, the clip could conceivably appear totally different. You can restack the order of multiple clips simply by clicking-and-dragging the effects up and down in the palette. When you do so, a double-headed arrow appears in the palette, which helps to guide you to a new vertical position in the palette.

Now that you know how to apply multiple effects, let's check out some other ways to modify these effects.

Keyframes and Video Effects

Adding single and multiple effects to a video clip is obviously easy to do. But, after a while, you might wonder if that's all there is to effects. In fact, if that's all effects were in Premiere, they'd be pretty limiting.

Remember, in the beginning of the chapter, we discussed animating effects? Well, effects applied to a clip can have keyframes in the duration of the clip. Positioning keyframes on the clip makes the effects animate over time. *Keyframes* are similar in concept to motion keyframes, where you can change the properties of a clip (position, zoom, rotation, and so forth) at a specific point in time (see Figure 10-6).

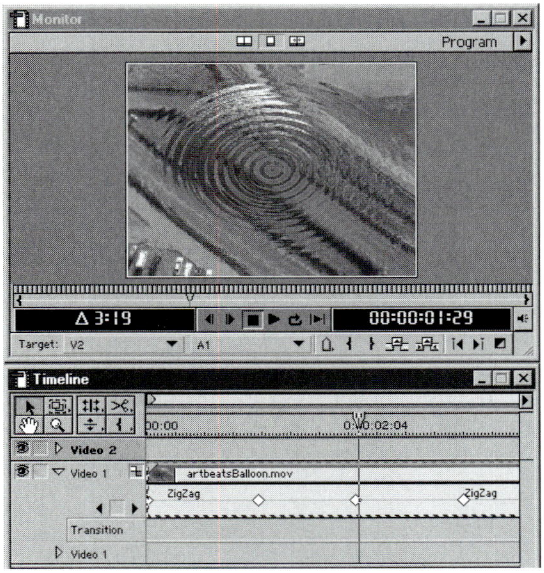

FIGURE 10-6
Keyframes on a clip in the timeline with a ZigZag effect applied

Depending on the distance/number of frames in between the two keyframes, the in between frames will change over time from one keyframe effect to the other.

As you can see in the previous figure, you can change the parameters of an effect over time and use keyframes to mark the points of change. In addition, you can set keyframes on multiple effects on the same clips. Sound complicated? Well, the concept is simple, but if your clips contain lots of effects with many keyframes, then you might need to do some planning up front.

NOTE Remember the two little icons to the left of the superimpose tracks? To refresh your memory, the diamond on the far left is used to display keyframes and the red rectangle is the Opacity Rubberband icon. You used the Rubberband feature when applying various levels of opacity to a clip in the last chapter. When an effect is added to the timeline, the Display Keyframe icon becomes active. You can toggle between the Display Keyframe icon and the Opacity Rubberband icon when an effect is applied to a clip by clicking either icon. This means you can also create various levels of opacity on your effects.

Another terrific feature of Premiere 6 is you can add keyframes right in the timeline. This makes the interface incredibly intuitive. You can see exactly what you're doing without having to open yet another dialog box and use a representation of the timeline to set your keyframes.

VIEWING KEYFRAMES IN THE TIMELINE

When an effect is applied to a clip in the timeline and the tracks are expanded, you can see the keyframe track on a clip in the timeline. In this track, you can set and manipulate the position of keyframes. But keyframes don't appear automatically. They have to be set in a certain way.

In Figure 10-7, there's a clip on Video Track 1 and Video Track 2, both with different effects applied to them. The clip on Video Track 1 doesn't have keyframes on it, but the clip on Video Track 2 does.

FIGURE 10-7
Keyframe tracks on Video Track 1 and 2

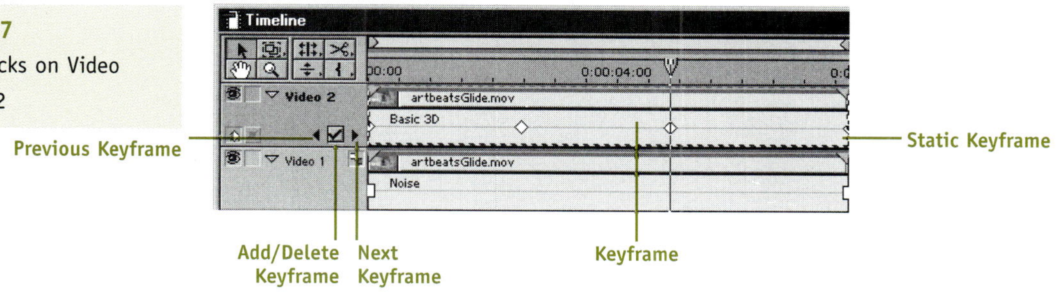

In the keyframe track for Video Track 1, there's a gray horizontal line with a white rectangle at its head and tail. Although you can drag these rectangles on the line, they're not yet recognized as keyframes. Rather, the effect appears static throughout the duration of the clip.

The clip on Video Track 2 has keyframes. Keyframes appear as diamond icons in the timeline and the clip on Track 2 has a total of four keyframes.

When you position the Edit line over a keyframe, the Add/Delete Keyframe box on the left of the track becomes checked, as shown in the previous figure. Also, you can navigate from keyframe to keyframe using the Previous and Next Keyframe arrows. Using these arrows to navigate is much simpler than dragging the Edit line through the timeline.

The other change in the workspace that's noteworthy when keyframes are applied to clips is that a stopwatch icon appears in the Effect Controls palette (see the illustration). This is the Enable Keyframing icon, which also serves as a reminder that keyframes are present on a track even if the keyframe track is collapsed.

Next, you learn how to create a keyframe on a track.

Creating Keyframes in the Timeline

Making new keyframes on a clip with effects applied is a little different from the way you add keyframes in the Motion Settings dialog box. This is because you can do it right in the timeline, which makes the process a lot easier. So, let's review the process of adding new keyframes to a keyframe track.

To Add keyframes to a keyframe track on a clip:

1. **Click a clip that has an effect(s) applied to it.**
2. **Make sure the clip's track is expanded.**
3. **Drag the Edit line to a place on the clip where you want to create a keyframe.**
4. **Click the Add/Delete Keyframe button to the left of that track.**
5. **A diamond will appear on the gray horizontal line in that spot on the timeline.**

If you scrub the timeline while pressing Alt (Windows)/Option (Mac) and you haven't changed the parameters of the effects on keyframes, no animation will appear. For example in the previous figure, the Noise effect applied to the clip on Video Track 1, the noise amount on all four keyframes is 25.6 percent. So, when the effect plays, it has the same properties throughout and the effect remains the same in time. So, let's look at how you can animate keyframes after you create them.

To Animate keyframes on the keyframe track of a clip:

1. **Select a clip in the timeline with keyframes.**
2. **Expand the track.**
3. **Click a keyframe. You can navigate to the next or previous keyframes using the directional arrow on the track.**
4. **In the Effect Controls palette, change the parameters of the effect on that particular keyframe (see Figure 10-8).**
5. **Select any additional keyframes and repeat the process.**
6. **While you scrub the timeline, depress Alt (Windows/Option (Mac). The effects now change in time, in between keyframes.**

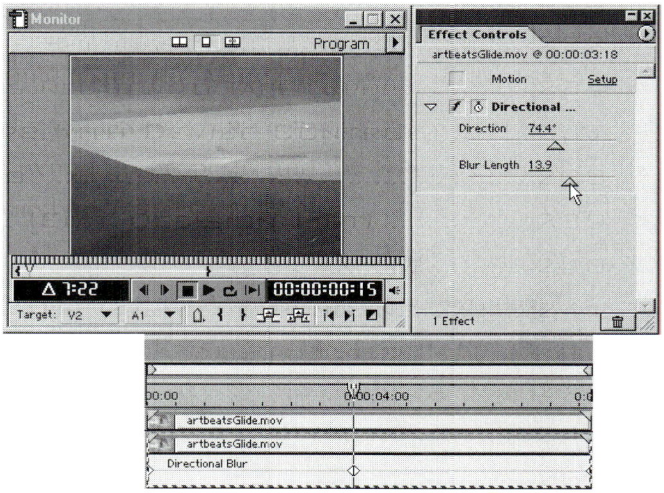

FIGURE 10-8
Animated effects are created in Premiere by changing the parameters of effects on keyframes in the Effect Controls palette

If you're changing the parameters on an effect that uses sliders, you might want to type in an exact numerical amount. Sometimes it's hard to select a specific amount from a slider.

To Manually INPUT NUMERICAL PARAMETERS OF AN EFFECT IN THE EFFECT CONTROLS PALETTE:

1. **Click a keyframe.**
2. **In the Effect Controls palette, click the number above the slider that's underlined. This number represents the numerical value of the slider.**
3. **A value dialog box for the effect parameter will appear (see the illustration).**

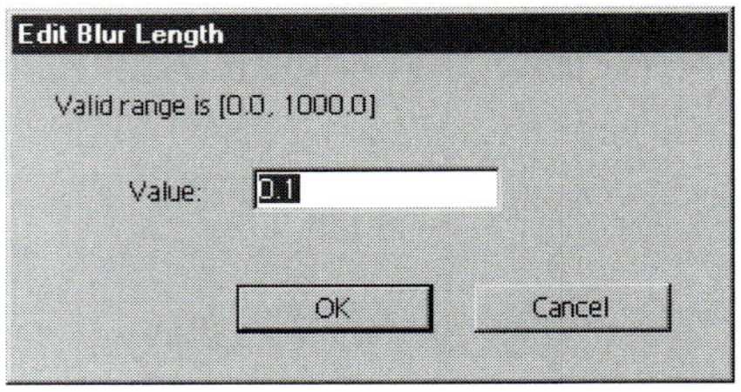

4. **Type in the value you want to assign to the parameter and click OK.**

Let's review the mechanics of the previous figure. The clip on Video track 1 has an additional keyframe on the keyframe track, for a total of three keyframes. The clip has a Directional Blur applied, taken from the Blur folder in the Effects palette. On the first keyframe, in the Effect Controls palette, the Direction and Blur Length sliders are both set to 0. On the second keyframe, the Direction slider is set to 74.4 degrees and the Blur Length slider is set to 13.9. On the last keyframe, the Direction and Blur sliders return to 0. The result is a dynamic, pulsating radial blur that changes from one extreme to another as the frames move through time.

CHANGING THE POSITION OF A KEYFRAME ON THE TIMELINE

After a keyframe is created, you can easily move it backward or forward in time on the keyframe track.

To Move A KEYFRAME ON THE TIMELINE:

1. **Click a keyframe and drag it to a new position.**
2. **When you do so, the pointer turns into an index finger.**

Not only can you move new keyframes, you can also reposition the first and last keyframes on the keyframe track of a clip. If you move the first keyframe on a clip forward in time, the effect won't begin until the frame with that keyframe is played. Concurrently, if you move the last keyframe backward in time, when the clip is played, the effect will end when that keyframe is played, even if it's shorter than the duration of the clip.

In Figure 10-9, the first and last keyframes were moved on the timeline. When the first keyframe is moved forward or the last keyframe is moved backward, the gray keyframe line turns black before and after the first and last keyframe. Additionally, the diamond turns into a half-black/half-white icon. The black line indicates the absence of an effect. The two-toned diamond alerts you to the fact that the first or last keyframe begins or ends before the natural duration of the clip.

To Delete A KEYFRAME:

1. **Navigate to the keyframe either with the previous/next arrows on the track or position the Edit line over the keyframe.**
2. **Click the Add/Delete Keyframe box in the track. When the box is empty, no keyframe appears. When the box is checked, it indicates a keyframe where the Edit line is positioned.**

As you can see, you can create thousands of incredible animated effects in Premiere on a single clip. Things become even more interesting when you animate more than one effect on a clip.

ADDING AND ANIMATING MULTIPLE KEYFRAMES ON A CLIP WITH MULTIPLE EFFECTS

Earlier in this chapter, we set more than one effect on a clip. Now that you've become familiar with keyframes and how they work, you're probably curious

FIGURE 10-9
When the first and last keyframe on a clip are moved, a black line replaces the gray line before the first keyframe or after the last keyframe

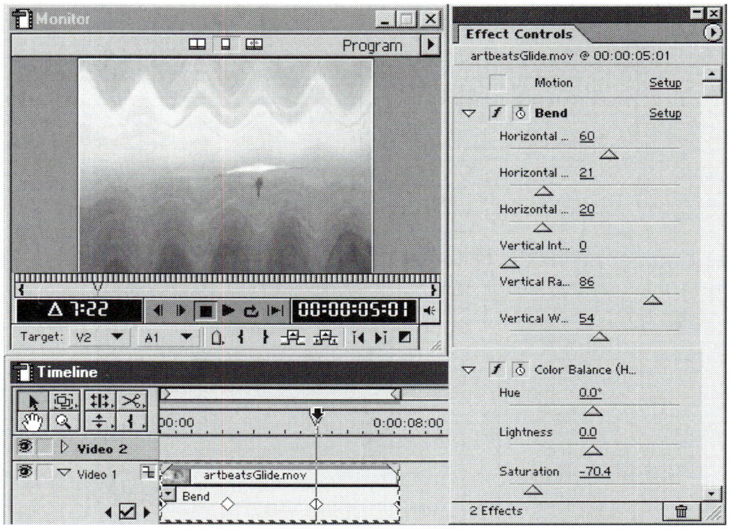

FIGURE 10-10
Two effects and multiple keyframes have been added to a clip

to know if you could animate keyframes on multiple effects. The answer is an unequivocal yes.

In Figure 10-10, two effects are on the clip named artbeatsGlide.mov. The effects used are Bend and Color Balance. In addition, four keyframes are on the Bend effect and three keyframes are on the Color Balance effect. On each keyframe in each effect, the parameters of the effect are changed in the Effect Control palette.

The Bend effect as you can see, distorts the clip and creates a wave-like effect by altering the horizontal and vertical pixels. The Color Balance effect adds or subtracts red, green, and blue from the clip, enabling you to create a custom-colored image. Both effects can be adjusted with various slider controls.

To Add MULTIPLE KEYFRAMES WITH MULTIPLE EFFECTS TO A CLIP:

1. **Select a clip-and-drag effect on to the clip from the Effects palette.**
2. **Set keyframes on the clip and change the parameters of the effect on selected keyframes.**
3. **Repeat this process for another effect on the same clip.**

4 Toggle back and fourth from one effect to another on the same keyframe track by clicking the pop-up arrow in the left corner. The currently displayed effect is the one on which you can set and modify the keyframes (see the illustration).

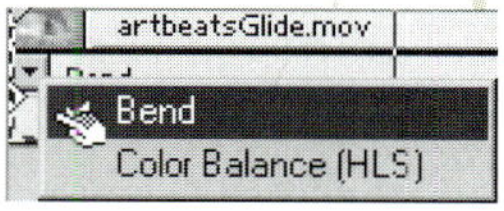

To Disable AN ANIMATION EFFECT ON A CLIP:

► Click the Stopwatch icon in the Effect Controls palette for that particular effect.

ADDING AND ANIMATING AN EFFECT ON A STILL IMAGE

So far, you've been looking at animating effects on video clips. You can also animate still images in the same way. Figure 10-11 shows a still image on Video Track 1 and another on Track 2. Both these images have animation effects applied.

The clip on Video Track 1 has a Bevel Edges effect applied to it and the clip's keyframes change over time. The effect doesn't begin until

> **NOTE** If you've worked in Photoshop, many of the Premiere effects should appear familiar to you, like the Noise, Distort, and Blur effects. In Photoshop, they're called *filters* and they can be applied to still images. Equivalent filters in Photoshop, and Effects in Premiere will, for the most part, yield the same visual outcome. So, familiarity with one application can boost your learning curve of the other

FIGURE 10-11
Two Photoshop files have been animated on Video Track 1 and 2

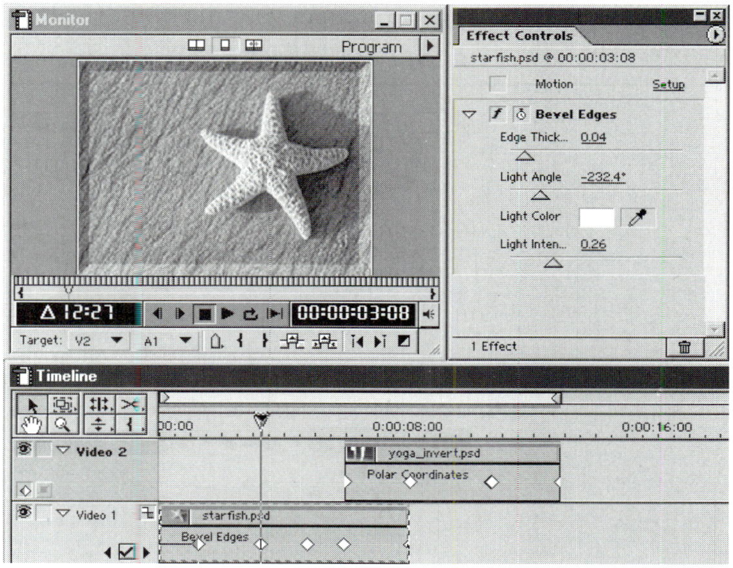

about one quarter of the way into the clip, as indicated by the black line on the keyframe track. The Bevel Edges effect creates a three-dimensional raised image. In the Effect Controls palette, you can control the thickness, angle, and intensity of the bevel.

The clip on Video Track 2 has a Polar Coordinates effect applied for the duration of four keyframes. This effect creates interesting distortions by moving the *X* and *Y* coordinates of each pixel to its polar opposite *X* and *Y* coordinate. You can adjust the percentage of distortion from a slider in the Effect Controls palette.

The Clip on Video Track 2 also has a fade applied to it. This enables you to see through the end of the first clip on Video Track 1 and the beginning of the last clip on Video Track 2. You can see the fade handles if you click the Opacity Rubberband icon to the left of the track.

So you can create some truly dynamic effects with still images as well as video clips in Premiere.

QuickTime Effects

You might have noticed that one of the folders in the Effects palette is a QuickTime folder. *QuickTime effects* are available to those systems that have versions of QuickTime 4.0 and later installed. A great number of QuickTime effects are already available as Premiere Effects, but they are certainly worth a look because you never know what you may find in here that may be of interest to you.

QuickTime Effects are applied from a dialog box. The Sepia tint selected in the Select Effect dialog box in Figure 10-12 casts a Sepia tone over the entire clip, using Sienna, White, and Black tonal values. You can also select another tint from the Tint Type pop-up, such as Black and White, X-ray, and Cobalt.

You can add more than one QuickTime effect the same way you would add multiple effects. To do so, simply drag another copy of the QuickTime effect on to a clip. You'll see the additional QuickTime effect appear in the Effect Controls palette. On the Mac, you'll also see the specific name of the QuickTime effect in the palette.

As you can see, effects are tremendously easy to apply, animate, and manipulate. Often, the name of the effect indicates what it looks like. Picking an effect

FIGURE 10-12
A Sepia QuickTime effect is applied to a clip using the QuickTime Select Effect dialog box

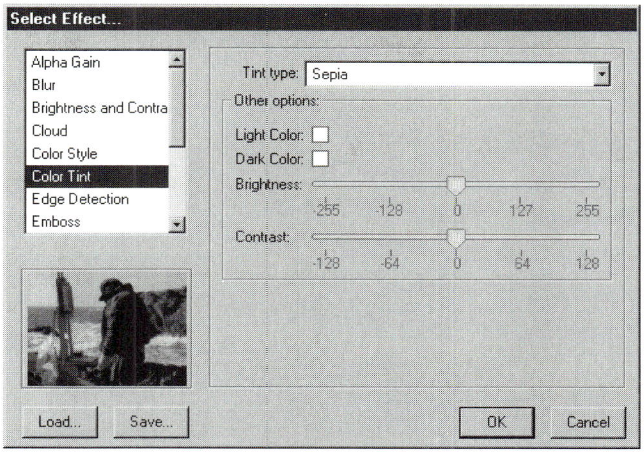

sometimes is like shopping for wallpaper. You bring one up, try it out, and either toss it or love it, and it helps jazz up your production. After you experiment with effects, you'll become familiar with their different categories and outcomes.

In the next chapter, we dive in to sound in Premiere to learn how it works. As you will see, there's a lot you can do with sound in Premiere to enhance a production.

ON THE VIRTUAL CLASSROOM CD-ROM **In Lesson 8, "Applying Video Effects to Clips," the instructor takes a look at the diverse selection of video effects in Premiere and shows you how to apply multiple effects on clips.**

11

Working with Audio in Premiere

Manipulating sound clips on audio tracks in Premiere is similar to manipulating video clips and still images on video tracks. As with video tracks, you have up to 99 audio tracks on which to place your audio. Like many tasks in Premiere, manipulating audio is quite simple once you get the feel for it. Premiere 6 comes with a new Audio Mixer that enables you to fade and pan tracks, as well as adjust multiple tracks in time. You can also apply audio effects to your sound that can alter the properties of the clip, to make the audio interesting. Premiere offers a plethora of audio effects that enable you to correct sound and to change its properties. Although Premiere doesn't possess all the intricate features of a full-fledged sound-editing program, in a pinch, it's a terrific tool.

Sometimes the importance of audio is overshadowed in a video production. Although audio tracks may seem to take a back seat to video, audio plays a major role in defining the mood of a production. The perfect combination of audio and video can create a genuine feast for the senses. While audio might seem to take a back seat to video, it has a subliminal effect on the way people experience your production. Now that you know how important audio is in Premiere, where do you start?

Audio in Premiere

If you're a beginner in Premiere, you might not know you can't create sound in Premiere. You can make adjustments to sound clips by trimming, mixing, panning, and animating sound. Just like video clips, sound is imported into Premiere. So, where does sound come from? If you want an immediate and quick solution to the sound issue, Premiere ships with a software package called SmartSound, which you need to install separately after you install Premiere. SmartSound provides a quick and easy way to create custom music tracks. It's a fairly simple and self-explanatory interface, prompting you along. If you're looking for sound effects or vocal tracks, you need to look elsewhere for more sophisticated sound.

TIP **Appendix B contains a listing of different sources for audio.**

You can convert sound from other digital and analog sources (like CDs) and capture audio in the Movie Capture window (with Audio only selected). Also your footage might have been recorded with sound, and you can capture the sound and video together. When you import a video clip with sound, the sound lays on an audio track and syncs with the accompanying audio clip, so you can acquire sound for your Premiere production in many places.

Once your sound is in Premiere, you can trim, mix, or modify it, just like any other clip. If your sound requires more doctoring than is possible in Premiere, then you need to turn to a more full-featured sound-editing program. When you're done editing the clip, you'd then import it into the Premiere Project window.

Choosing Audio Settings

You might not remember, but way back in Chapter 3, you learned about Project Settings. Settings are an important element in Premiere because the wrong settings can cause unexpected results. Sometimes, when you're all involved in creating a movie, you might forget the significance of settings. The correct audio settings up front ensure you get the audio results you want.

Although we previously covered audio settings, because they're relevant to this section, let's look quickly at the audio-related settings in Premiere.

> **NOTE** The materials used in the figures and illustrations in this chapter are located in the Chapter 11 folder on the CD. If you want to examine the source files, copy them over to your hard drive. The audio clips associated with this file are located in the sound folder in the Chapter 11 folder.

THE AUDIO SETTINGS DIALOG BOX

If you plan to incorporate audio in your Premiere production, you want to make certain your audio settings are correct. You navigate to the audio settings by selecting Project | Project Settings | Audio in an existing Premiere file. If you're creating a new file, in the Load Project Settings window, click the Custom button and navigate to the Audio settings panel in the Project Settings dialog box.

Let's review the settings in this box.

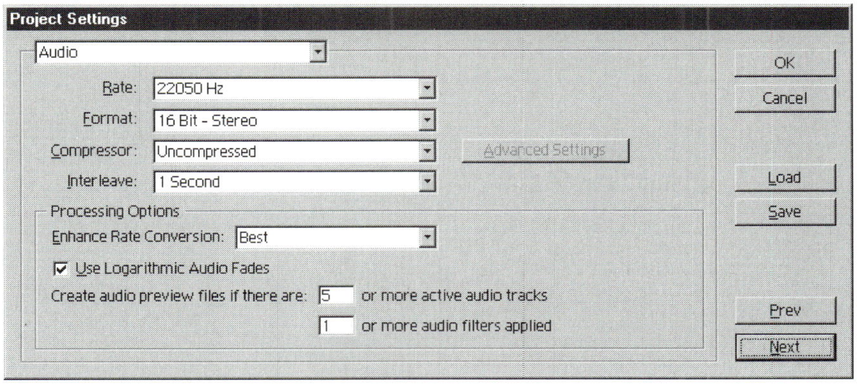

- **Rate** Rate refers to the audio sample rate. If you recall, a *sample rate* is when an analog sound is converted into digital sound and is measured, or sampled, at various intervals to create the digital equivalent of the analog sound. 48000 Hz is the DV standard and 44100 Hz is the CD standard; 22050 Hz is the standard computer sample rate, used on older computers. You should know the sample rate of the source sound being used before your production is started. If you're composing and editing your own audio in a sound-editing program, you can control the sample rate yourself.

- **Format** Format in this file is set to 16 Bit-Stereo, a typical setting used for CD-quality stereo sound. The format represents the audio bit depth or the number of bits in the sample. Just like in a bitmap picture, the lower the bit depth or format, the smaller the size and the lower the quality.
- **Compressor** Compressor enables you to select an audio codec (compression scheme) for your sound on export. For more information on this setting, refer to Chapter 3.
- **Interleave** This setting refers to the frequency in which audio is loaded into RAM. Generally you won't need to adjust the interleave. You may want to try adusting it for troubleshooting if your movie is experiencing audio problems during playback. For more information on this setting, refer to Chapter 3.

The Processing Options in the bottom half of the Audio panel include the following selections:

- **Enhance Rate Conversion** This refers to audio sample rates being sampled up or down. If you're going to work with sounds at different sample rates in the same project, combining 48 kHz DV audio with 44 kHz CD audio, for example, Enhance Rate Conversion should be set to Best.
- **Use Logarithmic Audio Fades** Logarithmic audio fades more closely resemble the way the human ear experiences sound. Use Logarithmic Audio Fades is checked in this project.
- **Create Audio Preview Files** The numbers in the Create Audio Preview file settings refer to how many audio tracks and audio effects Premiere will render in real-time when you play back the project. If your project contains more than these numbers of tracks and effects, Premiere will have to render a preview before you can hear your audio. If you have a fast computer, you can probably set these values higher and work a little more efficiently. The audio previews in this file are left at the default setting.

> **TIP** **If you select Window | Workspace | Audio, Premiere displays the audio default workspace and position windows in the workspace for you, including the Audio Mixer palette.**

Now that you know what these settings are, let's bring some sound into the Premiere workspace.

Importing Sound in Premiere

No real trick exists to importing sound in Premiere. Basically, it's the same process you use to import video clips and still images.

To Import a sound into Premiere:

1. Select File | Import File (or Folder) from the menu. You can also RIGHT-CLICK (Windows)/control-click (Mac) in the Project window to bring up the Import dialog box.
2. As you do with other media, navigate to the folder the media is located in and click Open or Import.
3. Premiere recognizes all the most popular audio formats, including .wav, .aif, .mov, .mp3, and .avi.
4. The sound appears in the Project window.

Audio in the Project Window

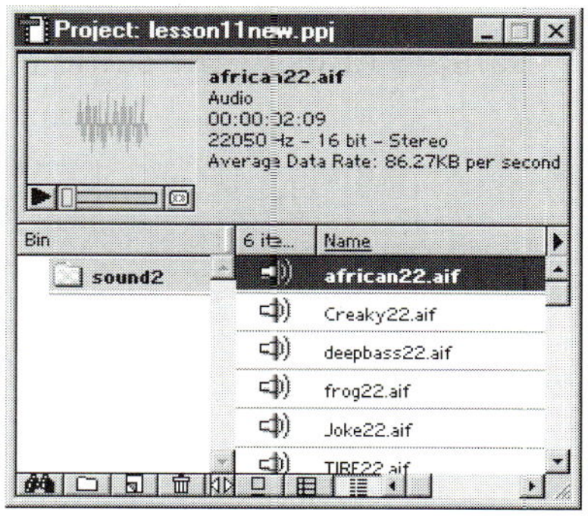

In the file named chapter11.ppj, there are several sounds in the file's Project window.

When you select a sound, a generic waveform icon appears in the Clip Preview in the upper-left corner of the window, telling you the selected clip contains audio only. A *waveform* is a visual representation of the digital file with peaks and valleys representing the high and low points of amplitude, or volume. Just like a video clip, you can preview the audio clip by clicking the Play control in the Clip Preview.

The information next to the Clip Preview also gives you the complete history on a clip. In the previous figure, note that to the right of the audio clip thumbnail, the length of the clip, as well as the sample rate and the format (stereo or mono), is indicated.

> **TIP** All the asset management features in the Project window pertain to audio clips as well or video clips. For example, audio clips can be organized in bins and the different views (Icon, Thumbnail, List) can also be used.

Once you test a sound in the Project window, you can drag it to an audio track in the Timeline or open it in a Clip window. If the sound needs further testing or trimming, or if you need to examine the waveform for mixing purposes, you'll generally open it in a Clip window. Let's look at some clips in the Clip window.

AUDIO IN THE CLIP WINDOW

The *Clip window* is a type of source window used for refining your clip before it moves to the Timeline.

To Open an audio clip in a Clip window with the Monitor window in Program view:

1. **Double-click an audio clip in the Project window.**
2. **The clip appears in its own window (see Figure 11-1).**

To Open a clip in a Clip window with the Monitor window displaying the Source and Program views:

1. **ALT + double-click (Windows)/OPTION + double-click (Mac) on a clip in the Project window.**
2. **The clip will appear in its own window.**

As mentioned in earlier chapters, you can also go to Edit | Preferences | General & Still Images and click Open Movies in Clip window to have clips open in a Clip window.

TIP Often, it's unnecessary to use the Source Monitor view with audio clips, so selecting Single view is usually the most efficient way to work with audio in Premiere. The waveform in the Source view is a smaller thumbnail version of the Clip window, minus some of the Clip window features. Clips can be difficult to trim in the Source view because you can't preview the real waveform of the sound. The Clip window also has a waveform zoom tool and a volume control you can use while previewing.

FIGURE 11-1
Audio Clip window

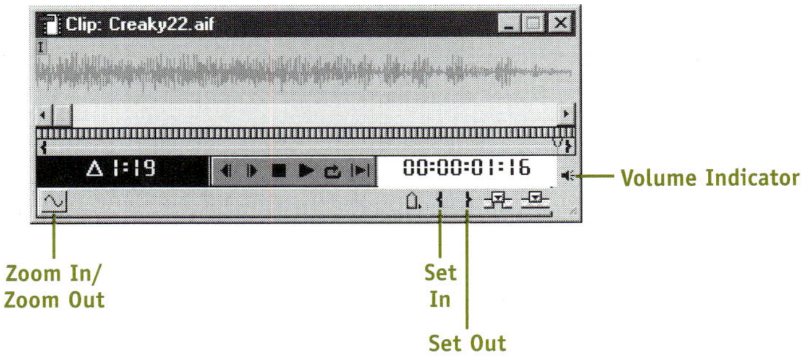

To Open an audio clip from the Timeline in a Clip window:

1. **Double-click a clip in the Timeline.**
2. **If the Source view in the Monitor window is displayed, ALT + double-click (Windows)/ Option + double-click (Mac) on a clip in the Timeline to open it in a Clip window.**

Features of the Clip window are similar to that of the Source window in the Monitor view with a few added features. It includes all the convenient transport features: Frame Forward and Backward, Stop, Play, Loop, Play In to Out, and so forth. If you manage to memorize the editing shortcut keys, the same keys work here as in the Monitor window. If you need a refresher on the Monitor window features and shortcut keys, refer to Chapter 4.

Let's look at the Zoom tool in the bottom-left corner of the Clip window available to you in the Audio Clip window. This tool enables you to scrutinize the waveform of an audio clip at various magnification levels. This tool is particularly helpful when you trim audio clips and when you need to examine the amplitude highs and lows to determine where the trimming is going to take place.

A volume indicator is also located on the bottom right of the Audio Clip window. This tool adjusts the volume on the source clip for previewing purposes. Three different volume levels—mute, loud, and louder—are indicated by cartoonlike waves emanating from a speaker icon.

You'll often use the Clip window to trim a clip. In and Out points on an audio clip are set the same way they're set on a video clip. When you trim audio, however, because you're now dealing with sound in time, you'll use a different set of criteria to decide how a clip will be trimmed. You'll examine the waveform to decide where the right place is to trim a clip, based on the highs and lows in the waveform—especially if you don't want an audio clip to sound as if it's beginning or ending abruptly. You'll want to take other issues into consideration, such as syncing the audio with a video clip. Although the process is similar, audio is a different animal and this must be figured into the equation when preparing and modifying sound clips.

In Figure 11-2, the In and Out points have been changed on the clip named TIRE22.aif. In the Clip window, the In and Out points are depicted on the

FIGURE 11-2
Trimming in an Audio Clip window

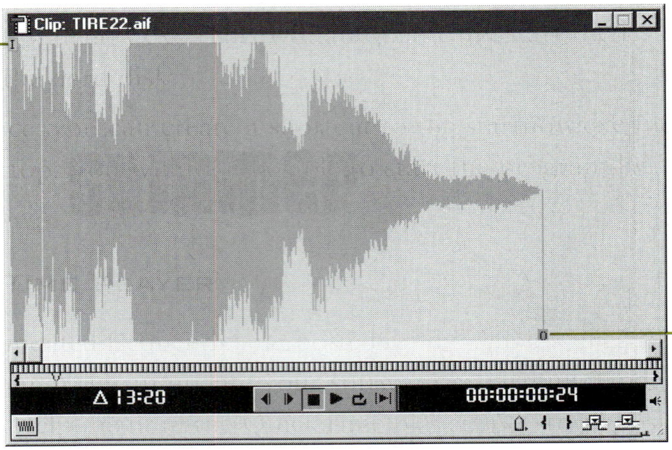

waveform as rectangles with the Letter *I* for the In point, within a green rectangle, and the letter *O* for the Out point within a red rectangle. Let's examine how this is done.

To Set new In and Out points on a clip:

1. **First play the clip in a Clip window to decide where it needs to be trimmed.**
2. **If you need to set an In point, identify the place in time where you want the new In point to start.**
3. **Click the In point icon or use the *I* key.**
4. **Repeat the process for the Out point.**

When you set In and Out points on sound clips, you'll use aural as well as visual cues to determine where to perform your trimming. For example, on the TIRE22.aif clip in the previous figure, the Out point is set to where the sound begins to fade in time. This can be heard on playback and is visually depicted by the spikes in the wave receding.

As you can see, setting In and Out points is a familiar and fairly simple process.

AUDIO IN THE TIMELINE

To assemble your movie, the source clips need to go into the Timeline. This can be done before or after trimming, either right from the Project window or from a Clip window. All you do is drag the clip into the Timeline to an audio track.

Audio clips reside on Audio tracks in the Timeline. The default Timeline displays three Audio tracks, but you can have up to 99 tracks.

To Create A NEW AUDIO TRACK:

1. **Select Add Audio Track from the pop-up Timeline menu.**
2. **You can also right-click (Windows)/OPTION-CLICK (Mac) to display the context menu and select Add Audio Track.**

You can add, delete, and rename audio tracks from the Track Options dialog box (see the illustration). Track Options can be accessed the same way you add a video track, that is, from the pop-up Timeline menu or by accessing the context menu in the Timeline.

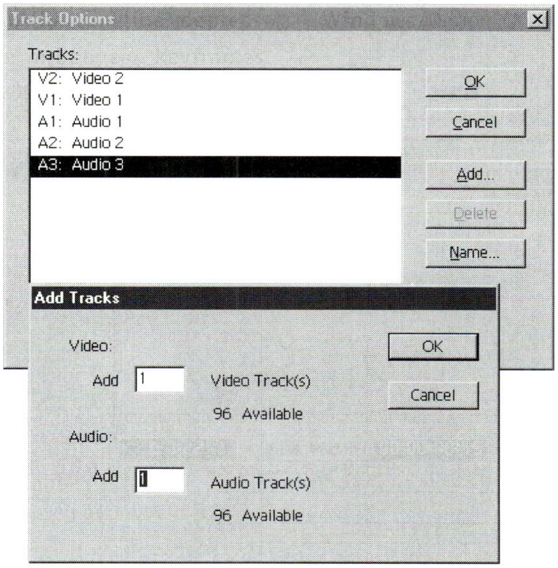

To add or rename a track in the Track Options dialog box, click the Add or Name button. When you do so, a dialog box prompts you for the appropriate information.

For adding tracks, indicate the amount of tracks you want to add. For renaming tracks, indicate the new track name. As you can see, this is a fairly straightforward method for managing your audio tracks.

Controlling Audio in the Timeline

Let's look at the various controls on an audio track. If you expand an audio track with a clip (Figure 11-3), you'll notice four icons in the bottom-left corner, many of which probably look familiar from the video track.

Let's look more closely at what the controls on the audio track do.

- **Audio Waveform** This button shows and hides a waveform on a track. Click this button on the bottom left to hide the waveform in the program. Click again to show it. All the controls are *toggle buttons*, meaning you click once to show a control, and then click again to hide a control.
- **Display Keyframes** This control displays keyframes if you added audio effects. Audio effects are discussed later in this chapter.
- **Display Fade Rubberbands** This control shows fade handles. Fade handles, or *rubberbands*, work the same way opacity handles do in the video tracks but, instead of fading opacity (which you obviously couldn't do on a sound), it fades the volume.
- **Display Pan Rubberbands** The *pan* refers to the left and right channel of a sound, and this track displays the pan. Sound can be shifted from one channel to another by adding pan handles, or rubberbands.

FIGURE 11-3
Controls on the Audio Track

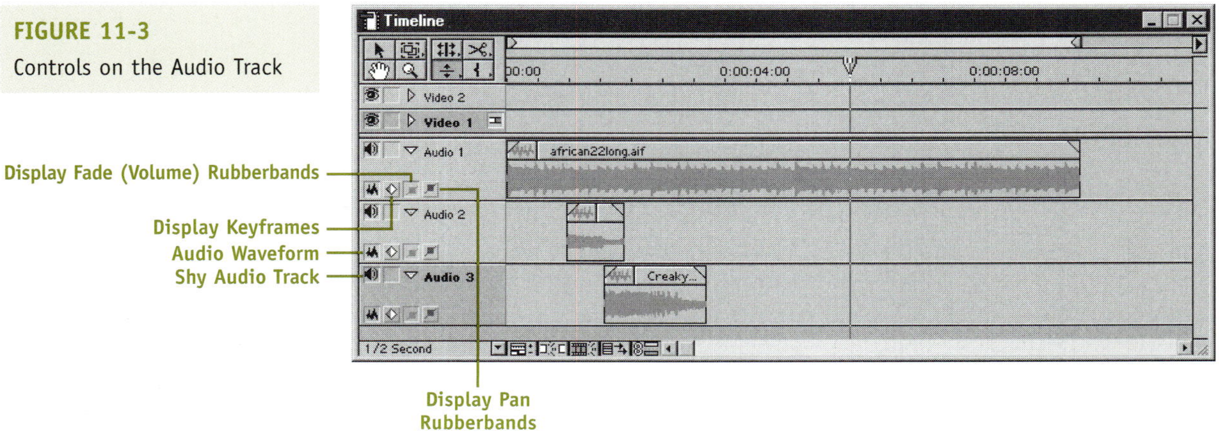

- **The Fade and Pan controls** Major components in audio mixing, these controls play a big role in adjusting sound in Premiere. They're also available in the Audio Mixer. In the next sections, you learn how to use these tools to get the sound mix you want. When the Audio Mixer is open, it overrides the rubberbands, which become inactive.
- **Shy Audio Track** When the speaker icon isn't visible, the sound won't play back. When the speaker icon is visible, it will play back.

USING THE FADE CONTROLS IN THE TIMELINE

As mentioned before, the major difference between audio fade controls and video fade controls (a.k.a. rubberbands) is this: instead of altering the opacity, you're changing the amplitude, or volume, of a sound clip. This is what fade controls are all about: varying the degree volume on clips in the Timeline. When you vary the volume on one or more clips on different tracks in the Timeline, you create a mix.

Let's look at how to set fade controls on a clip in the Timeline and examine how to add a few fade handles to an audio clip. To do this, the track must be expanded and the Display Fade Rubberbands button needs to be active to ensure the fade controls are showing.

Just like on the video tracks, the audio tracks display the fade line and handles in red. Note, in Figure 11-4, in the track named african22long.aif, three additional fade handles are added. These new handles are placed strategically in the area near the audio on the other tracks, which causes the fade (volume) on the top clip to drop over these clips. The fade line dips so the amplitude will be lower in these areas of the Timeline, allowing the other clips to be heard more clearly.

> **NOTE** **Make sure the Audio Mixer window is closed when you start experimenting with the fade rubberbands. The Audio Mixer overrides the fade rubberbands and, when it's open, Premiere ignores changes you make directly in the Timeline to the rubberbands.**

To Add A FADE RUBBERBAND TO AN AUDIO CLIP:

1. **With the Display Fade Rubberband button selected on the track, position the pointer over the portion of the line where you want a handle and click. Note, it turns into an index finger with a plus and minus sign.**

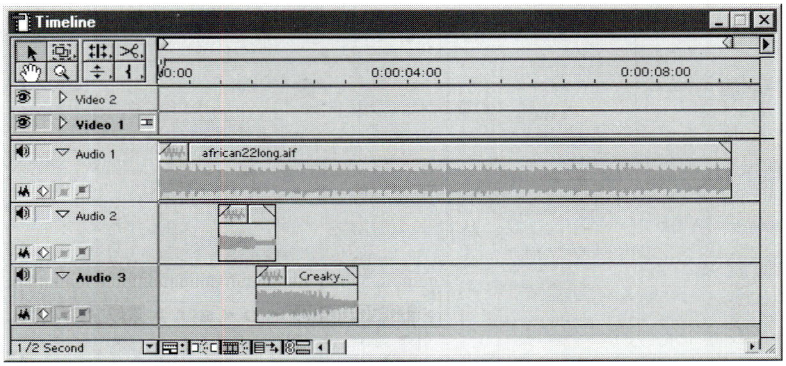

FIGURE 11-4
The audio clip named african22long.aif has several fade handles added

2 **As a result, a red rectangle appears on the fade line, indicating the presence of a fade handle.**

To Change THE POSITION OF A FADE HANDLE:

▶ **Click-and-drag on the handle in the Timeline.**

To Delete A FADE HANDLE:

▶ **Click-and-drag the handle outside of the panel and the fade handle will disappear.**

> **NOTE** **When you hover over existing handles to change their position, the pointer turns gray.**

Adding, deleting, and moving fade handles requires a lot of playing and replaying the contents of the Timeline to get the mix just right. You can playback the program or parts of the program right in the Timeline or using the controls in the Monitor Program window. This is a good opportunity for you to become acquainted with a few simple shortcut controls discussed throughout the book. For example, consider the following keys for efficient control:

- Play = Spacebar
- The JKL combination: J = Play in Reverse, K = Stop, L = Play
- LEFT/RIGHT ARROWS = One frame backward and forward

- A = Move Edit line to first frame
- S = Move Edit line to last frame

You can use many other shortcut keys to move around the Timeline or Monitor windows. If you forget which one is which, check Appendix A in this book or go to Help | Keyboard in Premiere for a quick rundown of all the shortcuts.

As your productions become more sophisticated, you'll be adjusting fade handles on multiple tracks, which can become quite complicated. Three tools in the Timeline toolbox can be helpful when you're dealing with multiple fade handles. Let's look at them.

TIP **Before you mix sound in Premiere, first make sure the volume control in the Monitor window is set to an acceptable level where you can hear subtle changes in each track. This volume control dictates the playback of the program in the Timeline. Second, make certain your computer's volume is also set to an acceptable level. You don't want to alter the volume controls in the middle of mixing because this could make the final mix incorrect. You want to maintain a consistent volume level in your workspace to ensure good results in your production.**

The Fade Tools in the Timeline

Three tools can be used in tweaking your audio fades: the Fade Adjustment tool, the Fade Scissors tool, and the Cross Fade tool. All three of these tools can add assistance in further adjusting fade handles. Of course, you might choose to do these techniques manually, by creating plain old handles and manipulating them. Personal preference prevails here.

TIP **Keep the Info palette displayed (Window | Show Info) if you want information on your fade rubberband, such as what frame it's on, the fade percentage, and how it fades in and out in time. The Info palette is also equally as useful for the pan rubberbands.**

The Fade Adjustment Tool The Fade Adjustment tool is located in the bottom row of the toolbox in a flyout menu (see the illustration). If you recall, this tool enables

you to move a segment in between two handles, as one unit.

TIP **The Fade Adjustment tool also works with the pan rubberbands. When the pointer is positioned over a pan line, the double-headed vertical arrow has a blue line in between instead of a red line as it does when you're adjusting a fade line.**

To Move an Audio Fade Segment in the Timeline:

1. **Select the Fade Adjustment tool.**
2. **Position the pointer over a fade segment. When you position the tool over a segment, the pointer**

turns into the Fade Adjustment icon, a double-headed vertical arrow with a red line in between.

3. **Click-and-drag the segment vertically in the track panel.**

To Fade a clip in one percent increments:

1. **Click a fade line while holding down the SHIFT key. This can be done while in the Fade Selection tool or with the Pointer tool.**

2. **The exact percentage of fade adjustment will appear next to the clip along with the clip's decibel level.**

The Fade Scissors Tool The Fade Scissors tool is located in the upper-right corner of the toolbox in a flyout menu with the Razor tools. This tool creates a segment with adjacent handles.

To Add a segment with adjacent handles:

1. **Select the Fade Scissors tool.**

2. **Position the pointer over an area of the fade line where you want to add a segment. When you do so, the mouse turns into the Fade Scissors icon.**

3. **Click the line. Two adjacent handles are then created. Drag on the handles to reposition them.**

The Cross Fade Tool The Cross Fade tool is located in the bottom of the toolbox in the same flyout menu with the Fade Adjustment tool.

The Cross Fade tool offers you a quick and simple way to create a cross fade technique. A *cross fade* is when two clips fade in and out of one another. With audio clips, the volume is adjusted, so one clip audibly fades out while the next clip audibly fades in.

Before you create a cross fade, you must overlap the two clips you want to fade (see the illustration).

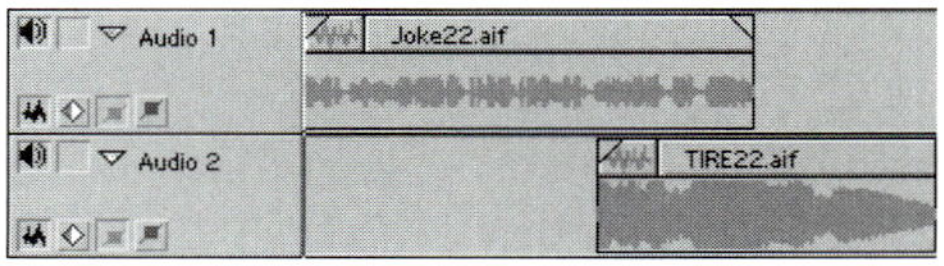

To Apply A CROSS FADE TECHNIQUE:

1. Select the Cross Fade tool from the toolbox.
2. Select the first audio clip to which you want to apply a cross fade technique.
3. Position the pointer over the second clip you want to fade into and click.
4. The first clip now fades into the other, as in the illustration.

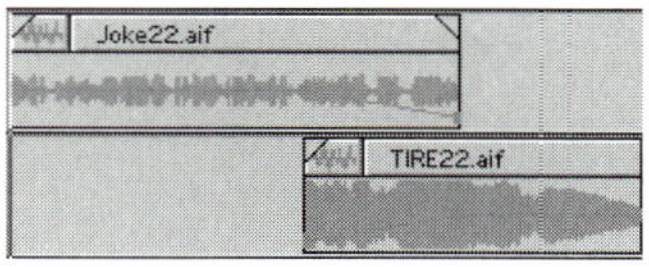

When you're done, test the results of your fade by playing the clips in the Timeline.

ADJUSTING THE AUDIO GAIN

You can use one other setting to adjust the volume on a clip and this setting is accessed from the menu. By setting the Audio Gain, you can adjust the volume globally on a particular clip.

To Set THE AUDIO GAIN ON AN AUDIO CLIP:

1. Select a clip.
2. In the menu, select Clip | Audio Options | Audio Gain. The Audio Gain dialog box appears. In this box, you can type in a percentage value for audio gain. For example, if you type in 50%, the volume of the clip is decreased by 50 percent.

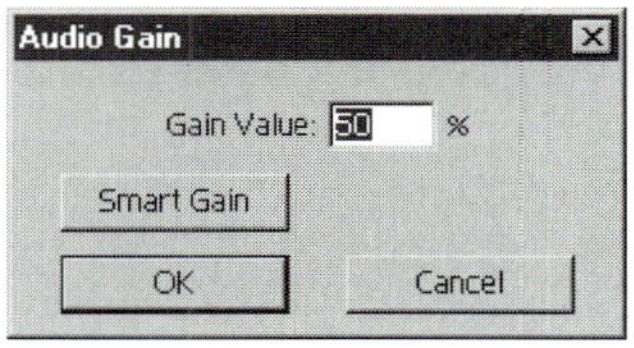

3. Clicking the Smart Gain button allows Premiere to do the calculation and determine how best to balance the clip's overall volume. This setting ensures a clip is at its maximum volume without causing sound distortion.

> **NOTE** You can change the speed of an audio clip just as you can with a video clip by selecting a clip and choosing Clip | Speed from the menu. This probably isn't the best solution to alter the speed of an audio clip, however, because it changes the pitch (too slow or too fast) and the duration of the clip (lengthens or shortens).

USING THE PAN CONTROLS IN THE TIMELINE

The *pan controls* enable you to adjust the left and right channels of an audio clip. You've probably surrounded yourself with stereo speakers at one time or another. Have you ever heard audio sound as if it's traveling from one speaker to another? This is because the panning, or balance, has been adjusted between the two channels (left and right) to create a special effect of sorts.

Panning refers to the redistribution of sound balance between left and right channels or speakers. When you adjust the pan handles on a mono clip, you can redirect the sound from one speaker to another. When you adjust the pan handles on a stereo clip, the sound rebalances in both speakers. Because Premiere doesn't let you see both a left and right track on a stereo audio clip, your options are somewhat limited in terms of what you can do with the redistribution of sound. Premiere does offer some menu commands for stereo audio clips. Let's look at them.

Adjusting Stereo Audio Clips

In Figure 11-5, the clip named african22long.aif is on Audio Track 1, and the clip named TIRE22.aif is on Audio Track 2. The african22long.aif clip is stereo and the TIRE22.aif clip is mono. Let's see what happens if we apply some commands to a stereo clip that enables us to manipulate channels separately. First, you need to select a stereo clip like the clip in Audio Track 1 (african22long.aif). If you have any additional sounds on other tracks, you can temporarily disable them by clicking the speaker icon. You generally want to make other tracks mute, so you can concentrate on the current track.

To Change A LEFT OR RIGHT CHANNEL ON A STEREO CLIP:

1. **With the clip selected, display the audio options either by selecting them from the menu (Clip | Audio Options) or right-click (Windows)/Control-click (Mac) to display the audio options in a context menu.**

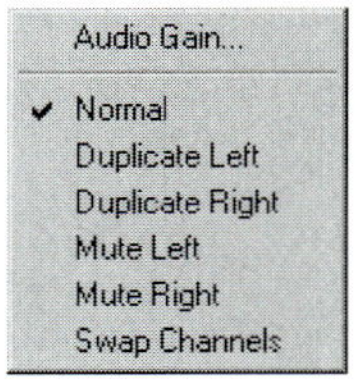

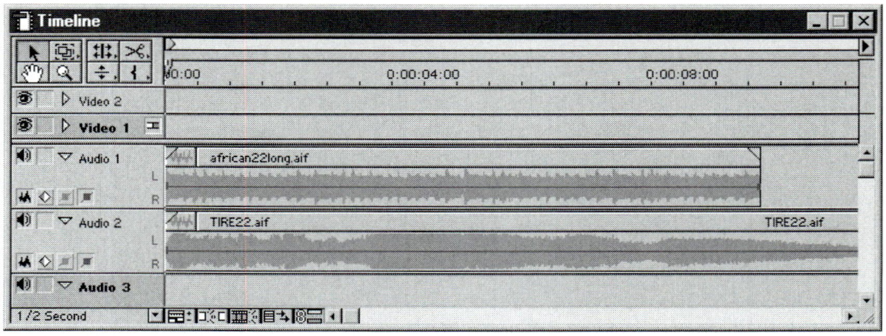

FIGURE 11-5
The clip named african22long.aif is a stereo clip

2 **Select one of the following commands:**

- **Duplicate Left/Right** This copies the channel on a stereo clip into the other channel and eliminates the original channel. In other words, if you choose Duplicate Left, the left channel is copied into the right channel and the original right channel is erased. This has the effect of putting the left channel into the center of the stereo image.
- **Mute Left/Right** This gets rid of the channel you choose.
- **Swap Channels** This copies the left channel into the right channel and vice versa, reversing the stereo image.
- **Normal** This returns a clip to its original state.

ALTERING THE PAN ON AN AUDIO CLIP

To alter the pan on an audio clip, you need to select the Pan Rubberband tool in the Timeline track. This is the little blue rectangle to the right of the Fade Rubberband tool. When you select this tool, if an audio clip is on the audio track, the pan control appears on the clip along with an indication of the left and right channels.

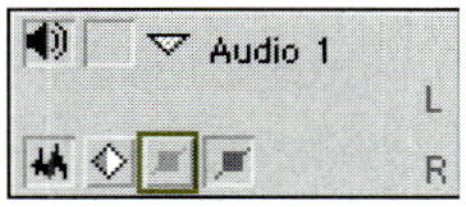

Pan handles are created the same way you create fade handles. In fact, some of the same tools in the toolbox you use to adjust fade rubberbands can be used for pan rubberbands. The difference, of course, is the pan handles adjust the left and right channels on a sound instead of the volume.

Let's see what happens when we change the pan rubberband on a clip. First, you need to select a mono clip. The audio clip in the Chapter 11 folder, named TIRE22.aif, is a mono clip, so you can use this clip if you want to experiment.

> **CAUTION** If you don't have stereo speakers on your computer, you won't be able to hear the results of your adjustments.

To Change THE PAN ON AN AUDIO CLIP WITH THE PAN RUBBERBAND:

1 **Make sure the Show Pan Rubberband icon is selected.**

2 **Select an audio clip.**

3 **Position the pointer over the first or last pan handle. When you do so, the pan handle turns into an index finger.**

4 **Drag the handle up (left channel) or down (right channel) to change the distribution of sound in the left and right channels.**

Add a pan handle the same way you add a fade handle. Simply click the pan line where you want the redistribution of channels to occur and reposition the handles. In fact, all the techniques used for manipulating audio fade lines apply to pan rubberbands so, for the most part, adjusting pan handles is self-explanatory. The trick to adjusting them is to listen intently to the results of your adjustments.

Both fading and panning can also be done in the Audio Mixer. The Mixer, new to Premiere 6, offers some additional features you can't do in the track alone. These additional features are a welcome addition to Premiere 6 and they give you a little more control over the audio. There will be times when one method works better for your project than another.

THE AUDIO MIXER

> **NOTE** **Each time you add a new audio track, it appears in the Audio Mixer.**

The Audio Mixer can be displayed by choosing Window | Audio Mixer. The Audio Mixer resembles a traditional audio mixing board, containing slide controls to adjust amplitude on each track. It also includes a master strip to the right, which controls the volume of all tracks combined (see Figure 11-6).

You can do several interesting things with the Audio Mixer. First, you can perform any of the functions you can do on an audio clip in the Timeline. For example, if you want to adjust the overall gain on a track, simply slide the volume fader for a track up or down. You can also set the pan in the Audio Mixer by selecting a track, and then clicking-and-dragging on the Pan/Balance control dial to the left or right. Be aware that your project's Audio Format must be set to Stereo (Project | Project Settings | Audio) to enable the Pan/Balance controls in the Audio Mixer. The

> **NOTE** **Mixing with the Pan/Balance control dial maintains the new volume and/or the balance throughout the playback of a program. The levels remain in a static position throughout, unless you automate the process. Automation is discussed later in this chapter.**

FIGURE 11-6
The Audio Mixer

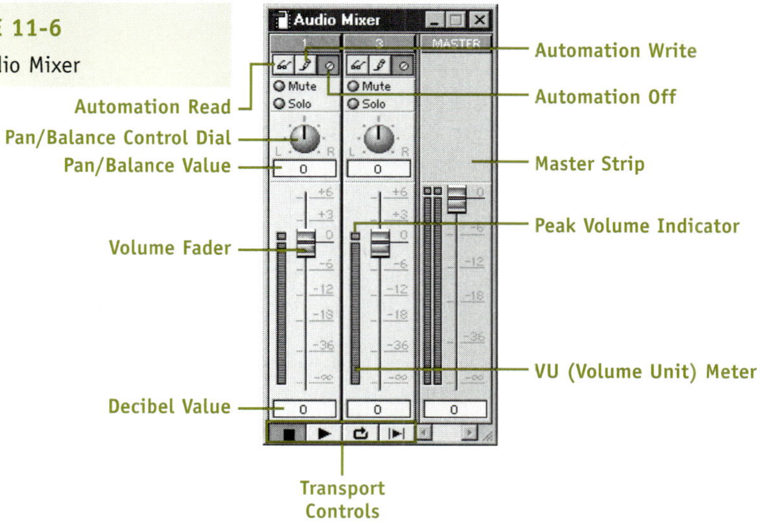

results of your adjustments can be played back right in the Audio Mixer using the playback controls at the bottom of the window.

> **NOTE** If your clip happens to reach the peak and turn red—indicating an unacceptable level of volume—when you adjust the fade volume again, the red indicator stays in place, even if the level is acceptable. To eliminate the red peak indicator, click it.

The Audio Mixer warns you if you also fade your track's volume out of an acceptable range. The Volume Unit Meter changes in color as a sound plays. If the volume on a sound reaches the very top (the Volume Peak Indicator) and turns red, this is an indication the volume has exceeded an acceptable limit and, as such, might contain artifacts. This helps you make decisions on how to mix the sound properly without causing distortion.

Sounds easy, doesn't it? All you do is slide the volume faders up and down for each track. For panning, slide the Balance disk to the left or the right. So, what happens if you adjust clips on multiple tracks? The settings will all work together, the same as they would do if you adjusted the settings separately in the Timeline.

> **TIP** When you disable an audio track in the Timeline by clicking its speaker icon, the track disappears from the Audio Mixer until it's enabled again.

Now that you have a basic idea of how the Audio Mixer works, let's examine some of its additonal features.

The Mute and Solo Buttons

NOTE **The Mute and Solo buttons are a monitoring feature only. In other words, they don't affect the actual mixing of tracks.**

The Mute and Solo buttons at the top of each track strip in the Audio Mixer are used to turn off the monitoring of selected tracks and to play others. The Mute button disables the playback of a track and the Solo button plays a track exclusively. This is an important feature because it enables you to isolate the monitoring of specific tracks while temporarily disabling others.

To Make a track mute:

1. **Click the Mute button of that track.**
2. **All other tracks will play back.**

To Make a track solo:

1. **Click the Solo button at the top of that track.**
2. **All other tracks will become mute.**

The Mute and Solo buttons are essential for creating a successful mixing of multiple tracks.

Mixer Automation

Up until now, we've been examining the static features of the Audio Mixer. I use the term "static" because the fade and pan settings you select on a track alter the clip for its full duration, and don't change over the course of the clip. So, what if you want to change the fade and pan on a clip in time, like you can do on the fade and pan rubberbands? You can this by using the automate write functions in the Audio Mixer. The advantage to setting fades and pans over time using this window is you can modify the settings in real time.

The three icons at the top of the Audio Mixer are for Automation Read, Automation Write, and Automation Off.

- **Automation Read (glasses)** This button reads the stored volume and pan data to control the level of playback on the track. 
- **Automation Write (pencil)** This button reads and records the stored fade and pan levels. Adjustments you make with the Write buttons are reflected as new handles in the fad/pan rubberbands in the Timeline. 
- **Automation Off (clock)** Use this button to disable automation. This is the default mode in the mixer. 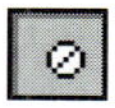

Before you use the automation features, you need to familiarize yourself with the settings in the Audio Mixer Window Options dialog box.

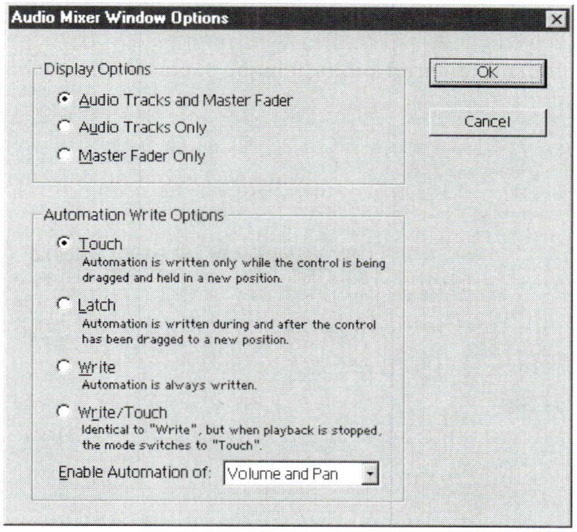

In this dialog box, you can customize the way your automation records by deciding how the fade volume and pan balance is going to work for you. The dialog box is split between two categories: the Display Options and the Automation Write Options. Let's review the various selections in the box and see how they might affect the outcome of your animation.

The Display Options relate to the way you want the mixer to appear and the choices are self-explanatory. The default setting is what you've seen in the Audio Mixer figures in this section, which includes the tracks, plus the Master fader, so this setting is purely subjective.

The second half of the Options dialog box enables you to select the way you want your automation to be recorded. In the dialog box, notice that under each selection is a description of the selection, in case you occasionally forget. The following is a clarification of these selections:

- **Touch** This is the default mode. When this is selected, the automation is only recorded when you click-and-drag the sliders. If you don't happen to be dragging a slider, it jumps back to a zero setting in the tracks VU meter. This setting obviously doesn't work well if you want to stop sliding the fader or the pan during the playback, and it could cause an abrupt change in the setting.
- **Latch** With this selected, the mixer stays wherever you put it. So, let's say you want to turn on the Automation Write for more than one track and change the volume or pan in time on these tracks. The Latch setting would leave one setting alone while you rush to the next setting, thus creating a real-time animated mix of sorts. Of course, you'd have to be a pretty fast juggler to accomplish this. Dragging on sliders with a mouse isn't exactly the same thing as sitting at a professional mixing board. Mixing tracks separately or ganging fade controls might provide a less-frenetic method for accomplishing a similar task.
- **Write** This is a continuous setting that always records automation, so when you stop the recording and start it up again, this picks up where it left off. You can easily overwrite recorded information using this.
- **Write/Touch** This offers a balance between the Write and Touch settings. It starts recording in the Write mode. When recording is stopped and started again, it goes on to the Touch mode.

> **NOTE** **To record the fade/pan, you need to be in Write or Write/Touch mode.**

- **Enable Automation** This is a pop-up menu. From here, you can specify whether you want to automate both the Volume and Pan or the Volume and Pan separately. The default, which seems to cover most bases, is Volume and Pan.

So now that you know all the whys, wherefores, and pitfalls of automation, let's actually do it. If you want, you can pretend you're sitting at the mixing controls in a big sound recording studio and mixing the next award-winning music video. Or, you can be real and get down to the business of mixing.

If you're following along with the lesson, let's rearrange our workspace so it resembles Figure 11-7. Notice also the tracks are expanded so you can see what's going on in the bottom half of the clip. In this figure, audio clips are on three tracks.

The Timeline is set up as follows:

- Audio Track 1—africanlong22.aif
- Audio Track 2—TIRE22.aif
- Audio Track 3—frog22.aif, creaky22.aif, and two more instances of frog22.aif. These four clips are disbursed throughout the Timeline to correspond with the tempo of the first clip, african22long.aif.

To Automate THE VOLUME OF A TRACK:

1. **Select the track in the Timeline (in this case, select the clip in Track 1) and move the Edit line to the point in time where you want the automation to begin.**

2. **Click the pencil tool (Automation Write) at the top of the track you're going to automate Track 1. Note, the other two tracks are set to Automation Off. You can also mute the other tracks if they seem audibly distracting to you.**

3. **Right-click (Windows)/CONTROL-click (Mac) on the Audio Mixer title bar to display the Write Options dialog box. For this project, select Write/Touch for Automation Write Options and click OK.**

4. **Select from the options in the Enable Automation pop-up menu (Volume and Pan or Volume Only).**

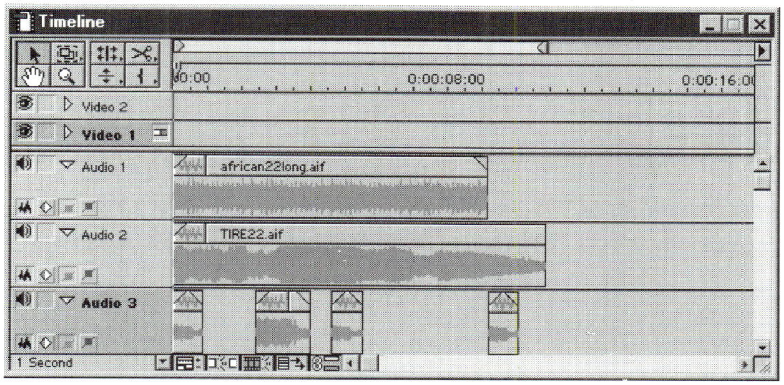

FIGURE 11-7
Tracks are being automated using the Audio Mixer

5 Make sure the edit line is at the begining of the Timeline. Click the Play button at the bottom of the Audio Mixer. Or, you can press the letter L on the keyboard.

6 Drag the Volume fader for the track up or down to increase or decrease the amplitude of the sound in real time, while the music plays. When you preview the results in the Timeline, you'll see the handles were automatically generated in time according to the way you dragged your slider (see the illustration).

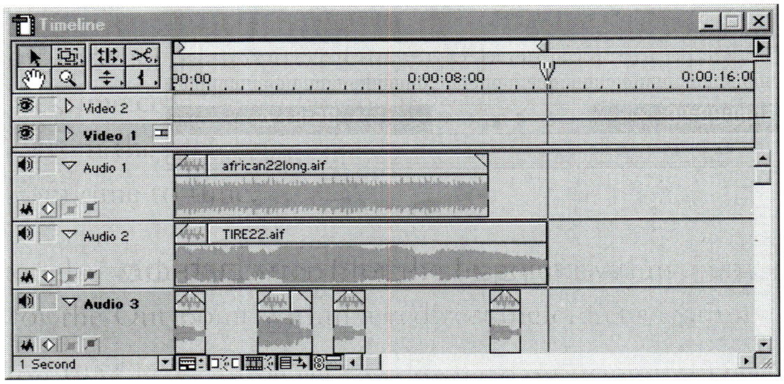

If you don't like your results, simply repeat the process. The new handles will write over the old.

Automating a pan is just as easy as automating a fade. Let's automate the pan of the clip on Audio Track 2 (TIRE22.aif).

CAUTION When automating with the mixer, don't get too close to the red peak in the VU meter because it will cause sound distortion.

To Automate a pan in the Audio Mixer:

1 First, select the track in the Timeline and click the Pan Rubberband icon. Move the Edit line to the point in time where you want the pan automation to begin.

2 Click the pencil tool (Automation Write) at the top of the track on which you're going to automate the pan.

3 If necessary, right-click (Windows)/CONTROL-click (Mac) on the title bar to display the Write Options dialog box. The Write/Touch for Automation Write Options is fine for this purpose, but you can experiment with other settings to check out the results. Sometimes, seeing results can help you comprehend the purpose of a setting.

4 Select from the options in the Enable Automation pop-up menu (choose Volume and Pan, or Pan Only).

5 Click the Play button (or the letter L) at the bottom of the Audio Mixer. Drag the Balance disc to the left and right to change the balance of the left and right channels as the clip plays in time. If you're using a mono clip, such as TIRE22.aif, you'll hear the sound go from one speaker to another if you have stereo speakers on your computer.

6 When you preview the results in the Timeline, you can see that pan handles were automatically generated in time on the pan rubberbands according to the way you dragged your slider.

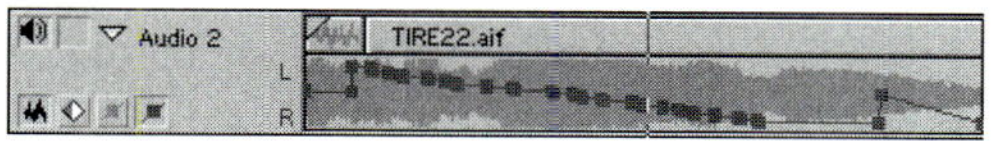

Once you automate the pan on this track, you can go back and use the same process to automate the fade. You could also fade and pan a group of tracks together in time by dragging the handles while they're automating, but this is kind of hard to do. Because of this, the Audio Mixer does offer a way to gang tracks together and automate them all at once. Let's look at this method.

Ganging Volume Faders in the Mixer

Ganging tracks together enables you to drag several clips up and down the fade slider in time to fade them all simultaneously. The difference between ganging and using the Master fader is this: before you gang the tracks, you can position the Volume faders on each track at any level you want. So, when you automate in time, the faders move together as a group, even though the Volume faders aren't aligned.

Another nice feature of ganging is when you need to drag a fader to the bottom of the VU to fade out sound completely on all tracks, the ganged sliders gradually equalize out toward the bottom. You can create up to four separate gangs.

Like all the other features in the Audio Mixer, this one is also easy to use.

To Gang several fade controls:

1 In the Mixer, adjust the Volume fade on all the tracks you intend to gang together.

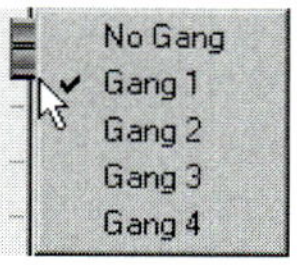

2 Right-click (Windows)/Control-click (Mac) on the Volume Fade control button to access the context menu.

3. **Select a gang number.**
4. **Repeat this process for all the fade controls you want in the same gang.**
5. **If you drag any of the Volume Fade controls that have been ganged, they'll all move together.**

To Animate a Gang:

1. **Turn on the Automation Write button on each track in the gang.**
2. **Make sure the Audio Mixer window options are set correctly for what you're about to do.**
3. **Press the Play button and drag one of the Volume Fade controls in the gang.**
4. **Play back the result and check out the Timeline to see the fade rubberbands that have been created in time.**

When you gang tracks and automate the fade controls, it changes the fade rubberbands on all the ganged tracks.

The Audio Mixer is a tremendous addition to Premiere. It provides you with some terrific features to make your sound mixing both more efficient and less tedious. Yet another sound-related feature exists in Premiere, which we touched on only briefly in the last chapter. These are audio effects. Let's look briefly at what they do.

Audio Effects

Once you know how to apply video effects, the concept behind audio effects will seem like a breeze. But audio is still a different animal than video. Where you were previously applying video effects to convey a certain experience in your production, audio effects can also create an experience, depending on which effect you select. As mentioned before, audio, often downplayed, is an equally important part of your production. As such, it must be treated as an important ingredient.

Premiere ships with a total of 20 effects. You access Audio Effects from the menu, Window | Show Audio Effects (see Figure 11-8).

FIGURE 11-8
The Audio Effects palette

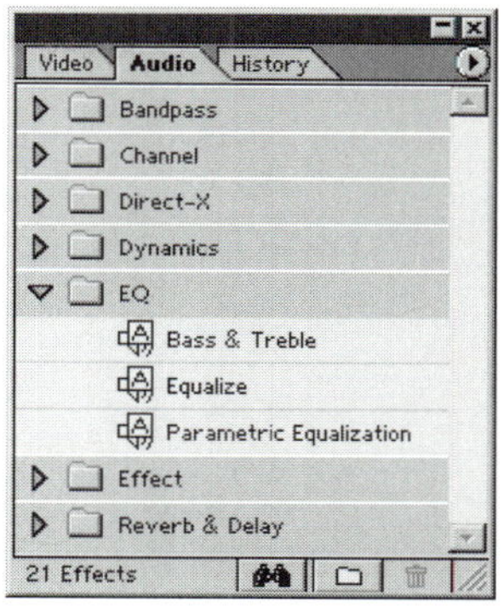

The palette navigates just like the other palettes in Premiere. In particular, it bears a striking resemblance to the Video Effects palette. In fact, both tabs are adjacent in a nested group palette.

The effects in this palette range from sound correction to sound distortion. They are organized in six groups and the titles of these filters are indicative of their function.

The six categories of audio effects are as follows:

- **Bandpass** Three different Bandpass effects exist, including Highpass, Lowpass, and Notch/Hum filter. These effects help to moderate or eliminate undesirable frequencies.
- **Channel** The settings for Channel are Auto Pan, Fill Left, Fill Right, Pan, and Swap. Use these effects to modify the left and right channels on a stereo clip.
- **Dynamics** These effects include Boost, Compressor/Expander, and Noise Gate. The Dynamics effects enable you to modify the peaks and valleys, or the dynamic range, of sounds.
- **EQ** The EQ effects are Bass & Treble, Equalize, and Parametric Equalization. Similar to the Bandpass effects, the EQ effects bring selected frequencies to the forefront and pull back on others.
- **Effect** Three Effects exist: Chorus, Flanger, and Multi-Effect. These special effects let you modulate the pitch and add delay to your clips. They add depth and motion to thin or static sounds.

- **Reverb & Delay** These effects include Echo, Multitap Delay, and Reverb. These sounds convey the sensation of sound in an enclosed space like a big concert hall or small room.

Just like the video effects, audio effects have parameters that can be set. Now, we'll apply a couple of effects to some clips to see what kind of results they yield. After all, hearing is believing.

To Apply AN AUDIO EFFECT TO AN AUDIO CLIP IN THE TIMELINE:

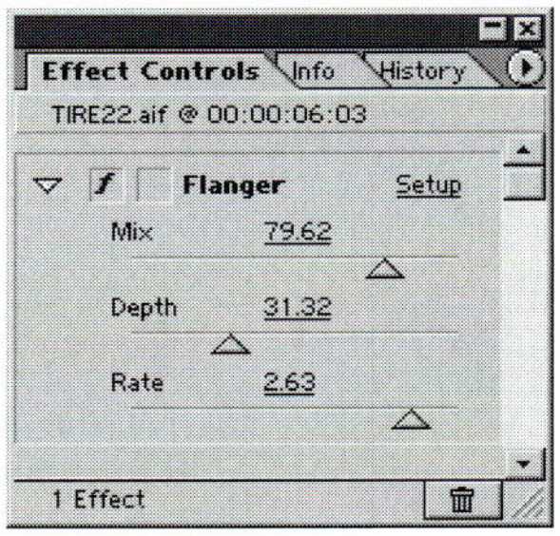

1. **Navigate to an effect in the Audio Effects palette.**
2. **Drag the effect onto a clip in the Timeline. When you do this, the Effect Controls palette will appear.**

In the Effects palette, you can set parameters for a selected effect. Just like the Effect Controls on a video clip, each audio effect has different adjustable parameters. In the case of the Flanger effect, you can adjust the Mix, Depth, and Rate of the Flanger.

If you click Setup in the Effect Controls (many effects will have a Setup, giving you more precise tools for the setting), you can preview the settings you selected on the sound to get just the right outcome. A Flanger effect, similar to the Chorus effect, gives the clip a warbling, "rushing" quality.

Basically all the effects are applied in the same way, offering effect-specific parameter adjustments in the Effect Controls palette for each one. Just like audio effects, you can apply more than one effect to an audio clip. To do so, simply drag multiple audio effects onto a clip. You can also access the Effect Controls palette by selecting Window | Show Effect Controls.

> **NOTE** **You can also disable an effect from the Effects palette. To do so, click the Effect Enabled button with the letter *f* to the left of the Effect title. To enable it again, click again and the *f* will appear.**

ANIMATING AUDIO EFFECTS

As with video effects, you can also animate audio effects. Again, the process for animating all audio effects is somewhat similar, with the exception of the effect-specific parameters that can be adjusted on each clip in the Effect Controls palette.

So, if you know how to animate one effect, the others will seem quite simple. To create an animated audio effect, you adjust the effect parameters over time on keyframes.

If you recall, when you expand an audio track, there is a keyframe icon just like in an expanded video track. To apply keyframes, the Display Keyframes icon must be checked. Let's examine the process involved in animating an audio clip by applying a filter and modifying the parameters of this effect on keyframes over time.

> **TIP** Third-party audio effects are available from various software manufacturers. For a list of audio-effect plug-ins available for Premiere, check out Appendix B. For additional plug-in information, visit the adobe.com web site.

In Figure 11-9, the audio file on Track 2, african22long.aif, has a Multitap Delay effect applied in time. Specifically, keyframes are added to the keyframe track—evenly disbursed—and totaling four keyframes.

To Animate AN AUDIO EFFECT ON THE TIMELINE:

1. **Select an audio clip and apply an effect using the method previously outlined.**
2. **Click the Display Keyframe icon and make sure the Effect Controls palette is displayed.**
3. **Drag the Edit line to the point in the Timeline where you want your first keyframe or click the previous frame/next frame arrows on the track and click the previous frame. Next, click the previous frame next, and then click the Add/Delete Keyframe button. Repeat this process to add more keyframes if desired.**
4. **Return to the first keyframe where you want the sound to change. In the previous figure, the parameters of the Multitap Delay effect were modified on the second and third keyframes.**

FIGURE 11-9
The clip named african22long.aif is animated in the Timeline

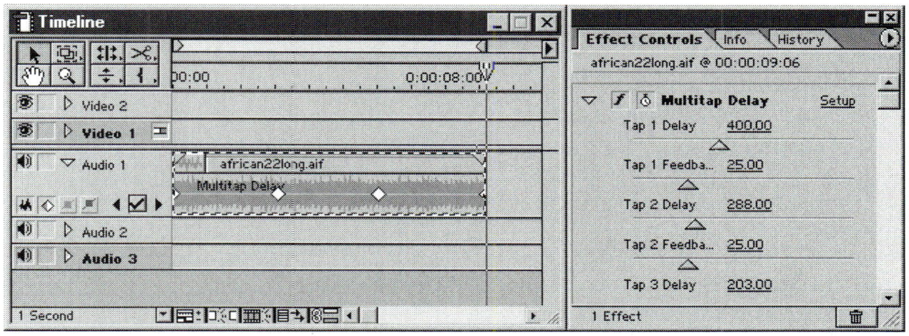

5 In the Effect Controls palette, either adjust the slider parameters for the clip you've chosen or, if there's a setup button, click it.

6 Repeat the process for the next keyframe, altering the parameters of the effect in the Effect Controls palette.

When you finish, play the sound to see what the results yield.

> **NOTE** You can play back audio effects in the Timeline without previewing a file. In the Audio Settings, under Processing Options, there's a setting where you can specify Create Audio Preview files if five or more audio tracks exist and if one or more audio filters are there. The default values can be made larger, depending on the speed of your computer.

To Add MULTIPLE EFFECTS TO AN AUDIO CLIP:

1 Repeat the previous process to add another effect.

2 When you include additional audio effects, just as with video effects, the additional effects appear in the Effects Control palette with the others. Also, a flyout menu appears in the bottom-left corner of the audio keyframe track, enabling you to toggle between the different effects (see the illustration).

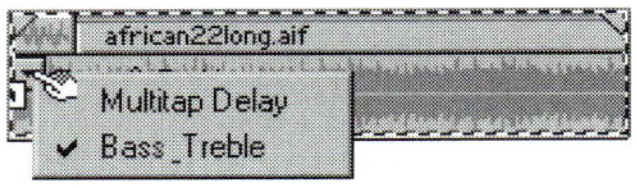

3 When you want to alter the keyframes on a particular effect, select it in the flyout menu. Alter the parameters on the keyframes according to the parameter selections on the Effect Controls palette.

The clip on audio Track 1 has two animated audio effects; Multitap Delay and Bass & Treble (Figure 11-10). These effects change over a duration of four keyframes. The settings on the Bass & Treble are exaggerated, so you can get an idea of what

FIGURE 11-10
The clip on Audio Track 1 has two effects applied to it

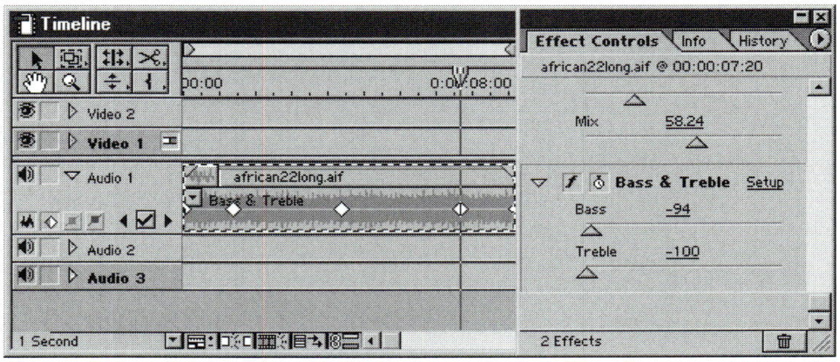

the effect does. If you play back these effects in the Timeline, it will give you an idea of how you can blend effects together and change their parameters in time. By experimenting, combining, and automating audio effects on a clip, you can achieve some pretty wild effects.

If you're a creative person, you can find many uses for audio effects. They can be used to change the feeling of a sound. For example, you can make an everyday audio clip sound like it was recorded in the Grand Canyon, or add some crackling ambient sound to an existing clip, so it sounds like a transmission from outer space. With all the new audio-editing features in Premiere, many near-professional quality mixing features and a slew of intriguing audio effects are now available for you to experiment with.

ON THE VIRTUAL CLASSROOM CD-ROM **The Audio Mixer is a versatile tool in Premiere. In Lesson 9, "Mixing Audio in Premiere," the instructor explains how to mix and balance multiple audio tracks.**

12

Preparing Your Video for Output

Outputting in Premiere means preparing your production to be introduced to the world, viewed, and, we hope, appreciated by others. Because your production can't live in Premiere forever, this is the last step in the Premiere process. It's perhaps the most exciting part, because seeing your production on a CD, the Web, or a TV screen gives you a sense of accomplishment and, along with it, a completely different perspective on what you've accomplished.

In this chapter, we cover the different output methods available for your projects. Whether your final production is output to video tape, audio, CD, the Web, or for use in another program (e.g., Flash, Director, Acrobat, or PowerPoint, to name a few), as you'll see, ensuring the best-quality output for your final goal takes some thought, care, and attention.

Putting Your Production on Tape

Recording your production to videotape is one of the most popular forms for showing and distributing video productions. Once you've set up your system correctly, moving your production to tape is straightforward.

Gigantic file size is the greatest challenge in exporting your movie to a tape device. A 10-minute digital video file can be more than 2GB. So a half-hour of video will be about 6GB. You can see why you need almost limitless (and ultra-fast) hard disk space if you plan to output your productions to tape. If you use your computer as a video-storage device, it's clear that even a 30GB hard drive would soon fill up with your video. Not only that, but frames drop easily when the hard disk can't keep up with the demands of the output.

There are two commands for exporting your Premiere video to videotape:

- **Print to Video** If your computer doesn't support device control, you can control the recording to tape in Premiere right from your device. For this, you can use Premiere's Print to Video command. This command is generic and fairly limited in its flexibility. However, if you're using an analog device, this is the only video output option available to you. You can also use this setting for multimedia screen presentations.
- **Export to Tape** If your configuration supports device control in Premiere, you'll use this command.

You can use either method on a single video clip, a portion of the Timeline as designated by the position of the work area bar, or the entire Timeline.

Exporting to Tape Settings

Before exporting your Premiere project to tape, it's a good idea to review the Project settings you've selected for your production. This will ensure the best-quality output possible to meet your project goals. Here are some settings you want to pay particular attention to before exporting to tape because they could significantly affect your final output.

KEYFRAME AND RENDERING

Your Fields setting is important when exporting to tape. We discussed fields in Chapter 3 on project settings. To quickly review, fields refer to interlaced video (TV standard), which displays two fields per frame as alternating scan lines. Each frame of a video is divided into two fields that display alternating scan lines. The choice between the two depends on which field your system expects to receive first. Your field choices are:

- No Fields
- Upper Field First
- Lower Field First

In general, when you output your movie as a file for use in another program or for playback on a computer screen, you should choose No Fields. If you will output to videotape for viewing on a TV monitor, you should choose one of the field settings. Your choice depends on your specific video output hardware. For DV output, choose Lower Field First.

Because different Preview options offer different playback speeds when working in Premiere, you must make sure that you view previews at the final playback speed. To do this, select From Disk from the Preview pop-up menu in the Rendering section of the Keyframe and Rendering Preferences dialog box (which you access via Project Settings), as in Figure 12-1.

GENERAL PANEL

The quality of your final tape will be only as good as the output from your Premiere production. For tape, you want the quality to be crisp and clear. One way you can ensure this is to review the Video, Audio, and Keyframe and Rendering settings and make sure you select the highest levels of quality available to obtain the best possible quality output.

FIGURE 12-1
Fields and Preview settings in the Keyframe and Rendering settings panel relate to your final output

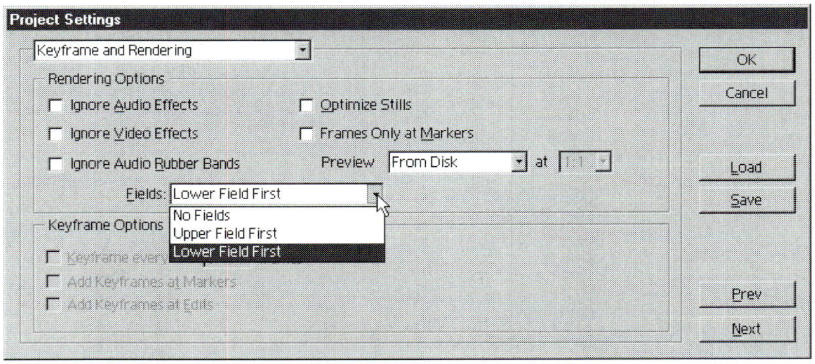

Scratch Disk and Device Control

The Scratch Disk Settings refer to the target disks where your assets and captured files are stored. The Device Control Settings are applicable if you're using a DV camcorder or tape deck to control the recording and playback of tape in the device. If you're outputting to tape, you should know whether your system supports device control because you can use this device feature to control recording in Premiere. We discussed device control in Chapter 6 on capturing. In the Scratch Disks and Device Control dialog box (accessed via Edit | Preferences), you can make sure that your scratch disks are set to the correct disks and folders and your device control options are properly installed.

If your hardware supports device control, from the Device pop-up menu in the Scratch Disks and Device Control panel, choose the Device Control option for your specific equipment. If you're working with DV equipment, you should choose DV Device Control 2.0 or whatever the latest version is (Figure 12-2).

By clicking the Options button, you can access the DV Device Control Options dialog box.

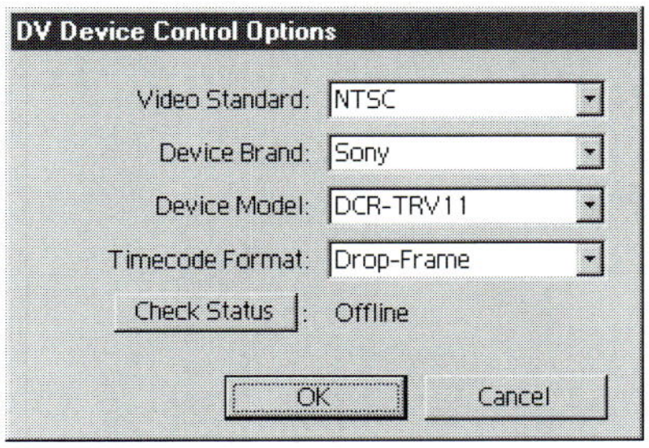

Here you should choose a Device Brand and Device Model. Next, pick the timecode format you want to use from the Timecode Format drop-down menu. This will almost always be drop-frame for NTSC productions.

Playback Options Related to Tape Export

After you've checked the relevant settings, you must make sure your playback options are set for optimal performance. Playback options refer to the method by

FIGURE 12-2
When you export your production to tape and the device you use supports device control, you can control the tape transport directly from within Premiere

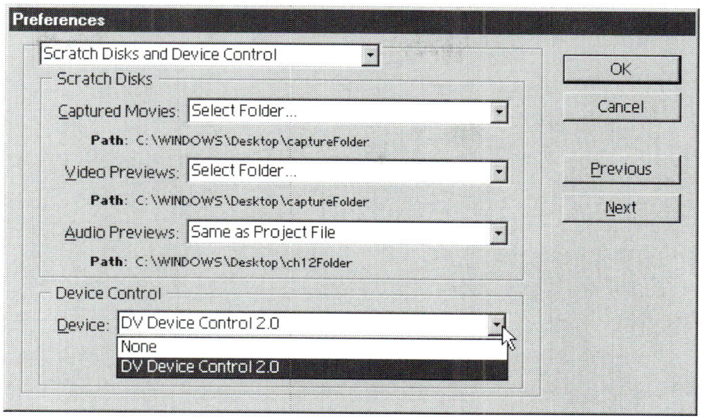

which the video is played back in various places during the process, such as your device or computer screen. Your choices are varied and, as always, contingent on your hardware configuration.

To Prepare FOR PLAYBACK OF YOUR VIDEO:

1. **If you're working with digital video equipment, connect the FireWire/IEEE 1394 cable, which attaches to your camcorder or tape deck, and plug it into your computer.**

> **NOTE** **For most Macs, the Editing Mode is set to QuickTime as the only choice available.**

2. **To set the playback to a digital video recording device, select Project | Project Settings.**

3. **While in the General dialog box, chose DV playback in the Editing Mode pop-up menu.**

4. **Click the Playback Settings button (Figure 12-3). Make sure your camcorder (if you're using one) is set to VCR/VTR.**

When you select DV playback in the Editing Mode pop-up menu in the General Settings panel, you can select the DV Playback Options dialog box. There are several playback options in this box. They are:

- **Playback on DV Camcorder/VCR** Select this if you want to play back on your camcorder or VCR.

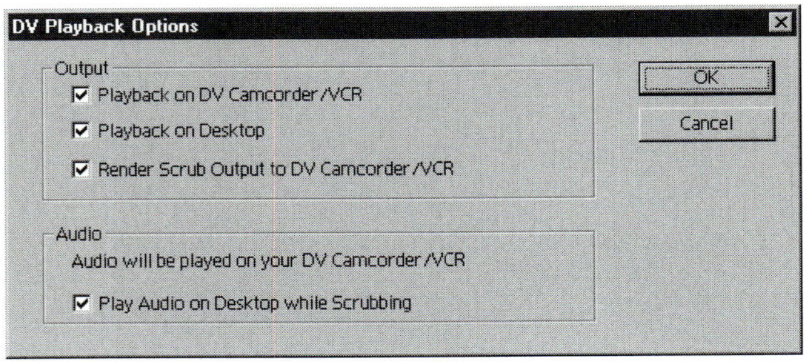

FIGURE 12-3
When you export to tape and use device control, you can set the playback options in the DV Playback Options dialog box

- **Playback on Desktop** This selection lets you see your output on your desktop and camcorder. Normally, this selection results in poor-quality output.
- **Render Scrub Output to DV Camcorder/VCR** If you feel it necessary to see scrubbing performed on your camcorder or VCR, choose this option.
- **Play Audio on Desktop while Scrubbing** If you want to play back audio on your computer while scrubbing, select this option.

If QuickTime is selected as the Editing mode and your computer has a FireWire interface, the following playback settings are available when you click the Playback Settings button:

- **Output Device** Select FireWire.
- **Output Mode** Choose between NTSC or PAL.

Mac users will see these options:

- **Apple FireWire NTSC or Apple FireWire PAL** You can also select frame size and rate while in this mode.
- **Play Audio on Output Device Only** Select this option to play audio on the output device only. If you do not select this option, audio in a video will play through your computer.
- **Sample Rate** For sound, you can specify an audio sampling rate. This should correspond to the sample rate of your audio clips.
- **Render Scrub Output to Output Device** Select this option if you want to view scrubbing on your camcorder or other output device.
- **High Quality Playback/High Quality Scrubbing** Select this option only if absolutely necessary because it will probably result in your video playing back very slowly on your desktop. Note that this setting affects playback only on

the computer screen; your DV output to a camcorder or DV deck will always be high quality.

- **Deinterlace Desktop Playback** Choosing this option sometimes enhances the quality of your video when playing back to the desktop. This setting has no effect on output.
- **Show Marker Comments** Check this if you want marker comments to appear on the output.

Exporting to Tape with Device Control

Device control is an amazingly helpful feature when you're outputting to tape. Let's explore how to use this feature.

To Use device control for export:

1. Turn on your videotape deck and load a blank tape. Make sure the tape has been striped (timecode already laid down) if you want to record your output to a specific timecode location.
2. Be sure to write down the timecode location of your production so you'll know exactly where the tape will begin and end on the blank tape.
3. Choose File | Export Timeline | Export to Tape. In the Export To Tape Settings dialog box, select Activate Recording Deck to tell Premiere to take control of the recording device (see the illustration). If you want to export only a single clip to tape, select the clip and go to File | Export Clip | Export to Tape.
4. At this point, if you have a specific timecode location where you want the recording to begin, check Assemble At Time Code and enter the timecode you jotted down from your previous notes.
5. In the Movie Start Delay field, enter a delay in quarter frames. Several devices require this delay to sync the recording device with the movie after starting the recording process.
6. In the Preroll field, enter the number of frames you want to back up or preroll before the specified timecode to let the tape attain the proper speed before starting to record. Some DV devices need extra preroll time before recording to prevent glitching or dropping frames.

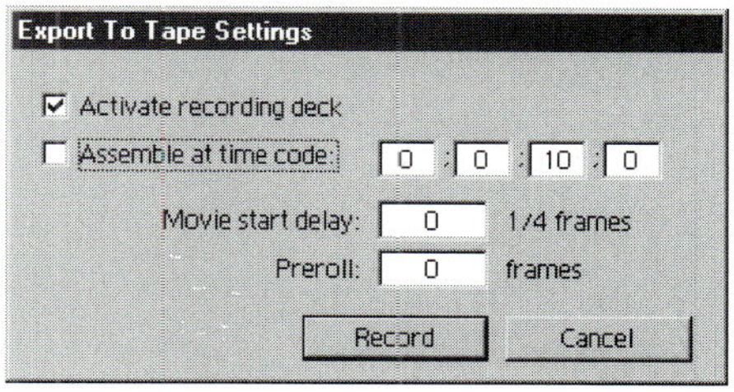

If you're using device control with an analog video output board, you must have an analog device control plug-in installed to control your device. If one is installed, select it in the Device Control pop-up menu in the Scratch Disks and Device Control dialog box and enter the options as suggested in your video board's documentation.

Printing to Video

If you don't have device control, you can use the Print to Video command (File | Export Timeline | Print to Video). This will play your Premiere video in the center of the screen on a TV, computer, or camcorder screen.

Should your frame size be smaller than the screen size, your video will sit against a black background. The bitmapped appearance will become more obvious the larger the ratio is between the original footage and output. If you want only to print a single clip to video, select the clip and go to File | Export Clip | Print to Video.

A nice feature of Print to Video is that it gives you the option of doubling the size of a frame when you export to videotape.

To Print to Video:

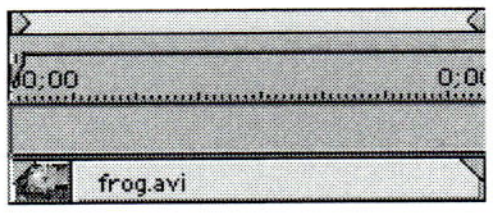

1. **The work area bar must appear above the Timeline section that you want to export to videotape.**

2. **To open the Print to Video dialog box, choose Print to Video from File | Export Timeline or File | Export Clip (see the illustration on the following page). Fill in the number of seconds of color bars and black you want to be recorded before your video is output. If you're outputting to tape, give yourself plenty of time to put your video recorder into record mode by entering in 10 seconds or so in either the Color Bars For or Play Black For Fields.**

3. **If you want to enlarge the frame to fill the screen, choose Full Screen or Zoom by 2 (Windows) or Zoom Screen (Mac).**

4. **If you want your video to play back in an ongoing, continuous fashion, choose Loop Playback. Click OK to start the output. Press the record button on your camera or tape**

deck. If you're producing a multimedia video on your computer desktop, you can skip this step. The image will appear on your computer screen.

5 If you enabled Loop Playback, you'll have to press ESC to discontinue playback. Otherwise, output will end when the clip or timeline ends.

Creating an EDL (Edit Decision List)

As a by-product of outputting your video, you can create an Edit Decision List (EDL) from your Premiere project (see Figure 12-4). An EDL is the recipe for your production, including all the trimmed clips and their locations on tape.

EDLs are used for offline editing. Offline editing is when you use low-resolution source materials to generate your video production. You can create a draft version of your project in Premiere, generate an EDL, and bring the EDL along with the source files to a video production facility. Here, they can generate a high-quality version of your production. Your EDL will contain all the instructions needed for the professional video editors to reproduce your video on a high-end workstation.

FIGURE 12-4
For offline editing in Premiere, you can output directly to an EDL

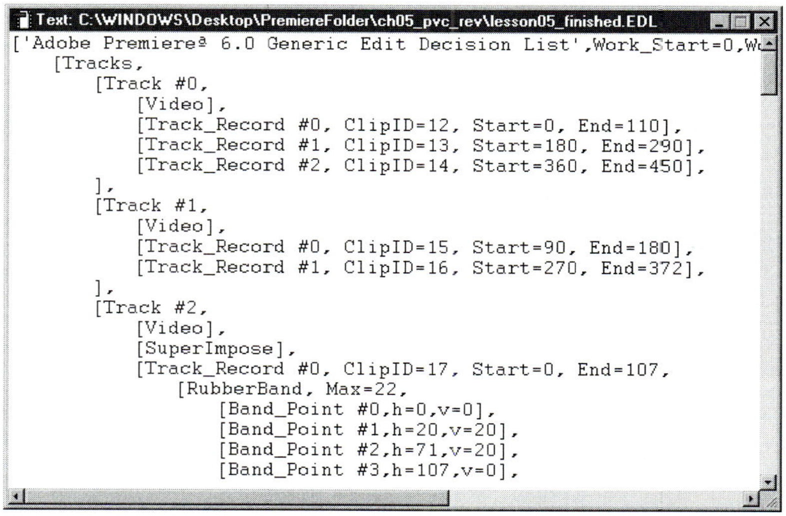
Text: C:\WINDOWS\Desktop\PremiereFolder\ch05_pvc_rev\lesson05_finished.EDL

```
['Adobe Premiere® 6.0 Generic Edit Decision List',Work_Start=0,Wo
    [Tracks,
        [Track #0,
            [Video],
            [Track_Record #0, ClipID=12, Start=0, End=110],
            [Track_Record #1, ClipID=13, Start=180, End=290],
            [Track_Record #2, ClipID=14, Start=360, End=450],
        ],
        [Track #1,
            [Video],
            [Track_Record #0, ClipID=15, Start=90, End=180],
            [Track_Record #1, ClipID=16, Start=270, End=372],
        ],
        [Track #2,
            [Video],
            [SuperImpose],
            [Track_Record #0, ClipID=17, Start=0, End=107,
                [RubberBand, Max=22,
                    [Band_Point #0,h=0,v=0],
                    [Band_Point #1,h=20,v=20],
                    [Band_Point #2,h=71,v=20],
                    [Band_Point #3,h=107,v=0],
```

If you will use an EDL file of your video, you should know that there are differences between Premiere's capabilities and those things that the EDL file can interpret. An EDL cannot translate certain video effects, audio-mixing features, and settings in Premiere. That said, an EDL can still be the most effective way to align original source files to a program that you created in Premiere, especially if your production is very large and your facility is not equipped to finish large-scale productions.

To obtain your desired results with an EDL that makes use of elements like audio mixing and special effects, you'll have to work closely with the video editor in the production facility you choose so you can communicate your design intentions that were not recorded in the EDL. For example, let's say you used a couple of special effects in your Premiere production that were very important to the overall design. You're now working with a video editor who's building the high-resolution version of the video. Let's say the EDL doesn't translate these particular effects. To resolve this problem you would either review the low-resolution version of the video with the video editor to show him what the effects are supposed to look like or describe these effects to him so he can replicate them on his high-end workstation.

To Create A GENERIC EDL FILE:

1. **Go to File | Export Timeline | EDL. Notice the long list of different EDL selections that address various formats (see the illustration).**

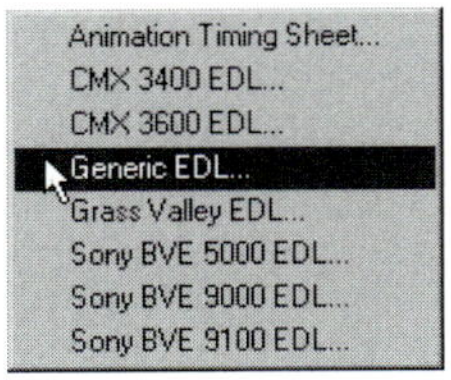

2. **Select the format named Generic EDL.**
3. **A Save dialog box prompts you for a file name and a Save location. The extension for this file will be EDL.**

Once you've created a generic EDL, it appears on screen for you to review. Other formats offer a variety of settings. Your video production house can best direct you on which settings to use. On the Adobe web site you can find more information about EDLs under Premiere support.

MOVIE FILE FORMATS FOR THE WEB

At some point, you'll probably want to show one of your Premiere productions on the Web. This may be on your web page, for a client's web site, or for a corporate intranet. In any case, because the Web has become a viable promotion vehicle, you'll want to become familiar with all of Premiere's web-export features. In keeping with this goal, let's look at various movie file formats you can use for web output.

To see video on the Web, the viewers of your web page must acquire the appropriate plug-in. You should provide a link on your web page to the URL of the plug-in in case the viewer doesn't have it installed. The following file formats require a plug-in installed in your browser software:

- **Audio Video Interleave (AVI)** All Windows computers can read AVI files; however, AVI is not often used on the Web because it isn't a cross-platform file format.
- **QuickTime** This is the most popular web video file format because it offers cross-platform capability with a good-quality playback. All new browsers and many older ones ship with the QuickTime plug-in.
- **Microsoft Advanced Streaming Format (ASF)** The Windows 2000 Server package includes a Windows media server to deliver ASF files. To save files in this format, when in Premiere, select the File | Save for Web command. If you're working on a Windows-only intranet video production, the ASF file format is a good choice because its output quality is high and it supports streaming video.
- **RealVideo** This streaming video format offered by RealNetworks is currently one of the most popular formats around. To use this format, you must export your Premiere movies in RealVideo format.

Exporting Using the Premiere Plug-ins

As we all know by now, slow connection speeds on the Web can turn away your audience and send them elsewhere.

To avoid this problem, you must create Premiere productions with small frame sizes and rates so that a home user with a slow modem and/or Internet connection can download your video in a reasonable amount of time. Of course, the quality then diminishes greatly, which alienates the other end of your global audience. So you're faced with a real dilemma: Do you go for small and crummy-looking or big and beautiful?

Once again, Premiere 6 comes to the rescue by providing essentially a total solution for outputting video to the Web with RealNetworks' Advanced RealMedia Export or Terran's Cleaner 5 EZ plug-in. Either of these utilities lets you optimize the output of your movie. These new plug-ins are one of my favorite features of Premiere 6.

These plug-ins are packed with export options. In addition to serving as an outstanding utility for exporting movies for CD-ROM and DVD-ROM output, Cleaner EZ is a great tool for the Web. It is assumed when you use these plug-ins that you want the lowest-bandwidth output that you'd need for Web and CD delivery. Therefore, the settings you select in these plug-ins will balance output quality with size/rate. There are some useful settings in these utilities for streaming media that let you accommodate both high and low bandwidths, which we also discuss in this section.

One of the greatest features of these plug-ins is that you can output in QuickTime format and create files for Windows streaming media while creating multiple versions of your movie so that every user can connect at their particular bandwidth to your Web site. Pretty amazing if you've been exporting video for the Web with limited resources up until now.

Exporting to the Web via Advanced RealMedia Export

The RealMedia format lets your web audience view your video production as it is downloaded to the web page. This is streaming video in action. Remember what used to happen before streaming video? Your web audience would have to wait until the entire movie was downloaded before they could actually view the video. Although downloadable formats are still widely used for smaller productions, streaming media is becoming increasingly popular.

To Use Advanced RealMedia Export:

- **Choose File | Export TimeLine | Advanced RealMedia Export to display the Advanced RealMedia Export dialog box (Figure 12-5).**

As before, you'll have to give some thought to deciding whether you want to export the entire timeline, a specific work area, or a clip. You must specify the following information:

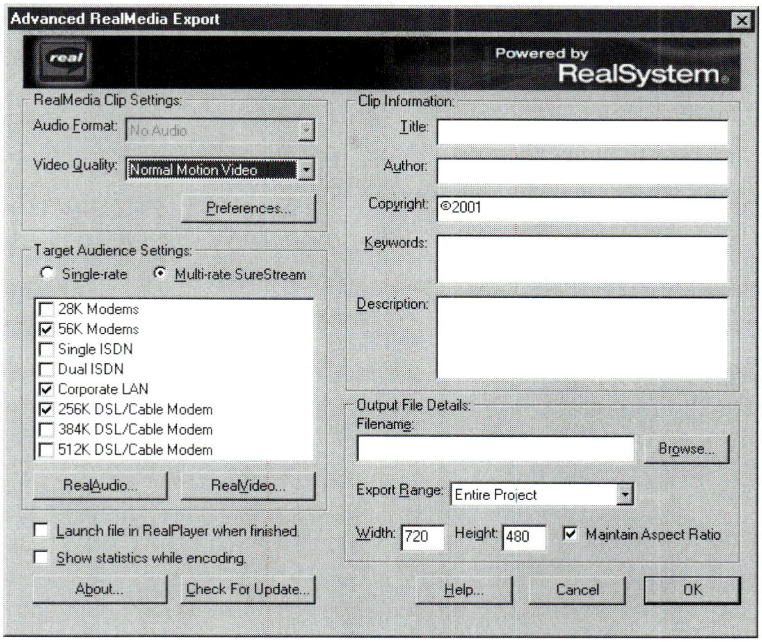

FIGURE 12-5 The Advanced RealMedia Export dialog box contains many settings for web and CD output

- **Audio Format** The Audio Format pop-up menu is located at the upper left of the dialog box. If you've included audio in your Premiere project, you should choose an audio format. By specifying the type of audio content in your clip, you can help the RealMedia exporter optimize its compression for the best possible output quality. Choose from the following formats:
  - Voice Only
  - Voice with Background Music
  - Music
  - Stereo Music
- **Video Quality** The Video Quality pop-up menu settings are at the top left of the dialog box under the Audio Format settings. As with specifying audio format, choosing a video quality helps give the best possible final output. The choices are as follows:
  - Normal Motion, when your video has motion and stills
  - Smoothest Motion, when your video has limited motion
  - Sharpest Motion, when your video has action or sports
  - Slide Show, when you want a series of still frames to appear in your video

- **Target Audience Settings** These settings are where you select a target audience for your media. Be aware that the Multi-rate SureStream setting usually provides the best viewing experience for your audience, but because the files are significantly larger than the Single-rate format, you'll have to provide (and pay for) more storage space on your RealMedia server. The distinctions are as follows:
  - **Single-rate** This is an ideal setting for a small movie. You'll also have to select a modem setting; the default is 56K for this setting.
  - If you want RealMedia to create different streams for a variety of bandwidths used by your web audience, you can select from the available bandwidth choices. The bandwidths range from 28K modems to 512K cable modems.
- **Clip Information** These fields let you add Title, Author, Copyright, Keywords, and Description information, or metadata, to your clip. The Keywords feature lets search engines locate the clip on the Web. The other information you included will appear as your movie plays on the Web. Obviously, if you don't enter anything here, this specific information will not appear in your movie.

Although selecting one of the default export settings usually works well for most projects, you may decide to change these settings, depending on the individual parameters of your video project. If this is the case, click the Preferences button to open the Preferences dialog box (Figure 12-6).

There are five tabs at the top of this box. Click a tab to display different options panels within Preferences.

FIGURE 12-6
The Preferences dialog box for RealMedia

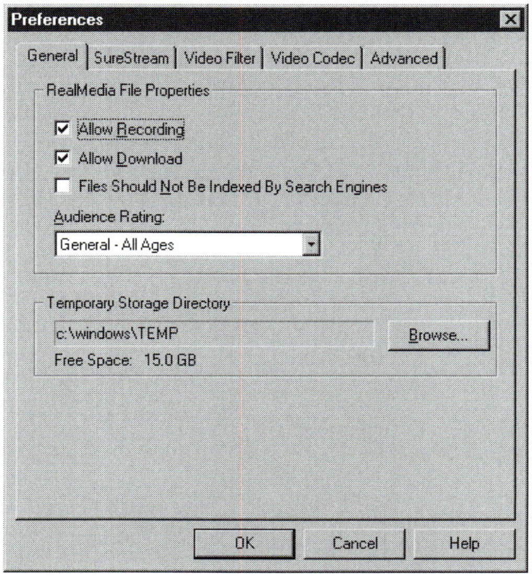

In the first tab, General, the following settings are available:

- **Allow Recording** Selecting this lets your viewers click a Record button to save the clip they're viewing on their computers.
- **Allow Download** Selecting this lets viewers save the clip to their hard drives before or after viewing.
- **Files Should Not Be Indexed By Search Engines** Selecting this prevents search engines from searching through your clips using specified keywords.

In the Audence Ratings pop-up list, you can also rate your clips for viewers to alert your audience of potentially objectionable content. The following settings are available:

- General - All Ages
- Parental Guidance Recommended
- Adult Supervision Required
- Children under 18
- Adults Only

The temporary storage directory lets you specify a particular drive or directory for the plug-in to cache files before exporting them.

Let's look at the next four tabs in the Preferences dialog box:

- **SureStream** The settings you select in this tab will determine how your SureStream clips are recorded. You can create an additional stream for older plug-ins. You can also specify an emphasis on audio or video, so when the viewing bandwidth drops, the remaining bandwidth will be allocated more to one than the other. SureStream is a RealMedia function that changes a viewer's data rate to accommodate multi-bandwidth users.
- **Video Filter** This tab lets you filter out noise from your movie files, which may have been produced by your capture card or camera.
- **Video Codec** Here you can select video compression format from a pop-up menu. RealVideo 8.0 will give you the highest-quality output.
- **Advanced** Advanced settings are available only in Windows. These settings provide additional ways to tweak compression. A dialog box in the panel suggests you don't mess with these settings, or else.

To Create AN EXPORT FILE AFTER YOU'VE CHOSEN ALL YOUR SETTINGS (FIGURE 12-7):

1. Click the Browse button.
2. Enter a file name, and click Save, then OK.
3. To create the export file, click OK in the Advanced RealMedia Export dialog box.

EXPORTING TO THE WEB USING CLEANER EZ

Without the capability of creating streaming files from your Premiere project, your viewer would have to wait until the entire production had been downloaded to view your video. With the proper settings selected in Cleaner EZ, your viewer can watch your video as it downloads. You can also export to CD-ROM and DVD-ROM with this plug-in. Cleaner EZ makes the export process very simple, providing a list of presets you can select from, plus a wizard which, as you'll see, is a great tool for new Premiere users.

NOTE For Mac users, Media Cleaner Pro by Media 100 is a great tool for web work. It's a more supercharged version of the plug-in that comes with Premiere. A Windows version is coming out in fourth quarter 2001.

Let's explore how to use this plug-in.

To Start EXPORTING A MOVIE WITH CLEANER EZ:

1. Select File | Export Timeline | Save for Web to open the Cleaner EZ plug-in (Figure 12-8).

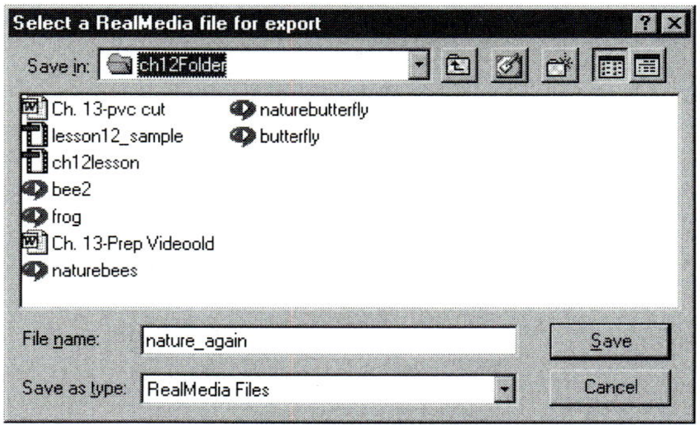

FIGURE 12-7
The dialog box for creating an export file in RealMedia

FIGURE 12-8
The Cleaner EZ dialog box

2 **In the Settings, choose a download option from the pop-up menu. The settings include QuickTime Progressive Download and MP3, among many others.**

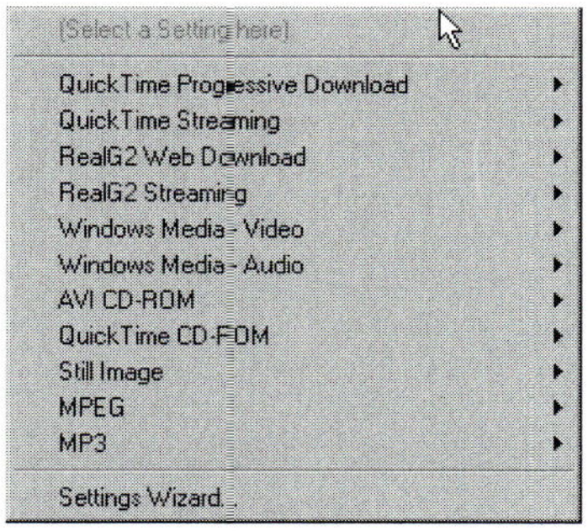

You'll notice an arrow to the right of all settings on this list. These settings have additional pop-up menus. Settings include still-image formats such as JPEG and Bitmap. The QuickTime Progressive Download lets you choose a progressive download, which lets a web viewer see the movie while it's downloading. There's also a QuickTime Streaming selection you can choose if you're using a QuickTime Streaming Server.

The Windows Media options are only for files served from a Windows Media Server. Many of the selections in this pop-up menu are self-explanatory and involve some experimentation on your part to test results.

If you're confused about the settings, it's best to use the Wizard feature (explained next). Once you've selected a setting, click the Start button. This will take you to a Save dialog box where you can save your new production.

The Export Wizard Feature in Cleaner EZ

The Export Wizard is an export sequence that prompts you for the correct settings. This is a great feature for beginners and seasoned users because the large number of export settings can be confusing (Figure 12-9). The Wizard helps decide settings for you based on your input. Let's take a brief look at this feature.

TIP **To export a single clip, select the clip and choose File | Export Clip. In the pop-up menu you'll be presented with the same options that are available when exporting a full timeline.**

FIGURE 12-9
The Delivery Medium panel in the Settings Wizard dialog box

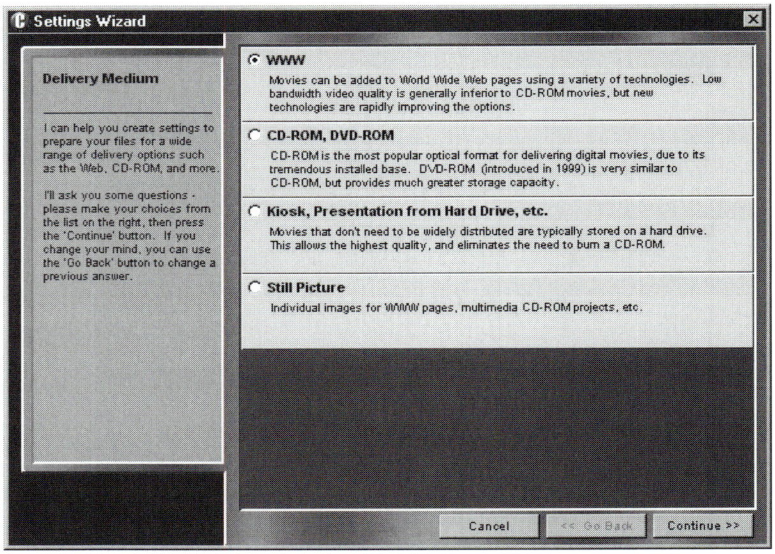

To Use THE SETTINGS WIZARD:

1. Choose File | Export Timeline | Save for Web to access the Save for Web dialog box. The Cleaner EZ plug-in is loaded through this dialog box.

2. In the Save for Web dialog box, select to Export the entire project or only the work area.

3. Click the Settings pop-up menu so you can access the export settings. Choose Settings Wizard at the bottom of the pop-up menu and click the Start button.

4. After Cleaner EZ is loaded, you will be given a series of choices in various panels for the best compression settings for your particular project. The first settings screen you'll see is the Delivery Medium definition and menu-style choices with descriptions under each category. Select a setting and then click Continue.

5. Which panels you see next depends on the delivery medium you selected. The panels are related to your choices. For example, in Figure 12-10, because in this example the WWW setting was selected as a delivery medium, the next panel that will appear is the Format panel. In this panel you can select between the following:

   - **QuickTime** For broadband and web streaming (from a web server)
   - **Real** Streamed from a RealServer
   - **Windows Media** Streamed from a Windows 2000 server

FIGURE 12-10
The Format panel in Settings Wizard

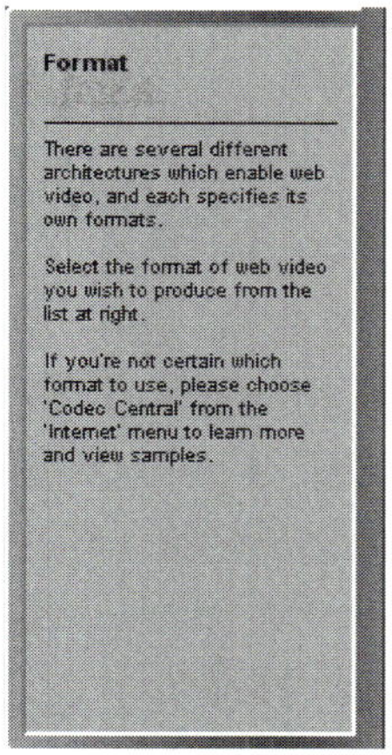

FILE FORMATS USED FOR EXPORT Premiere offers many different file export formats. Because of this, there are many different ways to use the materials you create in Premiere. You can export frames to still images or a series of frames as a still-image sequence. A still-image sequence can be imported into a program such as Flash or even ImageReady where you can transform your video into a Flash movie or an animated GIF file. Alternatively, you can export your video or audio to a digital format for the Web, CDs, or many other uses. Here is a list of the file export formats Premiere supports:

Video

- Animated GIF
- ASF
- DV Stream
- Microsoft AVI
- MPEG
- QuickTime
- RealMedia
- Windows Media

Audio

- AIFF (audio)
- MP3 (audio)
- Windows Audio Waveform (Windows audio)

Still Image

- Filmstrip
- FLC/FLI (Windows)
- GIF/GIF Sequence
- PICT/PICT Sequence (Mac OS only)
- Targa/Targa Sequence
- TIFF/TIFF Sequence
- Windows Bitmap/Windows Bitmap Sequence (Windows only)

Because each selection comes with a full description of what it is and does, it's almost impossible to select the wrong setting. Once you've made your selection, click the Continue button to go to the next panel.

Once you've selected the last possible settings, click the Finish button at the bottom-right corner of the final panel. After all your settings are compiled (Figure 12-11), Cleaner EZ compresses and exports the movie for you.

Exporting to CD-ROM Using Cleaner EZ

Although the Web is extremely popular for outputting digital movies, one of the most widely used mediums for digital video distribution is CD-ROM.

Much preparation work must be done to export movies to CD-ROM, which we cover in this section.

You'll want to use higher-quality settings when exporting a production to CD than you would for web delivery. In this case, your media limitations will be based on the speed of the viewing computer and its CD-ROM drive, rather than Internet bandwidth. If you know that your CD-ROM will be viewed on older systems, you'll have to use lower frame rates and smaller frame sizes than you will if your target audience has faster machines.

Cleaner EZ comes with some great settings for outputting to CD-ROM.

To Export to CD-ROM in Cleaner EZ:

1. **Preview the movie and select File | Export Timeline | Save For Web. In the Export dialog box pop-up menu, choose Entire Project or a specific work area. Click the Settings**

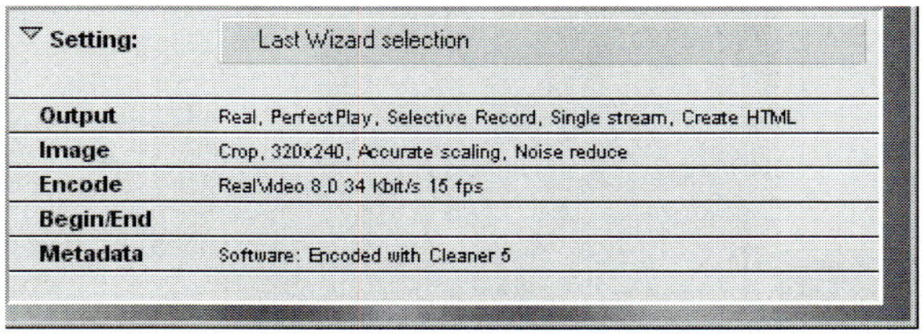

FIGURE 12-11 After you've finished selecting your settings, Cleaner EZ reviews all the settings in the Premiere NLE Source dialog box

pop-up menu and choose either QuickTime CD-ROM or AVI CD-ROM. Alternatively, you can always select the Wizard Settings, which can prompt you in saving to CD-ROM. For a rookie, this is the safest bet.

2 For both AVI and QuickTime, there are additional pop-up menu selections that let you choose from Cinepak, Indeo, or Sorensen (QuickTime only) compression formats, among others.

> **NOTE** If you select Cinepak compression and your Premiere production is lengthy, the compression process itself may take hours. So you might want to plan on your computer being tied up for a long time during this process.

3 When you are finished changing your settings in the Export Movie Settings dialog box, click OK. You'll be prompted to save your file.

Export to Movie Settings

If you're exporting a plain old movie for generic purposes, you can use the tried-and-true Export Movie function, File | Export Timeline | Movie. You can also export an individual clip with the Export Movie command (File | Export Clip | Movie).

When you select this option, if you're satisfied with the current video and audio settings in this dialog box, just name the file and click Save. Otherwise, click the Settings button in the Export Movie dialog box to access the Export Movie Settings panels.

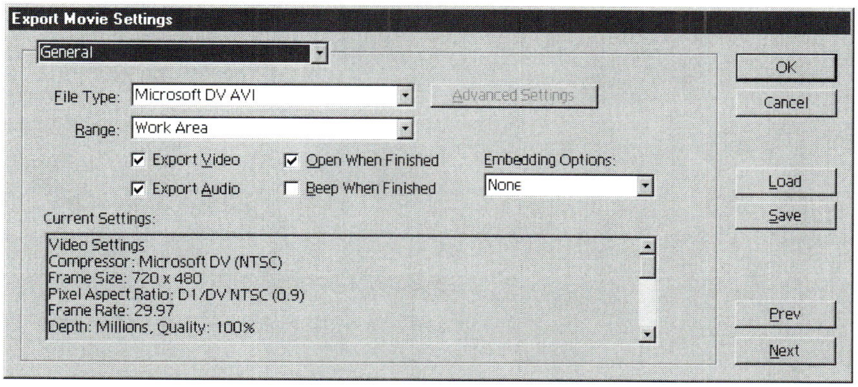

Click the Next button in the bottom right to navigate to the next panel. How long this whole process takes to render your final movie depends on several factors, such as the size of your movie, frame rate, frame size, and compression settings selected.

Keep in mind that although the video and audio settings you selected during the video-creation process might have seemed perfect for editing your movie at the time, they may not be the best way to go now for exporting and viewing purposes. For example, if you created a movie with a large frame size and high frame rate and now want to export it for web use, it may not play well at a typical home user's slow web-connection speed.

Thus, to obtain the best possible export of your movie for quality and relative speed in viewing on the Web, you may want to consider changing some of your export settings before exporting the file.

To Change EXPORT SETTINGS:

1. **Select the Settings button in the Export Movie dialog box to display the Export Movie Settings dialog box. You will be in the General settings panel as shown in the previous illustration. The selections are as follows:**
   - **File Type** Here you can select QuickTime, AVI format, still frames in GIF, TIF, or Windows Bitmap.
   - **Range** Depending on the final goal, you may choose to export the Entire Project or the Work Area specified in the Timeline.
   - **Export Video** This is an automatic default. If you don't want to export the video, deselect this.
   - **Export Audio** This is set to an automatic default. If you don't want to export audio, deselect this.
   - **Open When Finished** When this option is selected, your final movie will open in Premiere where you can play back the finished project.
   - **Save** By clicking Save, you can save and keep frequently used export settings.
   - **Load** When you click Load, you "load" those saved project settings.
2. **In the Video settings panel (click the Next button to access this), you can select from a wide range of compression schemes (codecs). Don't forget the goal: You must choose the best compression setting to produce the best quality with the smallest file size for your particular project.**

The following is a typical selection of codecs in the Compressor pop-up menu when QuickTime is selected in the General Settings dialog box. The selection will vary depending on your other settings:

- **Animation** Use this to create high-quality output. This setting works well for animation created in programs such as Photoshop. By setting the bit depth to Millions of Colors +, you are actually exporting an alpha channel with your movie.
- **Cinepak** Cinepak is a popular compression method because it works well for web and multimedia types of projects.
- **MJPEG-A, MJPEG-B** This choice is used for editing and capturing video; the compression provides good results.
- **Sorenson** This codec is great for high-quality desktop video for the Web and CD-ROM exporting. This selection offers better compression and quality than Cinepak.
- **Planner RGB** This choice can be used as an alternative to the Animation codec. It offers lossless compression and is suitable for work created in painting and 3D programs.
- **Video** Use this for video editing but not for exporting.
- **Component Video** Use this compression format for capturing analog video.
- **Graphics** Use this for graphics with 256 colors but not in desktop video.
- **Photo-JPEG** The image quality is good, but slow compression makes it unsuitable for desktop video.
- **H.263** This compression choice is used for video conferencing but is not recommended for video editing.
- **PNG** This setting is for still graphics and is included in QuickTime for the purpose of saving still graphics in PNG web format.
- **TIFF** This is a printing format for still images.
- **BMP** This is a Windows-compatible graphics format for use with still images.
- **DV-PAL and DV-NTSC** The choice depends on the geographic region for your audience and is used for transferring digitized data from DV camcorders into Premiere. This is primarily used for capturing video that will be transferred to another video-editing system.
- **None** This setting is for no compression used. You can create preview files very quickly in this setting, but the file sizes will be large.

When selecting any of these compression choices, you should always refer to the manufacturer's specifications because they relate to the hardware-specific codecs required for your capture board or computer.

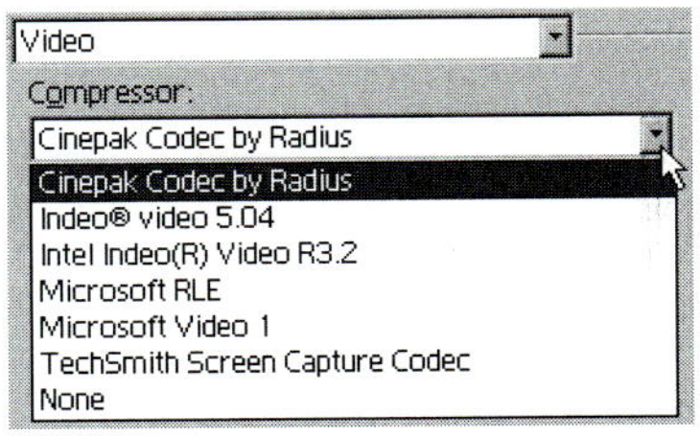

If you're exporting a Video for Windows file (AVI), the compressor choices in the Video panel include:

- **Cinepak Codec by Radius** Same as with QuickTime, a popular and common compression format because it works well for web and multimedia types of projects.
- **Indeo video 5.04** This codec offers good image quality and is often used for capturing raw data.
- **Intel Indeo® Video 3.2** Similar to the Cinepak codec, this scheme generates acceptable quality resolution. This is codec has been around for a while and it relies on older compression methods.
- **Microsoft RLE (Run Length Encoding)** Because the bit depth is restricted to 256 colors, it is suited only to animation created in painting programs with 256 colors. You can obtain lossless compression when you set the Quality slider to high.
- **Microsoft Video 1** This older codec generates low-quality output.
- **TechSmith Screen Capture Codec** Most likely, you won't see this codec in your compressor options because this codec is specific to my configuration. Depending upon your hardware and software configuration you may see additional codecs listed here.
- **None** Selecting this option will export the production without compression, resulting in a very large file size.

When you export your final movie, you'll sometimes want to change the audio settings as well as the video settings.

> **TIP** **For a more complete description of all codecs used in the industry, and some direction on when and how to use them, check out www.icanstream.tv/codeccentral.codecs.**

To Change AUDIO SETTINGS:

- **Choose Audio from the Export Movie Settings dialog box. From here, select one of the following:**

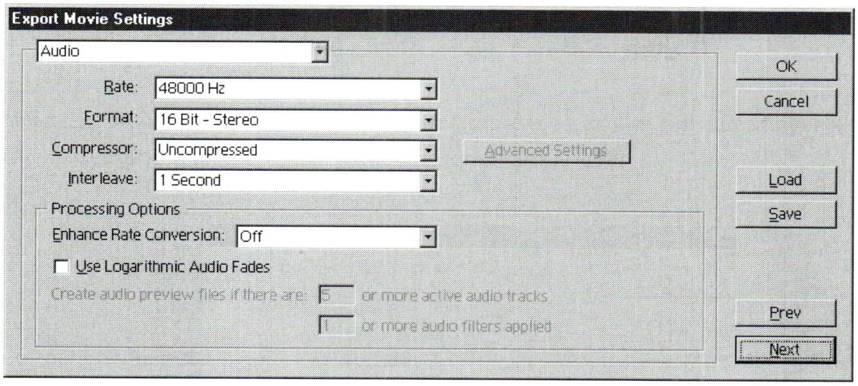

- **Rate** When you lower the Rate setting, you reduce the file size and speed up rendering. As you know, higher rates produce better quality and increase processing time.
- **Format** When you choose lower bit depths, you produce smaller files and reduce rendering times.
- **Compressor** In the Compressor pop-up menu, choose a compressor if you want.
- **Interleave** This choice determines how frequently audio will be inserted into the video frames.
- **Enhance Rate Conversion** This option controls audio quality.
- **Use Logarithmic Audio Fades** This selection allows for the most natural changes in the sounds.

If you want to compress a sound, you would choose among QuickTime audio codecs. In most cases on modern computers, audio compression is unnecessary. You normally need to work with compressed audio only when creating files for web delivery. These are your choices:

- **µLaw 2:1** This is a common audio format on the UNIX platform.
- **16-bit Endian and 16-bit Little Endian** Used primarily by hardware engineers and software developers.
- **24-bit integer and 32-bit integer soft** Used primarily by hardware engineers and software developers.
- **IMA designed by the Interactive Multimedia Association** Because this is a cross-platform format, it can be used to compress audio for multimedia.
- **32-bit floating point and 64-bit floating point** Used primarily by hardware engineers and software developers.

- **Alaw 2:1** Used for European digital telephony.
- **Qdesign Music** This is frequently used for high-quality web output.
- **Qualcomm Pure Voice** A speech format.
- **MACE 3:1 and MACE 6:1** These are Mac audio codecs used for QuickTime movies for both the PC and Mac.

Special Processing

Special Processing lets you further customize your movie settings. You can do things such as crop clips a certain way or apply some special effects that are geared toward really tweaking a file for low-bandwidth playback. You may never use this setting because of all the terrific new web/CD options offered in the new plug-ins. Nevertheless, it's good to know they exist in your Premiere bag of tricks because you never know when you may need them for a special situation.

You access Special Processing Options from the Export Movie dialog box.

To Select Special Processing options:

1. **Select the Settings button in the Export Movie dialog box.**
2. **Select Special Processing from the pop-up menu.**
3. **Click the Modify button to access the Special Processing dialog box. In this box, you can select from many settings. Also there's a Preview thumbnail at the top of the box to let you see your settings applied.**

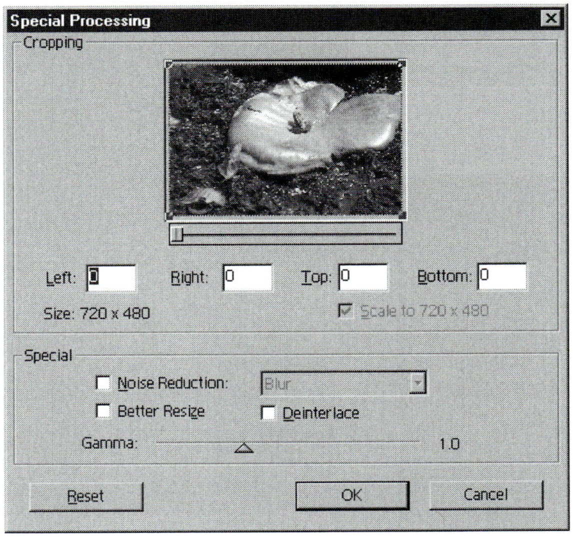

   - **Cropping box** **Lets you resize the movie to trim off black edges that might have occurred around the frames during capture or processing. To crop your output, drag the little handles in the corner of the Preview or type in the new dimensions.**
   - **Noise Reduction** **Blurs the image slightly, which may help improve the quality of low-resolution or noisy footage. When you check**

Noise Reduction, a pop-up menu is displayed from which you can select three different types of standard blurs.

- **Better Resize (under Special)** If the frame output size differs from the source clips, this setting resizes the movie while trying to maintain as much quality as possible.
- **Gamma slider** Adjusts the midtones of the clip. This setting doesn't affect the higher and lower levels of tonal value.

You may find the special processing options useful. One thing is for sure: You won't feel as if your output options are limited in Premiere.

Exporting to Various Still-Image Formats

This chapter wouldn't be complete without covering still-image formats. Often you'll have to isolate specific frames in your video for various purposes. This is easy to do in Premiere. What's more, after your still file is exported, you can import it into Adobe Photoshop to refine the image.

Let's examine some common popular file formats.

To Export a frame to a GIF file:

1. Drag the Edit line to a frame on the Timeline that you want to export.
2. Select File | Export Timeline | Frame.
3. In the dialog box, type in a name for the file and navigate to the place you want it saved.
4. Click the Settings button to specify the file type you want to save this to.
5. In the Still Frame Settings dialog box, select GIF from the pop-up menu. Other still-image selections include TIFF, TARGA, and Windows Bitmap. You can also select the Advanced Button to indicate transparency and dither options for the GIF.
6. When done, click OK to return to the main dialog box.

A sample still image is displayed so you can see what it looks like. Pretty simple, isn't it?

EXPORTING A SEQUENCE

You can export to an image sequence by selecting a clip or specific work area on the Timeline. A sequence is a series of still images that are generated based on the frame range selected. This might be the frame range in a clip or a work area. When this sequence is imported into an animation program such as Flash or a program that lets you assemble animated GIFs such as ImageReady or Fireworks, you can re-create an animated version of your video. To reduce file size, you can systematically eliminate frames in your program of choice. You can create some interesting effects using still-image sequences.

To Create A STILL-IMAGE SEQUENCE:

1. **Select a clip or work area in the Timeline.**
2. **Select File | Export Timeline | Movie.**
3. **In the Export Movie dialog box, click the Settings button.**

4 **In the General panel of the Export Still Frame Settings dialog box, from the File Type pop-up menu, select the sequence format you want to generate, as shown in Figure 12-12. You can choose among the following sequences:**

- **GIF**
- **Targa**
- **TIFF**
- **Windows Bitmap**

You can also select Animated GIF from the Settings menu. Doing this assembles the GIF sequence for you as an animated GIF.

Export in a Filmstrip Format

Because Premiere and Photoshop are "sister" applications in Adobe's world of computer graphics, web design, and animation, it's understandable that Adobe's design of the Filmstrip format was undertaken primarily to function as a bridge to facilitate interaction between these two programs.

When you create a video clip in Premiere and then load it into Photoshop as a Filmstrip file, you can view each individual video frame so that you can also use Photoshop's expansive color-correction tools and filters to adjust, correct, and/or retouch your individual frames.

You can also use this technique to create what's called "rotoscoping." This essentially means painting over a filmstrip to create some unusual effects (Figure 12-13).

FIGURE 12-12 In the General panel of the Export Still Frame Settings dialog box, you can export to a still image

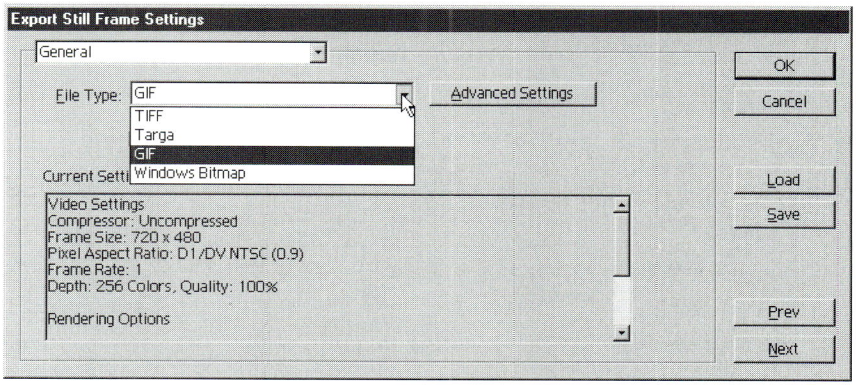

FIGURE 12-13
You can paint over filmstrip files to create interesting effects

The formidable masking features in Photoshop let you isolate areas and manipulate the shades, gradations, and colors of your video clips.

Additionally, once you've imported your filmstrip from Premiere into Photoshop, you can copy and paste images from one clip to another and take a piece from a photo and paste it into a frame in your video clip. You can also use the cloning tool in Photoshop to remove a person from a video clip.

If you want to use Photoshop to manipulate, color-correct, or retouch a video frame that was created in Premiere, you must convert the video clip to a Filmstrip format.

To export to a filmstrip, follow the same steps as for exporting to GIF Sequence (File | Export Timelines | Movie Settings | File type). For File Type, select Filmstrip from the pop-up menu.

To save a file in the Filmstrip format, you use the same procedure you used to export to a file sequence or an animated GIF. The file is saved with the .flm extension.

To Open a Filmstrip in Photoshop:

1. **Open a clip by choosing File | Open.**
2. **Navigate to the place on your hard drive where the .flm file is located and open it in Photoshop.**

FIGURE 12-14
When you open a filmstrip file in Photoshop, you can manipulate it as a still image and save it back out again when done; then reopen it in Premiere

3 **Use the tools in Photoshop to enhance or modify the properties of the filmstrip (Figure 12-14).**

4 **When done, save the file again and leave it in the .flm format.**

5 **Import it back into Premiere and add it to your Timeline to integrate it with the rest of your production.**

NOTE **Because a filmstrip contains all the frames in your clip in a single file, it can get really huge and you may need a lot of RAM dedicated to Photoshop to open and work with it.**

You may want to refer to your Adobe Photoshop software manual for a more specific review of the enhancement techniques, which you may choose to use.

With all these output options, you're certain to find one that works well with your particular production. Because exporting is the final destination of your production, it's important to get to know all the settings well to make certain you choose the one that fits the requirements of the production.

ON THE VIRTUAL CLASSROOM CD-ROM **In Lesson 10, "Getting Your Production on Tape," the instructor walks you through the process of exporting a production to tape using device control.**

Appendix A

Premiere Guide to Shortcut Keys

SHORTCUT KEYBOARD COMMANDS FOR CAPTURING VIDEO IN THE MOVIE CAPTURE WINDOW

COMMAND	WINDOWS	MAC
Play	SPACEBAR or L	SPACEBAR or L
Play slowly	SHIFT-L	SHIFT-L
Play Reverse slowly	SHIFT-J	SHIFT-J
Set clip In point	1	1
Set clip Out point	O	O
Record*	G	G
Record In to Out	ALT-record button	OPTION-record button
Go to capture In point	Q	Q
Go to capture Out point	W	W
Stop*	S	S
Pause	SPACEBAR or K	SPACEBAR or K
Fast forward (while playing or stopped)	F or L	F or L
Step forward 1 frame	RIGHT ARROW or 2	RIGHT ARROW or 2
Step backward 1 frame	LEFT ARROW or 1	LEFT ARROW or 1
Rewind (while playing or stopped)	R or J	R or J
Move through editable fields	TAB	TAB
Remove focus from all fields	ESC	ESC
Log	ENTER	RETURN
Eject	SHIFT-E	SHIFT-E

* This selection is available when capturing without device control; all others require device control.

SHORTCUT KEYBOARD COMMANDS FOR CAPTURING STOP MOTION VIDEO IN THE STOP MOTION WINDOW

COMMAND	WINDOWS	MAC
Record	SPACEBAR or G	SPACEBAR or G
Done	ESC	ESC
Capture 1 to 9 frames	Type number from 1 to 9	Type number from 1 to 9
Capture 10 frames	0 (zero)	0 (zero)
Remove most recent frame	NA	DELETE

SHORTCUT KEYBOARD COMMANDS FOR OPENING AND EDITING A CLIP IN THE PROJECT, BIN, STORYBOARD, OR TIMELINE WINDOWS

COMMAND	WINDOWS	MAC
Open clip in Trim mode (only in Timeline)	SHIFT-double-click clip	SHIFT-double-click clip
Open master clip (only in Timeline)	CONTROL-SHIFT-double-click clip	COMMAND-SHIFT-double-click clip
Edit original	Select clip, CONTROL-E	Select clip, COMMAND-E

SHORTCUT KEYBOARD COMMANDS FOR CHANGING VIEW OPTIONS IN THE TIMELINE WINDOW

COMMAND	WINDOWS	MAC
Cycle through icon sizes	CONTROL-[or]	COMMAND-[or]
Cycle through track formats	CONTROL-SHIFT-[or]	COMMAND-SHIFT-[or]
Specify area to fit in Timeline	Drag the Zoom tool	Drag the Zoom tool
Display entire project in Timeline	Slash (\)	Slash (\)

Shortcut Keyboard Commands for Moving Around in the Monitor, Timeline, or Clip Windows

COMMAND	WINDOWS	MAC
Move edit line to first frame	A, UP ARROW, or HOME	A, UP ARROW, or HOME
Move edit line to last frame	S, DOWN ARROW, or END	S, DOWN ARROW, or END
Move edit line forward 1 frame	2 or RIGHT ARROW	2 or RIGHT ARROW
Move edit line backward 1 frame	1 or LEFT ARROW	1 or LEFT ARROW
Move edit line forward 5 frames	4 or SHIFT-RIGHT ARROW	4 or SHIFT-RIGHT ARROW
Move edit line backward 5 frames	3 or SHIFT-LEFT ARROW	3 or SHIFT-LEFT ARROW
Move edit line to next edit point (not in Clip window)	CONTROL-SHIFT-RIGHT ARROW or PAGE DOWN	COMMAND-SHIFT-RIGHT ARROW or PAGE DOWN
Move edit line to previous point (not in Clip window)	CONTROL-SHIFT-LEFT ARROW or PAGE UP	COMMAND-SHIFT-LEFT ARROW or PAGE UP

Shortcut Keyboard Commands for Previewing in the Monitor, Timeline, or Clip Windows

COMMAND	WINDOWS	MAC
Preview	ENTER	RETURN
Play	SPACEBAR, tilde (~), or L	SPACEBAR, tilde (~), or L
Stop	SPACEBAR or K	SPACEBAR or K
Play from edit line to Out point*	ALT-~	OPTION-~
Play from In point to Out point	ALT-SHIFT-~	OPTION-SHIFT-~
Loop from In point to Out point	CONTROL-SHIFT-~	COMMAND-SHIFT-~
Play faster	Press ~ or L more than once as needed	Press ~ or L more than once as needed

* This keyboard command is not available if you use the Input Method Editor (IME) to type double-byte characters.

Continued

SHORTCUT KEYBOARD COMMANDS FOR PREVIEWING IN THE MONITOR, TIMELINE, OR CLIP WINDOWS *Continued*

COMMAND	WINDOWS	MAC
Play from preroll to postroll	CONTROL- – or ALT-click Play button	COMMAND- – or OPTION-click Play button
Reverse	CONTROL-ALT- – or J	COMMAND-OPTION- – or J
Scrub without rendering	Drag edit line in the Timeline time ruler	Drag edit line in the Timeline time ruler
Scrub with transitions, effects, and superimposing being visible	ALT-drag edit line in the Timeline time ruler	OPTION-drag edit line in the Timeline time ruler
Scrub with alpha channel visible only	ALT-SHIFT-drag edit line in the Timeline time ruler	OPTION-SHIFT-drag edit line in the Timeline time ruler

SHORTCUT KEYBOARD COMMANDS FOR SETTING IN AND OUT POINTS IN THE MONITOR, TIMELINE, OR CLIP WINDOWS

COMMAND	WINDOWS	MAC
Set In point at edit line	I, E, or CONTROL-ALT-UP ARROW	I, E, or COMMAND-OPTION-UP ARROW
Set Out point at edit line	O, R, or CONTROL-ALT-DOWN ARROW	O, R, or COMMAND-OPTION-DOWN ARROW
Clear In point	D	D
Clear Out point	F	F
Clear both In and Out points	G	G
Go to Clip In point	CONTROL-UP ARROW	COMMAND-UP ARROW
Go to Timeline In point	Q	Q
Go to Timeline Out point	W	W

Shortcut Keyboard Commands for Editing in the Program View or Timeline

COMMAND	WINDOWS	MAC
Target next track above current video target	CONTROL-+ (plus)	COMMAND-+ (plus)
Target next track below current video target	CONTROL-– (minus)	COMMAND-– (minus)
Target next track above current audio target	CONTROL-SHIFT-+	COMMAND-SHIFT-+
Target next track below current audio target	CONTROL-SHIFT-–	COMMAND-SHIFT-–
Go to next edit point	CONTROL-SHIFT-RIGHT ARROW or PAGE DOWN	COMMAND-SHIFT-RIGHT ARROW or PAGE DOWN
Go to previous edit point	CONTROL-SHIFT-LEFT ARROW or PAGE UP	COMMAND-SHIFT-LEFT ARROW or PAGE UP
Ripple edit 1 frame to left of edit line	ALT-LEFT ARROW	OPTION-LEFT ARROW
Ripple edit 1 frame to right of edit line	ALT-RIGHT ARROW	OPTION-RIGHT ARROW
Ripple edit 5 frames to left of edit line	ALT-SHIFT-LEFT ARROW	OPTION-SHIFT-LEFT ARROW
Ripple edit 5 frames to right of edit line	ALT-SHIFT-RIGHT ARROW	OPTION-SHIFT-RIGHT ARROW
Rolling edit 1 frame to left of edit line*	ALT-UP ARROW	OPTION-UP ARROW
Rolling edit 1 frame to right of edit line*	ALT-DOWN ARROW	OPTION-DOWN ARROW
Rolling edit 5 frames to left of edit line*	ALT-SHIFT-UP ARROW	OPTION-SHIFT-UP ARROW
Rolling edit 5 frames to right of edit line*	ALT-SHIFT-DOWN ARROW	OPTION-SHIFT-DOWN ARROW
Match edit-line frame with identical frame in master clip	T	T

* Using the rolling edit requires that you take extra footage beyond the clip In and Out points.

SHORTCUT KEYBOARD COMMANDS FOR EDITING ONLY IN THE MONITOR WINDOW

COMMAND	WINDOWS	MAC
Toggle between Monitor and Timeline windows	CONTROL-TAB	COMMAND-TAB
Toggle between Source and Program views	ESC	ESC
Insert source clip at edit line	, (comma)	, (comma)
Overlay source clip at edit line	. (period)	. (period)
Delete clip from Source view	View clip, then press CONTROL-BACKSPACE	View clip, then press COMMAND-DELETE
Lift the range of frames marked by In and Out points out of the project	/	/

SHORTCUT KEYBOARD COMMANDS FOR EDITING ONLY IN THE TIMELINE WINDOW

COMMAND	WINDOWS	MAC
Move selected clip left 1 frame	ALT-, (comma)	OPTION-, (comma)
Move selected clip right 1 frame	ALT-. (period)	OPTION-. (period)
Move selected clip left 5 frames	ALT-SHIFT-, (comma)	OPTION-SHIFT-, (comma)
Move selected clip right 5 frames	ALT-SHIFT-. (period)	OPTION-SHIFT-. (period)
Delete selected clip	BACKSPACE	DELETE
Delete selected clip using a ripple deletion	ALT-BACKSPACE	OPTION-DELETE
Delete preview file for selected clip	CONTROL-BACKSPACE	COMMAND-DELETE
Delete all preview files in the Timeline	CONTROL-ALT-SHIFT and click preview indicator	COMMAND-SHIFT-OPTION and click preview indicator
Cycle through timecode display format	CONTROL-click time ruler	COMMAND-click time ruler

Continued

SHORTCUT KEYBOARD COMMANDS FOR EDITING ONLY IN THE TIMELINE WINDOW *Continued*

COMMAND	WINDOWS	MAC
Set work area bar to full width of current window view	Double-click work bar area	Double-click work bar area
Set work area bar to continuous sequence of clips	ALT-click work area bar	OPTION-click work area bar
Set work area start	CONTROL-SHIFT-click work area bar	COMMAND-SHIFT-click work area bar
Set work area start at edit line	ALT-[(left bracket)	OPTION-[(left bracket)
Set work area end	CONTROL-ALT-click work area bar	COMMAND-OPTION-click work area bar
Set work area end at edit line	ALT-] (right bracket)	OPTION-] (right bracket)
Edit transition settings	Double-click transition	Double-click transition
Edit transition custom settings (if available for the applied transition)	ALT-double-click transition	OPTION-double-click transition
Slip selected clip left 1 frame*	CONTROL-ALT-LEFT ARROW	COMMAND-OPTION-LEFT ARROW
Slip selected clip right 1 frame*	CONTROL-ALT-RIGHT ARROW	COMMAND-OPTION-RIGHT ARROW
Slip selected clip left 5 frames*	CONTROL-ALT-SHIFT-LEFT ARROW	COMMAND-OPTION-SHIFT-LEFT ARROW
Slip selected clip right 5 frames*	CONTROL-ALT-SHIFT-RIGHT ARROW	COMMAND-OPTION-SHIFT-RIGHT ARROW
Slide selected clip left 1 frame*	ALT-LEFT ARROW	OPTION-LEFT ARROW
Slide selected clip right 1 frame*	ALT-RIGHT ARROW	OPTION-RIGHT ARROW
Slide selected clip left 5 frames*	ALT-SHIFT-LEFT ARROW	OPTION-SHIFT-LEFT ARROW
Slide selected clip right 5 frames*	ALT-SHIFT-RIGHT ARROW	OPTION-SHIFT-RIGHT ARROW

* To use slip and slide, you will require extra footage beyond the clip In and Out points as well as clips that are adjacent in time.

SHORTCUT KEYBOARD COMMANDS FOR WORKING WITH MARKERS IN THE MONITOR, TIMELINE, OR CLIP WINDOWS

COMMAND	WINDOWS	MAC
Set numbered clip marker at edit line	CONTROL-ALT- (0–9)	COMMAND-OPTION- (0–9)
Set unnumbered clip marker at edit line	CONTROL-ALT- = (equal sign)	COMMAND-OPTION- = (equal sign)
Go to first clip marker	CONTROL-SHIFT-UP ARROW	COMMAND-SHIFT-UP ARROW
Go to last clip marker	CONTROL-SHIFT-DOWN ARROW	COMMAND-SHIFT-DOWN ARROW
Go to previous clip marker	CONTROL-LEFT ARROW	COMMAND-LEFT ARROW
Go to next clip marker	CONTROL-RIGHT ARROW	COMMAND-RIGHT ARROW
Go to numbered clip marker	CONTROL- (0–9)	COMMAND- (0–9)
Clear a clip marker	Go to marker, then press CONTROL-SHIFT-C	Go to marker, then press COMMAND-SHIFT-C
Clear all clip markers	CONTROL-ALT-SHIFT-C	COMMAND-OPTION-SHIFT-C
Set numbered Timeline marker at edit line	ALT-SHIFT- (0–9)	OPTION-SHIFT- (0–9)
Set unnumbered Timeline marker at edit line	* (asterisk on numeric keypad) or ALT-SHIFT- =	* (asterisk on numeric keypad) or OPTION-SHIFT- =
Go to first Timeline marker	CONTROL-SHIFT-UP ARROW	COMMAND-SHIFT-UP ARROW
Go to last Timeline marker	CONTROL-SHIFT-DOWN ARROW	COMMAND-SHIFT-DOWN ARROW
Go to previous Timeline marker	SHIFT-Q	SHIFT-Q
Go to next Timeline marker	SHIFT-W	SHIFT-W
Go to numbered Timeline marker	SHIFT- (0–9)	SHIFT- (0–9)
Clear a Timeline marker	Go to marker, then press CONTROL-SHIFT-G	Go to marker, then press COMMAND-SHIFT-G
Clear all Timeline markers	CONTROL-ALT-SHIFT-G	COMMAND-OPTION-SHIFT-G

SHORTCUT KEYBOARD COMMANDS WHEN WORKING IN TRIM MODE

COMMAND	WINDOWS	MAC
Toggle between Monitor and Trim views	CONTROL-T	COMMAND-T
Go to next edit point	CONTROL-SHIFT-RIGHT ARROW or PAGE DOWN	COMMAND-SHIFT-RIGHT ARROW or PAGE DOWN
Go to previous edit point	CONTROL-SHIFT-LEFT ARROW or PAGE UP	COMMAND-SHIFT-LEFT ARROW or PAGE UP
Trim left of edit line by 1 frame	LEFT ARROW	LEFT ARROW
Trim right of edit line by 1 frame	RIGHT ARROW	RIGHT ARROW
Trim left of edit line by 5 frames	SHIFT-LEFT ARROW	SHIFT-LEFT ARROW
Trim right of edit line by 5 frames	SHIFT-RIGHT ARROW	SHIFT-RIGHT ARROW

SHORTCUT KEYBOARD COMMANDS WHEN WORKING IN TITLE WINDOW

COMMAND	WINDOWS	MAC
Add to text size by 1 point	Select text-CONTROL-ALT-RIGHT ARROW	Select text-COMMAND-OPTION-RIGHT ARROW
Decrease text size by 1 point	Select text-CONTROL-ALT-LEFT ARROW	Select text-COMMAND-OPTION-LEFT ARROW
Add to text size by 5 points	Select text-CONTROL-ALT-SHIFT-RIGHT ARROW	Select text-COMMAND-OPTION-LEFT ARROW
Decrease text size by 5 points	Select text-CONTROL-ALT-SHIFT-LEFT ARROW	Select text-COMMAND-OPTION-LEFT ARROW
Increase kerning by 1 unit	ALT-RIGHT ARROW	OPTION-RIGHT ARROW

Continued

SHORTCUT KEYBOARD COMMANDS WHEN WORKING IN TITLE WINDOW *Continued*

COMMAND	WINDOWS	MAC
Decrease kerning by 1 unit	ALT-LEFT ARROW	OPTION-LEFT ARROW
Add to leading by 1 unit	ALT-DOWN ARROW	OPTION-DOWN ARROW
Decrease leading by 1 unit	ALT-UP ARROW	OPTION-UP ARROW
Add to leading by 5 units	ALT-SHIFT-DOWN ARROW	OPTION-SHIFT-DOWN ARROW
Decrease leading by 5 units	ALT-SHIFT-UP ARROW	OPTION-SHIFT-UP ARROW
Move selected object by 1 pixel	UP ARROW, DOWN ARROW, LEFT ARROW, or RIGHT ARROW	UP ARROW, DOWN ARROW, LEFT ARROW, or RIGHT ARROW
Move selected object by 5 pixels	SHIFT-UP ARROW, DOWN ARROW, LEFT ARROW, OR RIGHT ARROW	SHIFT-UP ARROW, DOWN ARROW, LEFT ARROW, OR RIGHT ARROW
Set background to black	B	B
Set background to white	W	W
Reset color and shadow swatches to default colors	Z	Z
Turn draft mode on or off*	~	~
Select next object lower in stacking order	, (comma) or < (left angle bracket)	, (comma) or < (left angle bracket)
Select next object higher in stacking order	. (period) or > (right angle bracket)	. (period) or > (right angle bracket)

* The ~ (tilde) is not available if you are using the Input Method Editor (IME) to type double-byte characters.

Shortcut Keyboard Commands When Working in the Audio Mixer Window

COMMAND	WINDOWS	MAC
Reset pan to default or 0 (zero)	ALT-click pan control	OPTION-click pan control
Reset volume to default or 0 (zero)	ALT-click volume control	OPTION-click volume control

Shortcut Keyboard Commands in Timeline Tool Toggles Window (to Temporarily Activate a Related Tool)

IF YOU WANT THIS TOOL	WHEN IN THIS TOOL	WINDOWS	MAC
Selection	Any tool except Selection	CONTROL	COMMAND
Link/Unlink	Selection tool	ALT-SHIFT (with a clip selected)	SHIFT-OPTION (with a clip selected)
Block move	Block Select	CONTROL-ALT	COMMAND-OPTION
Block copy	Block Select	ALT	OPTION
Multitrack Select	Track Select	ALT	OPTION
Multirazor	Razor	ALT	OPTION
Slide	Slip	ALT	OPTION
Fade Adjustment tool	Selection	CONTROL-ALT-SHIFT when over a rubber band	COMMAND-OPTION-SHIFT when over a rubber band
Precise pan or volume	Selection	SHIFT-drag pan or volume rubber band	SHIFT-drag pan or volume rubber band
Add default transition at cursor (A/B Editing mode only)	Selection	CONTROL-ALT-SHIFT-click transition area	COMMAND-OPTION-SHIFT-click transition area

Appendix B

Premiere Virtual Classroom Web Resource Guide for Premiere and Digital Video

Today, digital video overflows into so many other disciplines, including digital video (DV), the Web, animation, and audio, that it's helpful to know at least a little about all related topics to see the complete picture. This is important because if you're going to be integrating animation, video, text, graphics, and sound to create multimedia projects, you'll no doubt have many questions along the way. Questions may include what software do you use for various types of output and what kind of file formats work in conjunction with other applications. If you're new to nonlinear editing and the world of multimedia, there's a whole world out there full of information and resources for you to explore. The following is a list of web resources on various topics for your reference.

NOTE **At the time of this writing, the following sites were all up and running. Because of the transient nature of the Web, sites are here today, gone tomorrow. If you happen upon one that no longer exists, know that it did at one time and move on to the next.**

Training/Tutorial/Technical Sources

This list includes places you can turn to for additional training as well as answers to various technical issues.

www.adobe.com

This is probably the first place you want to start. Adobe lists all sorts of training and technical sources for Premiere. This site is a little hard to navigate, so it isn't always easy to quickly find what you're looking for. Adobe does offer excellent user forums for Premiere (adobe.com/support/forums).

www.apple.com

Apple's site offers plenty of related tutorials, such as creating in QuickTime tracks, creating video and audio tracks, and streaming media. Many animation programs such as Flash and GoLive now support QuickTime tracks, and Premiere QuickTime formats can blend nicely with these other applications.

www.equip.zdnet.com

This site offers outstanding tutorials and technical notes on all aspects of Premiere.

WWW.DVDDEMYSTIFIED.COM

DVD's FAQs section is highly informative and definitely worth a visit.

WWW.VIDEOFILE.COM

This is a good place to look for articles and a video discussion board to obtain more information about DV and video production.

WWW.DV.COM

This site is a useful resource for free downloads, such as making a digital video appear as if it's on film, and a free subscription to an online newsletter.

WWW.DVWEBVIDEO.COM

This site provides the scoop on streaming video, tips, and web-animation tutorials using QuickTime movies.

WWW.DVCREATIONS.NET

Need a boot camp on the entire modern DV-creation process from camera to lighting to editing and delivery to get you up to speed? This is the place to find this type of information.

WWW.ARTSCHOOL.COM

This site is for the Center for Digital Imaging and Sound (CDIS), and it offers tutorials, forums, and other topics of DV interest.

WWW.STREAMINGMEDIA.COM

This all-inclusive site provides tutorials, a glossary of DV terms, product reviews, and a section of featured videos, case studies, and a job board.

WWW.DIGITALVIDEOEDITING.COM

Through this site's Techniques section, you will find tutorials in Premiere and a Market Directory for everything from audio to digital cameras to post–video-production hardware. Get out the credit card!

WWW.VIDEOGUYS.COM

This site not only sells equipment at discount prices but also offers a discussion forum providing answers to questions regarding DV capture cards, tips, tricks, a FireWire Q&A with a comparison chart, and issues related to Premiere 6.

WWW.SHURE.COM

This site offers downloadable technical publications such as *Guide to Audio Systems for Video Production* in addition to information about Shure's audio products.

WWW.INDIECLUB.COM

A filmmakers' networking site.

WWW.SONICNET.COM

This is the place to listen to audio and watch videos using RealPlayer.

WWW.NDIC.COM

Here you'll find informative articles about maximizing output quality of digital video, DV tips and tricks with Premiere, cool Premiere shortcuts, editing faster in Premiere, and online classes.

WWW.ONLINEFILMFESTIVAL.COM

This site offers resource buttons with links to sites on animation, equipment, and practically anything you can imagine related to the capture of motion pictures and music.

WWW.PLANETPOINT.COM

Looking for a job in the profession? Check out the online resume service. Directors, designers, editors, and other related professionals can post samples of their work. There are also plenty of high-quality QuickTime professional spots for viewing and assessing.

WWW.MOVIE.MAC.COM

This site offers articles, reviews, and sound. Although it's slanted toward Mac users, there's a lot of useful information that Windows users can apply in their movie-making pursuits.

www.knowpath.com

The Digital Institute of Video Arts site offers a plethora of tutorials, articles, forums, and other information.

www.digitalmediashopper.com

This site sells all kinds of DV equipment and offers free subscriptions to great DV trade newsletters such as *Digital Media Newsletter*, *WaveForm*, *TimeLine*, *DMN*, *Loud!*, *StreamLine*, and *Levels* with links to sign up for the newsletters.

www.bmrc.berkeley.edu

This is the Berkeley Resource Center, offering resources and how-to guides with more than 15 Premiere subjects and projects.

Audio (MP3, WAV, AIFF)

Readers looking for additional sound sources for their Premiere productions can explore these sites.

www.wavcentral.com

Be sure to check out this site for a database of the best sound available on the Web.

www.soundrangers.com

This site offers an expansive, downloadable sound library priced from $1.25 to $2.95.

www.webtechniques.com

This is a daily e-magazine that offers sometimes useful information and examples of video, audio, animation, and other kinds of multimedia seen on the Web. There are also job listings for professionals in the field.

www.sputnik7.com

This site offers MP3 downloads.

WWW.PLAYSTREAM.COM

Playstream offers pay-as-you-use streaming media services for streaming audio and video. They work with individuals as well as companies. You can stream in popular formats like Real Media, QuickTime, and MP3.

The following are some MP3 sites worth checking out:

WWW.LISTEN.ZDNET.COM

This expansive section of zdnet's site contains free music downloads from 75,000 bands.

WWW.EMUSIC.COM

Here you can download music for one low monthly fee.

WWW.MP3.COM

Check out this site for a wealth of information from CD burning to MP3 gadgets. The site also offers free music of many types and reviews of software and hardware.

WWW.BESONIC.COM

At this site you can play and download music. Also available are a forum, chat, and topics of interest.

WWW.AUDIOGALAXY.COM

Here you can download MP3 music and obtain players and plug-ins to alter your MP3 music. Of particular interest are the numerous utilities you can download to facilitate your MP3 playback. Also offered on this site is lots of music for you to browse through.

WWW.INSOUND.COM

This great site provides reviews of musical videos, film shorts, and the ability to download thousands of free MP3 tracks from your favorite artists and labels.

WWW.HOLLYWOODEDGE.COM

Want free sound effects for your movie-editing project? On this site you can obtain many sound effects—anything from landing a spaceship to hitting a baseball. The site also has an extensive library where you can download sound for a fee.

www.vitaminic.com

This site offers a sizable and eclectic collection of quality music.

www.epitonic.com

This site specializes in current and popular music. Here you can peruse tracks, subscribe to an online newsletter, download files, and stream their music pages. You can also stream entire albums.

Audio-Editing Applications and File-Conversion Links

Obviously, you can do a little sound mixing in Premiere. For those of you who want to get serious about editing your digital audio, depending on your configuration, you'll need an audio-editing application. Here are some selections for both Mac and PC platforms.

For the PC:

- www.goldwave.com (Goldwave)
- www.soundforge.com (SoundForge)
- www.syntrillium.com (Cool Edit 2000)

For the Mac:

- www.kagi.com (Sound Maker and Convert Machine)
- www.macromedia.com (SoundEdit 16)

For those of you who want to create and mix your own techno sounds for Premiere productions, try any one of these sound-mixing applications:

- Rebirth from Propellerheads
- MixMan from Sonic Foundry
- Groovemaker from Sonic Foundry
- Acid from Sonic Foundry

These sound-mixing programs are so much fun, you'll feel like you're at an all-night rave!

Tips and Techniques

As a high-profile tool for DV editing, Premiere employs the best of tools to finely craft your production and then output to leading formats for many types of media. Because Premiere offers such a comprehensive mix of professional video-editing tools, you may want to review some of these sites and take a look at "the bag of tips and techniques" for working with some of these sophisticated tools.

www.ndic.com/videotricks.html

This site offers great tips and techniques for video editing, including how-tos on a textured look, layering movies, panning across a still image, speeding up editing in Premiere, and shortcuts in Premiere.

www.videomaker.com

Here you can find NLE (nonlinear editing) information about videography.

www.adobe.forum.com

This is a user forum from Adobe about Premiere.

Inspirational Video Sites

Sometimes the best way to get ideas on how to develop a video production is to review video sites that either inspire you or drive you nuts because they're in such bad taste. Here is a wide selection of sites that offer much inspiration and idea-generation in case you need that one little spark of an idea and can't seem to find it.

www.bmwfilms.com

This site is extremely interesting and currently one of the most popular around. Here, you can download the free BMWPlayer plug-in, which enables DVD-like playback of BMW movies and allows access to larger-format films. BMW films feature short works from award-winning movie directors.

www.altpick.com

Altpick offers previews of artists who create moving images, animations, films, and videos and also features interviews with artists from all types of media. This site also offers neophyte videomakers the opportunity to post new and experimental work for viewing and critiquing by others in the field.

www.storyfarm.com

This is a small but growing company of musicians, artists, videographers, and designers using digital media to tell their stories. A special feature is a short film entitled *The Eye of Rudra*, a DV production.

www.thewomb.com

This site offers what they call a "digital rebirth of sound" with all sorts of strange and inspiring digital music.

www.itworld.com

This site runs video and audio combinations for review and critiques on various business subjects relevant to the Web, video production, and business-to-business sites (B2B).

www.billabong-usa.com

This award-winning site is a feast for the creative eye. It combines the best of all popular media: video, sound, Flash animation, and interactivity. The site includes many frame-by-frame images edited in Premiere that create a rhythmic pulse. Pickled, the Movie, offers an online moviemaker, where you can throw together a movie on the actual site and e-mail it to your friends. How'd they do that? Read about it in the book called *Flash Deconstruct* (New Riders, 2001).

Movie Streaming and Film Sites

The Internet is changing the way movies are made and distributed through a relatively new phenomenon called streaming movies. These sites provide streaming films for you to watch and critique. Most of these sites let users stream feature-length and short films on demand. In some cases, you may have to download a media player if you don't have it on your computer. These sites are especially useful for those of you making videos on the Web.

WWW.IFILM.COM

This site offers online movies to review and a great place to put up your movies.

WWW.REELMIND.COM

On this site, you can put up an 18-minute film, animation, or music, as a living resume. Your work of art can contain up to 5MB of supporting visuals and artwork. This company will take care of compressing and encoding of your video when you send in a tape.

WWW.ONLINEFILMFESTIVAL.COM

This site offers a film database along with message and discussion boards.

WWW.ATOMFILMS.COM

This site is for the short-film market. You can submit your file or VHS tape, and, if they like it, they'll give you an exclusive contract for production.

WWW.EVEO.COM

This site is also for the short-film market. It's about three minutes long and applies to all skill levels.

WWW.ZEROONEFILMS.COM

This is another film site offering a database of films for viewing.

WWW.FILMFILM.COM

This is another film site offering a database of films for viewing. This should help get your creative juices flowing.

WWW.SPUTNIK7.COM

This site has mostly music videos; however, it also features video stations, videos on demand, MP3 downloads, and related content.

WWW.CINEMANOW.COM

This site allows viewing by genre of movie with downloads and other items.

QuickTime

QuickTime, a popular editing format on both the Mac and Windows platforms, lets users with the QT plug-in play back high-quality audio and video on their computers. Because QuickTime has become a universal format, there are many sites devoted to the subject of QuickTime and movies viewed in QuickTime.

www.apple.com/quicktime/download

This site features movie trailers and hot picks where you can tune into QuickTime TV to see streamed live or on-demand music and videos, gaming videos, and a cubic VR gallery.

www.iarchitect.com

This site, from Isys Information Architects, offers a solid review of QuickTime Player and a list of related articles that provide complete information about QuickTime.

Stock Video Footage

These sites offer prerecorded video for incorporating into a video production that might require a video clip you can't digitize yourself. Much of the higher-priced footage was shot on film, so the quality is incredible. They also offer libraries of online and instantly accessible databases of thousands of hours of stock footage from around the world on every topic and subject.

www.videouniversity.com

This site offers a $19.95 guide to public domain footage (generally not as good quality as fancy stock footage) and articles about producing video.

The following are all excellent sources for stock digital footage:

www.artbeats.com

Artbeats clips are used throughout this book, so we have a special affection for their collection.

The following are also excellent resources for hard-to-find footage:

- www.busybox.com
- www.corbisimages.com
- www.eyewire.com
- www.dv-stock-footage.com
- www.k5kj.net
- www.oddballfilm.com
- www.photospin.com
- www.stockart.com
- www.stockmarket.com
- www.stormvideo.com
- www.videosource.com
- www.videostate.com

Trade Shows/Conferences and Special Events Related to Digital Video

To keep your skills polished and your overall knowledge of the field up-to-date, check out the trade shows and conferences that are offered for digital video. You can also preview the latest equipment and software at these special events.

- www.aftereffectswest.com (After Effects West Conference)
- www.aiga.com (The National Design Center)
- www.bdaweb.com (Broadcast Designers Association)
- www.beaweb.org (Broadcast Education Association)
- www.dvexpo.com
- www.flashforwardinstitute.com (Flash Forward 2001)
- www.nab.org/conventions (National Association of Broadcasters)
- www.produceresconferences.com (Producers Conferences)
- www.siggraph.org

Associations

Membership in various associations relevant to your industry is usually helpful for staying in touch and in tune with your field of endeavor—especially if you're new to the field and need to learn how to jump into it. These organizations provide information, tutorials, links, forums, chat links, and much more to keep you abreast of the latest in DV technology.

www.dvpa.com (Digital Video Professionals Association)

When you join this organization ($15 membership), you gain access to a stock video collection. There are also links to desktop video, DV clips, and video-editing information.

www.dvda.org (DVD Association)

This is a DVD developers networking association for educators, trainers, fine artists, and professionals of many other disciplines.

www.ibcnews.com (IBC News)

This association offers a WorldWide Users Group Digital Media Techniques Library—with articles on Premiere, After Effects, and other software. Also, there are examples of works from various videographers and samples from current video festivals.

Equipment

These sites offer a plethora of information about equipment used in digital video such as video-capture cards, DV camcorders, and cameras.

www.adobe.com/premiere

This site offers, among other things, links to companies that sell Premiere-approved hardware such as capture cards. From the Adobe site, under Premiere, click the Capture Cards link.

www.videoguys.com

Videoguys sells all sorts of DV-related equipment, such as FireWire cards, DV camcorders, and fast SCSI drives. The company also offers compatibility charts to help you determine the best configuration for your system.

www.equip.zdnet.com

This site offers product reviews for DV equipment.

www.apple.com

Apple's web site offers a wealth of information on compatible equipment and peripherals suitable for doing DV on your Mac workstation.

www.dvdirect.com

This site offers featured product reviews and a subscription to its *DV Direction* newsletter.

www.canon.com

Canon's site offers much information about DV cameras and camcorders and the best fit for your computer's configuration.

www.dell.com

Dell's web site offers information and pricing regarding Dell's DV computer configurations.

www.jvc.com

JVC's site offers information and pricing on its line of DV capture cards.

www.photovideo.com

Here is a large selection of new and used video-related equipment and peripherals.

Miscellaneous Resources

These sites cover the gamut from writers' resources to tools and reviews on DV.

www.digitalmedia.net

This extensive site offers a variety of information, including writers' information, a Hot User Forum that's highly informative and educational, and a trade show and convention calendar for DV enthusiasts.

WWW.IDGNET.COM

This site offers downloads, tools, reviews, and how-tos.

WWW.ADOBE.COM/SUPPORT/DATABASE.HTML

This section of the Adobe web site provides a searchable database for support knowledge about Adobe Premiere.

WWW.HELPTALK.NET

This site offers support forums, information about suitable books, and training.

DOWNLOADS

For downloads of sound files, tutorials, shareware software, and more, check out these sites.

WWW.ADOBE.COM

Here you can get free tryouts for Premiere and After Effects.

WWW.DV.COM

This site offers numerous downloads of sound files, Premiere tutorials, and shareware.

BOOKS

Planning to produce your own movies? You'll want to get your hands on reading materials. There are many excellent books that can point you in the right direction.

- *The Filmmaker's Handbook: A Comprehensive Guide for the Digital Age*, by Steven Ascher (NAL, 1999), is an excellent resource.
- *The IFilm Digital Video Filmmaker's Handbook 2001*, by Maxie Collier (Lone Eagle Publishing, 2001), is a great instructional guide on the basics of digital filmmaking.
- *The Digital Filmmaker Handbook*, by Ben Long (Charles River Media, 2000), is an outstanding book for learning about the production process of filmmaking.

- *The Guerilla Filmmaker's Handbook*, by Chris Jones (Continuum Publishing Group, 2000), covers all aspects of making low-budget movies; a sound investment.

ADDITIONAL TRAINING RESOURCES

If you want to stay current with the changes in technology and software driving it, you'll have to know where to find the training best suited to your needs and budget, whether online or facility-based.

WWW.TOTALTRAINING.COM/MISC/TRAINING.HTML

This organization offers highly acclaimed video training that covers the multimedia gamut. Taught by seasoned professionals, this series is especially useful for the intermediate to advanced user looking for information you just can't find anywhere else. They offer tapes for Premiere, After Effects, and Photoshop, to name a few.

WWW.ADOBE.ELEMENTK.COM

This site offers online training for Premiere and After Effects. If you have a busy schedule and are looking for a self-paced class, this provides you with an alternative approach.

PLUG-INS FOR ADOBE PREMIERE

As mentioned in Chapter 10, Premiere has many enhancement plug-ins available for purchase and download. These plug-ins include transitions, audio effects, video effects, and processing. Here are a few of the many available plug-ins.

WWW.ADOBE.COM/PRODUCTS/PLUGINS/PREMIERE/MAIN.HTML

This section of the Adobe web site has all sorts of enhancements available for download that complement Premiere.

Here's a list of several of the plug-ins to provide you with a wide range of Premiere enhancement tools.

Access Fx, Inc.

- **Lord of the Wipe** This plug-in is a dynamic, exciting gradient-based transition that offers fully customizable options such as image interpolation, rotation, scaling, edge softness, screen, and rotation placement.
- **Translux** This is a pixel-based transition plug-in allowing customization to a wide array of parameters, such as changing height and width, density, transparency, and movement of pixels in the transition.

Arboretum Systems, Inc.

- **Hyperprism** For real-time sound effects processing, this software is the way to go. It's an excellent add-on to the tools already used in post-production, broadcasting, and games. It offers 23 effects, such as reverb, pitch shifting, sweepable resonant filters, modulation, stereo enhancers, and dynamic compression.
- **Ray Gun 1.2** For noise reduction that automatically cleans up noisy vinyls and tags, check out this plug-in.
- **Ionizer 1.3** Ionizer is a multiband dynamic processor offering fast spectral analysis and 512 bands of gated EQ per channel. It's great for noise reduction, equalization, limiting, compression, and expansion, all at 32-bit floating-point internal precision.
- **Boris FX** Boris is a well-known and fun 3-D special-effects plug-in for nonlinear editing with 3-D text.

Crystal Graphics

- **Crystal 3D Vortex** This plug-in offers a collection of 3-D transition effects for video that lets you integrate cutting-edge broadcast-quality 3-D transitions between some video clips.

Inscriber Technology

- **TitleMotion** With this plug-in, you can create dazzling video titles and motion graphics directly from the Premiere workspace. It offers more than 200 predesigned templates and more than 200 new text styles.

Pinnacle Systems, Inc.

- **Hollywood FX** This is a 3-D effects and transitions plug-in for Premiere and After Effects with such offerings as transparency, shadows, shine, trails, and motion blurs.

Pixelan Software

- **SpiceMasters** This is a top-rated plug-in that applies and customizes super-soft-enable transitions in Premiere.

Check out the Adobe Web site for a complete list of Premiere plug-ins.

Appendix C

Premiere System Requirements

To use Premiere 6, your computer configuration must meet the following minimum requirements:

For a Macintosh:

- PowerPC processor
- Apple OS 8.1 or later operating system
- Minimum of 32MB of application RAM (48MB or more is recommended)
- 50MB of available hard-disk space for installing Premiere 6
- Large-capacity hard disk or disk array
- CD-ROM drive
- Apple QuickTime 4.0 or later (installed with Premiere)
- QuickTime-compatible video-capture card
- 24-bit color display adapter

Additional requirements for Editing in DV Format on a Mac:

- PowerPC processor (minimum 300 MHz)
- Apple FireWire 2.4
- QuickTime-compatible FireWire (IEEE 1394) interface
- Large-capacity hard disk or disk array capable of sustaining 5 MBps
- Additional requirements for third-party capture cards:
    - Adobe Premiere-certified capture card. For a complete list of these cards, go to www.adobe.com.

For a PC:

- Intel Pentium II-class processor, 300 MHz or faster (or 100 percent-compatible processor)
- Windows 95, 98, 98SE, NT 4.0, or 2000 or Windows ME operating system
- 64MB of RAM (128MB is recommended)
- 85MB of available hard-disk space with 40MB for installing Premiere

- 256-color video display adapter and compatible monitor
- Large-capacity hard disk or disk array at least 7200 rpm
- CD-ROM drive

NOTE **Adobe recommends not using external FireWire or USB drives, even at 7200 rpm.**

Additional Requirements for Editing in DV Format on a PC:

- Intel Pentium III, 500 MHz or faster (Pentium III 700 MHz is recommended)
- Windows 98 Second Edition, Millennium, or 2000 operating system
- 128MB of RAM (256MB or more is recommended)
- Dedicated large-capacity 7200 rpm UDMA 66 IDE or SCSI hard disk or disk array
- Microsoft-certified OHCI IEEE-1394 interface
- Apple QuickTime for Windows 4.0 or later or Microsoft DirectX Media 5.1 or later (optionally installed with Premiere), or other video software that is supported by video-capture hardware
- Sound card (if your video-capture card does not have onboard sound circuitry built into the configuration)

Additional requirements for third-party capture cards:

- Adobe Premiere-certified capture card

Index

Symbols

A

D

E

F

G

H

I

J

K

L

M

N

O

P

Q

R

S

T

U

V

INTERNATIONAL CONTACT INFORMATION

AUSTRALIA
McGraw-Hill Book Company Australia Pty. Ltd.
TEL +61-2-9417-9899
FAX +61-2-9417-5687
http //www.mcgraw-hill.com.au
books-it_sydney@mcgraw-hill.com

CANADA
McGraw-Hill Ryerson Ltd.
TEL +905-430-5000
FAX +905-430-5020
http://www.mcgrawhill.ca

GREECE, MIDDLE EAST, NORTHERN AFRICA
McGraw-Hill Hellas
TEL +30-1-656-0990-3-4
FAX +30-1-654-5525

MEXICO (Also serving Latin America)
McGraw-Hill Interamericana Editores S.A. de C.V.
TEL +525-117-1583
FAX +525-117-1589
http://www.mcgraw-hill.com.mx
fernando_castellanos@mcgraw-hill.com

SINGAPORE (Serving Asia)
McGraw-Hill Book Company
TEL +65-863-1580
FAX +65-862-3354
http://www.mcgraw-hill.com.sg
mghasia@mcgraw-hill.com

SOUTH AFRICA
McGraw-Hill South Africa
TEL +27-11-622-7512
FAX +27-11-622-9045
robyn_swanepoel@mcgraw-hill.com

UNITED KINGDOM & EUROPE (Excluding Southern Europe)
McGraw-Hill Publishing Company
TEL +44-1-628-502500
FAX +44-1-628-770224
http://www.mcgraw-hill.co.uk
computing_neurope@mcgraw-hill.com

ALL OTHER INQUIRIES Contact:
Osborne/McGraw-Hill
TEL +1-510-549-6600
FAX +1-510-883-7600
http://www.osborne.com
omg_international@mcgraw-hill.com

Learn Web Site Design!

Video Lessons from Laurie Ulrich and Brainsville.com

FrontPage is a useful tool to create Web sites quickly and easily. But you need to decide for yourself how you want your site to look, feel, and act. I'm Laurie Ulrich, author of *Web Design Virtual Classroom*, and I've created a video CD showing you the vital information you need to create sharp-looking sites. It's called the **Web Design CD Extra**, and it covers key areas like these:

Graphics and Design Tools
Photoshop, Flash, and Dreamweaver help speed development and produce better-looking images faster

Web Site Critiques
Frank opinions about other people's mistakes--plus simple principles for sharp-looking sites

HTML Basics
Learn the language of the web to make your sites work the way you want

Structuring Pages
See how tables and frames let you control text and image placement

Creative Page Balancing
Eye-pleasing colors, layouts, and designs to keep your site visitors coming back

...And more! The complete contents are listed at www.Brainsville.com.

The lessons on the **Web Design CD Extra** use the same easy-to-follow video presentation style as the CD included with this book. I'm right there on your screen, talking to you about Web design in the same practical, understandable way.

The **Web Design CD Extra** is an essential tool for learning Web design. Check it out at www.Brainsville.com.

Best Wishes,

Laurie Ulrich

Name: Laurie Ulrich

Project: Web Design CD Ext

Order the Web Design CD Extra at

Brainsville.com™

The better way to learn.™